CW01022536

Roman Conquests
Mesopotamia & Arabia

Roman Conquests Mesopotamia & Arabia

Lee Fratantuono

(with illustrations by Katelyn McGarr and Caroline Hamlin)

Pen & Sword
MILITARY

First published in Great Britain in 2020 by
Pen & Sword Military
An imprint of
Pen & Sword Books Ltd
Yorkshire – Philadelphia

Copyright © Lee Fratantuono 2020

ISBN 978 1 47388 326 0

The right of Lee Fratantuono to be identified as Author of this work has been asserted
by him in accordance with the Copyright, Designs and Patents Act 1988.

A CIP catalogue record for this book is
available from the British Library.

All rights reserved. No part of this book may be reproduced or transmitted in any
form or by any means, electronic or mechanical including photocopying, recording
or by any information storage and retrieval system, without permission from the
Publisher in writing.

Printed and bound in the UK by TJ Books Limited, Padstow, Cornwall.

Pen & Sword Books Limited incorporates the imprints of Atlas, Archaeology, Aviation,
Discovery, Family History, Fiction, History, Maritime, Military, Military Classics,
Politics, Select, Transport, True Crime, Air World, Frontline Publishing, Leo Cooper,
Remember When, Seaforth Publishing, The Praetorian Press, Wharncliffe Local
History, Wharncliffe Transport, Wharncliffe True Crime and White Owl.

For a complete list of Pen & Sword titles please contact

PEN & SWORD BOOKS LIMITED
47 Church Street, Barnsley, South Yorkshire, S70 2AS, England
E-mail: enquiries@pen-and-sword.co.uk
Website: www.pen-and-sword.co.uk

Or

PEN AND SWORD BOOKS
1950 Lawrence Rd, Havertown, PA 19083, USA
E-mail: Uspen-and-sword@casematepublishers.com
Website: www.penandswordbooks.com

For Professor Roland Boecklin,
Professor of Classics,
Ohio Wesleyan University
1948–1971

Contents

Preface and Acknowledgments

The present volume is a specimen of that strange genre known as 'popular' scholarly literature. That is to say, it is an introduction either for the general reader who may be interested in learning something about Roman involvement in Mesopotamia and Arabia, or for scholars – even in Classics and Ancient History – who may wish a convenient *précis* of a difficult and perennially interesting topic – indeed, one that is not laden down with scholarly apparatus.

That said, we should dispense at once with what this book is not. It is not a source of original insights into what happened in the Roman Near East. It is not a comprehensive history of its subject – not by any means whatsoever. Glen Bowersock provided the world of classical scholarship with the groundbreaking *Roman Arabia* (Harvard University Press) in 1983. That volume remains foundational to any study of Roman involvement in much of the region under consideration in the present book. A decade later, the same university press released Fergus Millar's *The Roman Near East, 31 BC – AD 337*. That study is comprehensive and covers such diverse and yet inextricably interrelated areas as Asia Minor, Syria, Armenia, Mesopotamia and Persia. Likewise, Peter Edwell's 2008 Routledge monograph *Between Rome and Persia: The Middle Euphrates, Mesopotamia and Palmyra under Roman control* is an exemplary source of much relevant information. David Potter's Routledge volume *The Roman Empire at Bay* is perhaps the best comprehensive study available for the history of Rome from AD 180–395. The volumes of the *Cambridge Ancient History* offer unfailingly reliable coverage of their subjects. And there are countless other books that can be cited for plentiful historical, literary, archaeological and numismatic analysis of the regions under concern. Kaveh Farohk's Pen & Sword title *The Armies of Ancient Persia: The Sassanians* (2017) has been immensely helpful and a pleasure to read on the vast subject of the Persian military (especially in the crucial fourth century AD). Equally valuable has been John Harrel's *The Nisibis War: The Defence of the Roman East, AD 337–363* (2016), from the same library of ancient military history. My work is a survey; the existence of such detailed studies as these has obviated the need for me to go into details that would duplicate existing monographs.

Scholars will of course need to consult copiously annotated academic works, studies that reflect intense research into the manifold problems posed by a study of Rome's involvement in lands that today include the the countries of Syria, Jordan and Saudi Arabia. Since this volume is intended primarily for an anglophone audience, I have consciously avoided citing work in other languages. I have deliberately eschewed my normal practice of including copious footnotes, all in an effort to make this book both as accessible and as reliable as possible to a wide audience. Failure to cite something does not indicate either ignorance of the source or implicit criticism.

I am wholly ignorant of Arabic, Armenian, Turkish and Persian sources, except in English, French or German translations (and through the kind offices of friends and colleagues), and through scholarly commentaries and apparatus thereon. Conversely, all Greek and Latin translations are my own.

This book appears in the Pen & Sword series devoted to 'Roman Conquests'. It is a natural companion volume to Richard Evans' 2012 study in the same series on *Asia Minor, Syria, and Armenia*. By necessity, much of the story of the two volumes overlaps. It was purposely designed that the two volumes would be roughly the same length, and that they would complement each other insofar as possible.

A word must be said too about the temporal scope of this volume. I have chosen to commence the present study with the reign of Augustus, in part because with Augustus a number of important threads in the story of Roman Mesopotamia and Arabia may first be identified, both as part of Rome's military history and as part of its imperial propaganda. The book closes before the 'fall' of the western Roman Empire in AD 476, a convenient if somewhat artificial chronological marker. Coverage is extremely cursory after Julian the Apostate and his short-lived successor Jovian, mostly because a definitive chapter break in Roman–Persian relations occurs in 363, ushering in a period that would remain more or less stable for well over a century. A more comprehensive study would have included the work of Lucullus and Pompey the Great among others (not to mention the history of the great Byzantine–Persian wars of the sixth century) – but their exploits are already covered elsewhere in the Pen & Sword 'Roman Conquests' series. To go through almost five centuries of Roman history is also quite enough for one book of deliberately brief compass. One must choose both start and finish points. Augustus and Julian the Apostate represent deliberate choices that reflect my understanding of Roman imperial relations with the Near East. Others would make other choices – mine are conditioned for both practical and philosophical reasons.

My approach seeks to provide a readable history of Roman involvement in the East, with a deliberate avoidance of too much in the way of technical study of the Roman Army and Roman military operations. I provide a start to a vast subject, and offer a general appraisal. Throughout, I have been conscious of the possible interest of the subject to those interested in the contemporary history of the Middle East.

I am grateful to Philip Sidnell, my editor at Pen & Sword, for his customary exemplary advice and guidance. My retiring provost Charles Stinemetz is a great supporter of Classics at our college, and an eager student of military history – I write every book for this press with Chuck in mind.

I owe a special debt of gratitude to the two freelance photographers whose work illustrates the volume – Katelyn McGarr and Caroline Hamlin, both Delta Gamma alumnae of Ohio Wesleyan University. Due to the realities of political and military life in the early twenty-first century, the locations of photographs for this volume have been chosen first and foremost out of concern for the safety of these photographers. I am deeply appreciative of the excellent professional work that both Katelyn and Caroline contributed to the enrichment of this volume.

It is my hope throughout that this book will encourage study of an inherently fascinating aspect of Roman expansion, warfare and provincial organization. Few of my projects have been as pleasurable, or as difficult – difficult mainly in that throughout I was tempted to do the necessary research to write a far more detailed book, indeed to focus my work on the career of Julian the Apostate in particular. That would, however, not serve the needs of the admirable series for which it was designed – and certainly not of the intended audience of general readers. In that latter regard, throughout I have been conscious of and inspired by my excellent lecture class groups in the history of the Roman Empire that I offer biannually. Those students regularly delight in the study of Rome's eastward expansion, and its many wars and machinations with Persia and other neighbouring powers. To them I owe a debt of thanks for the inspiration to agree to compose this study.

This volume is dedicated to the memory of my predecessor in the Department of Classics at Ohio Wesleyan, Roland Boecklin. Boecklin was an excavator at Dura Europos in Syria during the great Yale University archaeological excavations of the 1930s. From 1948–71, he served – much like myself today – as a one-man Department of Classics. Some of Boecklin's own books line the shelves of the Classics Department today, a gift from one of his last students at the college, alumnus David Watts of the class of 1970. Especially in light of Boecklin's important work on the Roman Near East, this volume is fittingly offered in his honour.

Chapter 1

Introduction to Roman Arabia

The Expedition of Aelius Gallus against Arabia Felix, 26–25/25–24 BC; the Putative Arabian Expedition of Gaius Caesar, AD 1

The history of the Roman conquest of Arabia – if indeed it can be said that Rome ever did such a thing – is a subject of intrinsic interest, not least for the ongoing importance of that region of the world in contemporary military and political affairs. It is a topic that also poses significant problems for the would-be student or researcher, whether professional or amateur. Our sources are relatively limited, and even the reigns of such great and well-known Roman emperors as Trajan and Septimius Severus – to name but two who are of great significance in the history of Rome's involvement in Arabia – are not particularly well documented. Some of our ancient sources survive only in later abridgment; sometimes, what sources we have are quite likely wrong in their statements. And perhaps fundamentally, one is challenged by the fact that 'Arabia' never seems to mean quite the same thing to our individual ancient authors and sources. What one author might label 'Arabia' could refer to anything from territory bordering on contemporary Iran in the east down to the Sinai Peninsula of modern Egypt, through Iraq, Syria, Jordan – and of course the Arabian Peninsula. The history of Roman Arabia is inextricably linked to that of its neighbouring Roman provinces and territories, to Roman Syria, Mesopotamia, Egypt and Judaea.

Today, that vast Arabian Peninsula is home to a number of nation states, of which the largest by far is the Kingdom of Saudi Arabia. Saudi Arabia and the United Arab Emirates are the only contemporary nation states on the Arabian Peninsula whose names reference this storied ancient land of Arabia; the other countries as of this writing are the State of Kuwait, the Kingdom of Bahrain, the Sultanate of Oman, the Republic of Yemen and Qatar. In antiquity, the peninsula was home to a variety of peoples, with nomadic populations and scattered kingdoms marking its immense territory.

In the records of classical antiquity, we have no evidence that there was ever a unified control of this huge swathe of largely desert land. Greek and Roman historians and other writers not only regularly refer to 'Arabia' without always providing a reference as to the specific area or people they are describing, but also sometimes seem to mislabel even particular regions of Arabia. 'Arabia' was a name applied potentially to the entire region, just as today the label 'Arab world' is often employed to refer to areas as disparate as Morocco and Kuwait, and likewise 'Arab' is commonly employed as a sometimes quite imprecise ethnic label.

Consideration of 'Roman Arabia' as a discrete territory of the ancient Roman world is thus difficult for a variety of reasons, not least the fact that 'Arabia' was never precisely defined geographically by either the Greeks or the Romans. When historians speak of 'Roman Arabia', they often mean the province of Arabia Petraea, established in AD 106 by the great emperor Trajan. This province did extend into territory now held by the Kingdom of Saudi Arabia, but it also included extensive portions, for example, of modern Jordan and Syria. Indeed, its very name 'Petraea' refers to the great settlement of Petra that was located in modern Jordan.

When we speak of 'Roman Arabia', we are referring to one of the more remote regions of the Roman Empire as it existed at its greatest extent early in the second century AD, during the reign of Trajan. The Romans never succeeded in subjugating the entire peninsula – indeed, they never sought (at least in practice if not in imperial propaganda) to capture the entire region, the majority of which is inhospitable desert. It is difficult if not impossible to identify with precision the borders of what constituted 'Arabia' for the Romans; we are left ultimately (and as ever) with the need to rely on ancient Greek and Roman sources that reference the region, as well as the archaeological record. The very remoteness of the region contributed to the problems that plague our sources. 'Arabia' – whatever part of it one meant – was simply not as well known to our Roman imperial sources as was Gaul, Spain or even Britain.

'Arabia is a vague word,' Glen Bowersock notes on the first page of his seminal work on Roman involvement in this region, *Roman Arabia* (Harvard University Press, 1983). Few scholars have done as much for the study of Roman Arabia as Bowersock, and the inaugural sentiment of his influential book on Roman involvement in the region properly highlights this core problem that confronts us as we begin our desert trek with the ancients.

Depending on the source, historical references to Arabia could include territory beyond the confines of the peninsular Asian subcontinent of Arabia. For the purposes of our story in this second part of our work, we shall focus particular attention where possible on the peninsula – though of necessity that part will include overlap with neighbouring areas.

One ancient source that does attempt to define 'Arabia' is the great work of Diodorus Siculus (c. 80–20 BC), a Greek writer from Sicily who wrote a vast compendium of world history in forty books. Diodorus is a sometimes underappreciated treasure trove of information about the ancient world. He is not nearly as famous as such ancient historians as Herodotus, Thucydides, Livy or Tacitus, and few would consider ranking him with those luminaries of ancient history. But he does do what relatively few others attempted: he offers a 'complete' history of the ancient world, an omnibus view from the perspective of a late first-century BC scholar, and we would be much the poorer in our knowledge of antiquity minus his surviving work.

At Book 2.48–49 of his history, Diodorus offers a general overview of ancient 'Arabia'. For him, it was a region between Syria and Egypt, with the eastern part inhabited by the Nabataeans. Diodorus' Nabataeans live a life of thievery and plunder that is based on their extensive knowledge of where to find water in the inhospitable desert of their realm. Fiercely independent, the Nabataeans were exceedingly difficult to surpass in war, in large part because they knew the territory so well and the territory they mastered posed extreme conditions for any would-be conqueror. Besides this unforgiving region of vast eastern desert, there was a comparatively more fertile and fruitful southern zone, the 'Arabia Eudaimon' of Greek lore ('Arabia Felix' for Latin speakers). This was the storied land of spices, of myrrh and cinnamon. At 19.94–100, Diodorus records invaluable information about the Nabataean Arabs as part of his account of the efforts of Alexander the Great's one-time general Antigonus' attempted campaign against them. The Nabataeans live the ultimate nomadic life; indeed, for these Arabs, to plant grain or fruit-bearing trees, to cultivate wine or to construct a house is a capital offence. These Arabs, Diodorus notes, believe that to engage in such acts of domestic civilization would render them subject to the domination of others. Instead, they focus on the desert pasturage of camels and sheep. Though only some 10,000 in number, the population is by far the wealthiest in Arabia because of access to the spice trade. Diodorus thus presents what we shall find to be recurring themes in the history of Arabia: wealth and commerce, trade and riches from spices and incense, all of which contribute to an eventual surrender to luxury and decadence – a common theme of the moralizing historians.

At some point in their history, the Nabataeans – or at least some of them – abandoned a primarily nomadic life and became more settled. There was soon the apparatus of a monarchy, with a king and an attendant luxurious life in such settlements as the famed Petra in modern Jordan. Scholars have speculated that one reason for the marked change in Nabataean life was the inevitable result of economic prosperity for a kingdom at the very crossroads of important commercial exchange between Rome, India, Mesopotamia, Egypt and Syria. 'Arabia' soon became a realm of conspicuous wealth, with a power that was rooted more in economic strength than military might. Places like Petra and Bostra (in modern Syria) were opulent by ancient standards, and they were on the very border of Roman Syria. By the time of Trajan, the Nabataean Arabs did not constitute any real military threat to Rome, but they did pose an inviting target for Roman expansion at a cheap price. Petra was given the special status by Trajan as *metropolis Arabica* – the Arabian metropolis or Arabian 'mother city'. Petra was of undeniable importance to the region, even if Bostra became the base of the eventual single Roman legion in Arabia. The city of Philadelphia was transferred from Roman Syria to Roman Arabia under Trajan; it was located on the site of the modern capital of Jordan, the city of Amman. Arabia became 'urbanized', we might say, even if such 'urbanization' was on a scale far less grand than that seen in other quarters of the empire.

Alexander the Great himself had intended a conquest of Arabia before death cut short the continuation of his ambitious plans for Macedonian expansion and ever-increasing empire. Indeed, quite literally at the time of his death, his main workload consisted of reviewing plans for the proposed operations. The Romans would succeed in winning appreciable victories in the region, and would eventually see the setting up of a province under the emperor Trajan. But Arabia was always a hinterland for Rome, yet one of romantic allure from Alexander to Augustus and beyond, and a region of economic significance even in times long before the advent of oil, as well as ever-increasing strategic importance in the defence of the eastern empire and the eastern Mediterranean coast in particular. Arabia thus held a dual fascination for the Romans: it was on the one hand a romantic realm of imperial association with conquest of the 'ends of the world' and the dreams of the great Alexander, but it also represented a significant military and economic strategic region of interest, especially as Rome faced increasing and indeed sometimes perennial challenges from its eastern neighbours

Parthia and Persia. Arabia was a region that demanded attention for very good economic and strategic reasons. It was also a relative backwater of empire, a place all too easy to ignore without a crisis.

A major element of the propaganda for Rome's first emperor, the celebrated Augustus (63 BC – AD 14), was that he had brought peace to the world by his defeat of Cleopatra of Egypt and her lover Mark Antony at the naval Battle of Actium in 31 BC; that victory was cast as a triumph of West over East, of the forces of the sober Roman world against the drunken madness of barbarians. Augustus had helped to spread Roman peace and order from west to east – including to Arabia. Such grandiose considerations of empire and glory played very well in the arena of political propaganda and poetic reflections on the splendid restored Golden Age of Augustus – whatever the historical reality behind the epic veneer. Augustus came as the last figure in a long history of Roman civil wars, and a major element of his approach to winning power in Rome was his casting of his conflict with Antony as a foreign one. Rome was fighting not so much a great Roman commander like Antony, but his Eastern paramour and her Eastern allies. It was a fight between the sober, traditional forces of the Italian West and the decadent, indeed drunken excesses of Cleopatra's East (an argument that was only aided by Antony's notorious bibulousness). It was a clash of civilizations, a recurring theme in history of interactions between West and East, Europe and Asia, Rome and its distant neighbours. And Arabia was part of that equation.

Augustus would come to present himself as having done what Alexander the Great had not lived long enough to accomplish: the capture of Arabia. It was a bold claim, ridiculous on its face in so many regards. But it made for excellent press coverage, as it were, of what the new Roman *princeps* had achieved in his settlement of the East. And it was not entirely the stuff of fantasy.

The historical justification for this ambitious claim of global conquest with respect to the Arabs was an expedition that resulted in several military engagements in 26–25 or 25–24 BC (there is some uncertainty as to the precise dates). Luca Grillo offers the following summary of the episode in his entry on 'Arabia and Arabi' in the vast *Virgil Encyclopedia* of Richard Thomas and Jan Ziolkowski: 'Aelius Gallus (not to be confused with his predecessor as prefect of Egypt, Cornelius Gallus), on behalf of Augustus, conducted an uneasy expedition in Yemen (25–24 BC), which Augustus could not quite call a victory (Augustus, *Res Gestae* 26.5; compare Cassius Dio 53.29.3–8). By Virgil's time, then, Arabs were identified with worrisome people living in the Arabian peninsula.' Arabia was one of the hotspots of early Augustan imperial military strife.

The years after Actium were not years of uninterrupted peace for Rome. Admittedly, Augustus' achievements had put an end – at least for the time being – to the grim spectre of civil war that had for so long haunted the Roman political and military scene. There is good reason for the celebrated reference in the evangelist Luke's gospel to the peace that prevailed in the world under Caesar Augustus at the time of the birth of Christ.

But foreign wars and engagements continued apace, even during the years of his intended *Pax Augusta*, or 'Augustan Peace'. And Arabia was a theatre for such engagements, albeit not nearly as famous or celebrated an arena as Spain or Germany would be. Arabia was one of the classic 'Eastern' territories that played such a key part in the unfolding development of Augustan propaganda. India was as well, though the Romans never made it anywhere near even the borders of where Alexander's Macedonian army of conquest was able to venture. Arabia was the most exotic and indeed fantastic of the areas referenced in Augustan propaganda that actually saw the presence of Roman military units. The dusty sands of Arabia constituted a legitimate arena for Roman adventurism and attempted conquest. The drama that would unfold would not, however, serve to provide a particularly glorious page in the annals of Roman conquest. Propaganda would often trump reality for the Romans and Arabia.

No complicated, highly original thesis is needed to explain the impetus for the Aelius Gallus campaign. Wealth and the dreams of Arabian treasure would be enough to motivate Augustus to authorize the expedition. Awareness that Alexander had planned a conquest of Arabia centuries before would only have served to provide even more encouragement in the increasingly irresistible mix of motivators. The fact that Augustus' notorious foes Cleopatra and Mark Antony had extensive dealings in the East, and had used the East as a base of operations aimed against Italy, would also have been a consideration. This was an expedition designed to explore and to establish friendly economic and military ties; to conquer recalcitrant foes only if need be.

We may begin our consideration of Roman involvement in Arabia and Rome's conquest of Arabia with a note from Augustus' *Res Gestae*. Augustus therein provides a reference to a military expedition that was conducted during his reign in the far south of the peninsula. It was not the first Roman operation in 'Arabia', though it was apparently the first in the southern part of the vast peninsula (we shall later reference some of the earlier Roman military engagements, in particular the operations of Pompey the Great against the Nabataean Arabs in the north-west, though the account of Roman Republican military operations under Pompey in this region are covered by Richard Evans' companion volume in this series, *Roman Conquests: Asia Minor, Syria and Armenia*). The Romans had had dealings with Arab peoples in the process of the conquest of Asia Minor and Syria; there had never been an actual expedition to the southern part of the peninsula until Augustus, and there was never any (at least successful) attempt under either Augustus or his predecessors to set up a lasting Roman presence.

The *Res Gestae* is an account of the deeds of the emperor Augustus that was intended to be inscribed on his mausoleum in Rome. Because of its preservation (mainly from the so-called *Monumentum Ancyranum* from modern Ankara in Turkey), we are fortunate to have the text of the inscription in its original Latin, which deserves to be quoted here (with my translation appended). Arabia is mentioned once, in a passage that has occasioned significant critical commentary:

'*Meo iussu et auspicio ducti sunt duo exercitus eodem fere tempore in Aethiopiam et in Arabiam quae appellatur Eudaemon, magnaeque hostium gentis utriusque copiae caesae sunt in acie et complura oppida capta. In Aethiopiam usque ad oppidum Nabata perventum est, cui proxima est Meroe; in Arabiam usque in fines Sabaeorum processit exercitus ad oppidum Mariba.*' (*Res Gestae* 1.26.5)

'At my order and under my auspices two armies were conducted almost at the same time into Ethiopia and into the Arabia that is called Felix [i.e., Fertile], and great forces of the enemy of both races were slain in battle, and very many towns were captured. In Ethiopia there was progress to the town of Nabata, which is the closest to Meroe; in Arabia the advance proceeded up to the territory of the Sabaeans, to the town [of] Mariba.'

Augustus thus provides a tantalizingly (and characteristically, for the work) brief account of his purported achievements. Mariba, the modern Mar'ib in Yemen, was the capital of the Sabaean kingdom. The Sabaeans are perhaps best known in the popular imagination for lingering cultural references to Solomon's encounter with the Queen of Sheba (which may be identical with 'Saba'), and to the references to the gifts and incense of the Sabaeans in the Christian liturgy for the Feast of the Epiphany/Theophany. The very names are redolent with the mystique of the East: Arabia, the Sabaeans. The propaganda value of mentioning these distant lands as fodder for Augustan conquest was immense.

For the Romans of the Augustan Age, then, Mariba was one of the most distant landmarks of Roman expansion and domination. Mariba was a fabled city of the Far East, as it were, a fabulous locale to which relatively few Romans had ever ventured. What Augustus does not reveal is just how successful the venture was. 'Arabia' and the 'Arabs' are referenced in the great epic of Augustan Rome, the *Aeneid* of Virgil; certainly Arabia figured in the propaganda of the Augustan regime. But the actual extent of Roman rule over any territory in the modern Yemen or Saudi Arabia was a different story altogether from the poetic dreams of conquest and subjugation. The Augustan Age involvement in Arabia was not so much a story of glory as of almost desultory disappointment and failure.

Indeed, Augustus' laconic note about Arabia Felix references what some might reasonably think was a fiasco: an expedition launched from Roman Egypt all the way to modern Yemen. It was an expedition that was not destined to add territory to the burgeoning Roman Empire; it was not even to secure a lasting economic benefit that we know about in terms of trade and financial profit for Rome. It was, however, eminently suitable for conversion into propaganda. Arabia Felix mattered in large part because it was so distant and remote; it mattered for geographical as well as economic reasons. It was all too easy for the propagandists of Augustan Rome (especially the poets) to transform the operations of Aelius Gallus into material for celebrating the spectacular achievements of the Augustan Peace. 'Arabia' was also a region the notorious Cleopatra had demanded from Antony as part of the price of her sexual and other favours (cf. Josephus, *Jewish Antiquities* 15.92 ff.); Augustus would secure what his one-time foreign enemy had demanded from her deluded Roman paramour. His attempted conquests would not be against the Nabataeans, who were already clients of his rule, but instead against the more southerly Sabaean Arabs of Arabia Felix.

We possess some details of this Augustan era expedition from other surviving ancient sources, references that can provide some details to supplement the laconic record in Augustus' *Res Gestae*. A quite valuable account is extant from the histories of Cassius Dio Cocceianus (*c.* AD 150– 235). In 53.29.3–8 we read that the governor of Egypt, Gaius Aelius Gallus, conducted an operation in Arabia Felix in 24 BC (as we shall see below when we consider the evidence of Strabo, it appears that the expedition actually departed for Arabia in 25 BC, with the military operations taking place the following year). There is a noteworthy reference to the expedition in the Roman poet Horace's Odes (1.29), where he asks one Iccius if he is preparing to join the campaign against Sheba (i.e., the Sabaean Arabs; cf. the same poet's *c*. 1.35.38–40, with reference to military operations against the Arabs). Horace is not interested in providing specific historical details about the campaign; there is no way to know what or how much information he had about the expedition.

Cassius Dio wrote a massive history of Rome that surveyed some thousand years of Roman triumphs and defeats in eighty books. We possess a significant portion of the work; it fills nine volumes in the Loeb Classical Library (the most convenient text and translations available). The immense coverage of the work has seemingly deterred critical commentary, but slowly, an Anglophone project sponsored in part by the American Philological Association (now the Society for Classical Studies) has seen the publication of volumes of historical commentary on Dio's *magnum opus*. We are fortunate in that the relevant sections of the work that deal with the reign of the emperor Augustus survive in an appreciably respectable condition: Books 36–54 have survived in an essentially complete state, Book 55 has not fared so well, while Books 56–60 are extant. Much of the Augustan and Julio-Claudian period is thus able to be studied through Dio's lens. As with any ancient historian, there are the inevitable questions of reliability and quality of information. Dio has rarely been honoured as one of the premiere historians of ancient Rome; he is never mentioned in company with Livy or Tacitus. That said, like many relatively 'minor' figures in surviving classical literature, reappraisal and closer study have served largely to improve his reputation. He has been criticized more often than not by those who have not read him. Careful study reveals that he is a thoughtful, talented student of history. And we do well to remember that we have exceedingly little of the literature produced by the classical Greeks and Romans: even second-rate classical history is of inestimable value.

We may turn to a paraphrase and commentary on Dio's text regarding the situation in Roman Arabia under Augustus and the Gallus expedition. Sabos was king of the region. At first, Dio notes, the Romans encountered no one (a testament, we might think, to the desolate nature of the country). Most of Gallus' army was destroyed by the weather and the so-called odd nature of the available local water; at first it was the very land and water that assaulted the Roman expeditionary force, not any human enemy.

Those who fell ill were afflicted with head complaints, while survivors found that the disease settled in their legs (skipping the rest of their bodies). The only treatment was to take wine and olive oil, both as a drink and as a salve for their weary, broken bodies. Needless to say, Dio notes, there was an insufficient supply of both wine and oil to treat the army. Arabia was a hellish landscape for the invading Mediterranean armies; this might as well have been the end of the world, and for many of Gallus' men, it would indeed be the demise of whatever dreams of wealth and glory were fondly cherished.

At this dismal juncture, the Arabians attacked. On all previous occasions, the Romans had proven victorious in any engagements (although Dio provides no details of these encounters), but now nature was fighting as an ally of the Arabians (who were obviously more acclimatized to the harsh region). Sabos' forces took back all that the Romans had captured, and succeeded in expelling the expeditionary force entirely from their territory. Dio records that this force under Gallus was the first Roman expedition that came to this region of Arabia for the sake of conquest. They advanced to a place he names as 'Athlula' (the modern location is probably Baraquish in Yemen).

Alongside Dio's relatively cursory account, we may also note the longer record of the expedition preserved by the Augustan Age geographer Strabo (64/63 BC – c. AD 25), who was a contemporary of Gallus (*Geography* 16.4.22–23). Strabo was not what we would call a military historian, but the locale of Gallus' military adventure was of obvious enough interest to Strabo's geographical subject. His *Geographica* – like Dio's history – is available in the Loeb Library, where it fills eight volumes. The Ohio State University classicist Duane Roller has done exemplary work on Strabo for Oxford University Press, producing a two-volume set with translation and copious annotations. Strabo was apparently an inveterate world traveller, who had first-hand knowledge of many of the locations of which he writes.

Strabo records that Gallus was sent to explore both Arabia and Ethiopia. Augustus is said to have desired to conquer the region in part because of the report of its extreme wealth; the Nabataean Arabians were said to be ready to ally with him in his plans against Saba. The Nabataean leader Syllaeus (a deputy of the king, Obodas) deceived Gallus, however, leading him on circuitous, pointless routes through the wilderness and on water under the guise of offering expert guides. Gallus is said to have made the tactical error of preparing for a naval engagement, even to the point of constructing no fewer than eighty ships at the shipyard of Cleopatris (the modern Suez). Strabo notes that the Arabians were very good at cheating customers in the emporium, but very bad at fighting on land – let alone on the water. Gallus expected a naval battle, or at least naval resistance from the Arabians; it is possible that Syllaeus had led him to believe that such a peril was more than likely.

Gallus set out to prepare an additional 130 vessels to transfer a large army of some 10,000 infantry, which included 500 Jews and 1,000 Nabataeans under Syllaeus. After fourteen days of hardship, his forces landed at Leucê Comê, Greek for the 'White Village'. The modern site is unknown, but it may well be identified with Yanbu' al Bahr in Saudi Arabia. The journey was difficult, with many of Gallus' ships lost at sea. Syllaeus had lied that there was no easy way to travel to Arabia Felix by land. For Strabo, Syllaeus' plan was to use the Romans as his aid in conquering the region, with the intention of taking power for himself. Like Dio, Strabo records that Gallus' men were afflicted with a disease on account of the local water. Gallus spent the summer and winter at Leucê Comê, waiting for his surviving forces to recover. Strabo identifies *stomacacce* as one of the diseases, a sort of paralysis of the mouth. The other ailment was *scelotyrbe*, a weakness in the legs (we may recall that Dio referenced both head and leg afflictions among Gallus' men). Bacteria in the water could have been the culprit. We may compare ulcerative stomatitis (the German *Mundfäule*); malnourishment would not have helped with whatever mischief the local water engendered for Gallus' hapless men.

Water was carried by camels, and Syllaeus' guides were once again in the practice of delaying the Romans' journey and creating unnecessary hindrances and delays to enervate the army. Gallus' force arrived at the territory of one Aretas, a kinsman of Obodas. Aretas was friendly and provided presents, but Syllaeus continued to be treacherous. Thirty days were spent travelling through a country by trackless ways, with precious little in the way of natural resources for refreshment. Next was a nomadic desert region, Ararenê, where the king was the aforementioned Sabos. Fifty more days were spent passing through this country, again often by routes that lacked roads or ease of conveyance. The Romans arrived at the city of Negrana, the modern Najran in south-western Saudi Arabia on the border with Yemen. King Sabos fled, not wishing to engage directly with the Roman forces, and Negrana was captured. Six days later, battle was joined, and some 10,000 of Sabos' men are said to have died, compared to but two Romans. Sabos' men are said to have been utterly unfit for battle and seriously inexperienced; they used bows and spears, swords and slings, though most employed a double axe.

Gallus next seized the city of Asca, which had been abandoned, then advanced to Athrula (cf. Dio's Athlula). A Roman garrison was placed here after another bloodless victory. Arrangements were made for supplies of grain and dates to be readied for the continuing Roman advance. The next target was the city of Marsiaba (i.e., Mariba), which was controlled by the Rhammanitae under Ilasarus. This city resisted a siege of six days, after which lack of water forced Gallus to end his operations. Captives reported that the Romans were now only two days' march from the country that produced the rich spices and aromatics for which the Romans were greedy. Now at last he learned that he had wasted six months in pointless travels around the peninsula because of the bad faith of Syllaeus. He arrived back at Negrana, then at Hepta Phreata (i.e., the 'Seven Wells'), Chaalla, then Malotha and through a desert region to Egra, a village in the land of King Obodas. The return journey – far more efficient – took sixty days instead of six months. The army was then conveyed across the Myus Harbour in eleven days, following which there was a march to Coptus (modern Qift in Egypt) and then at last home to Alexandria.

Strabo notes that Gallus returned with those who were fortunate to have survived one of the perhaps most unappreciated adventures of the Augustan Age – an extraordinary journey from modern Egypt through Saudi Arabia and into Yemen and back. A total of seven men are said to have died in actual fighting; the rest were lost to disease and the hardships of the journey. Strabo wryly notes that the expedition did not, in reality, add much to knowledge of the geography of Arabia, though a slight contribution was made. Syllaeus ended up decapitated for his treachery against Rome. Strabo does not blame Gallus at all for the whole matter, and he even credits him with the ability to have conquered all of Arabia Felix, had he not been deceived by Syllaeus.

It is easy enough to see how the expedition of Aelius Gallus could have been turned into a propaganda triumph for the Augustan principate. Gallus had indeed seized several cities, though there was no permanent settlement. Furthermore, he had lost almost no men to hostile action, and much of the territory that was involved in the expedition was inhospitable desert that no one except nomads wished to inhabit. Nature was the fiercest enemy in the region, and it is likely that Augustus decided that it was not worth any additional Roman lives to venture back in the hope of a more systematic conquest. How, after all, could anyone in Rome have entertained serious hopes of setting up a reliable system of communication and reinforcement to so distant and harsh a land at anything approaching a reasonable benefit relative to the cost?

Aelius Gallus has entered the annals of Roman history primarily for his involvement in this ill-fated adventure. His relative obscurity has even caused him sometimes to be confused with his predecessor in the prefecture of Egypt, the doomed elegiac poet and suicide Cornelius Gallus (cf. 70–26 BC), the exact nature of whose offence against the good will of Augustus remains a popular subject of scholarly debate.

In his celebrated encyclopedic work the *Natural History*, Pliny the Elder (AD 23–79) praised Aelius Gallus as the only Roman to date to have carried Roman military armaments into Arabia; Gaius Caesar (the son of Augustus, not the far more famous Gaius Julius Caesar) had only glimpsed the region. Gaius' expedition (if it merits that appellation) into Arabia is of uncertain provenance and purpose. There may have been efforts to gain control of the spice trade for Rome, but this cannot be proven without further evidence (cf. further Pliny the Elder, *NH* 2.168, where it is noted that Gaius Caesar conducted operations on the Arabian Gulf; 6.141, where reference is made to King Juba of Mauretania and his volumes on Arabia that were dedicated to Gaius; 6.160, of how unlike Gallus, Gaius only glimpsed Arabia; 12.55–56, where Gaius' expedition is referenced in connection to a description of the incense tree, with *another* mention of Juba's writings on Arabia; and 32.10, with yet another citation of Juba's *Arabica*). Was there an Augustan Age province of Arabia? Possibly; perhaps probably. Gaius Caesar, in any case, was ill-fated. Born in 20 BC, he would die in February of AD 4, having enjoyed a consulship in AD 1 – the likely year of his Arabian expedition. Gaius accomplished quite a lot in the short span of his life: he concluded a peace treaty with the Parthian Empire and launched an invasion of the Kingdom of Armenia after a rebellion there. He was wounded in the ensuing confrontation, a wound that proved to be the beginning of the end for his military and political career: he was soon in a state of total weakness and near despair (some have speculated that the long reach of Augustus' wife Livia may have seen to his elimination as a potential threat to the power and future imperial prospects of her son Tiberius). His death was one of many blows to the succession plans of Augustus. Gaius Caesar conducted operations in Arabia, and may have penetrated as far as the Gulf of Aqaba, but we are sorely in want of more detailed information about what the young scion of Augustus accomplished.

Pliny in any case lists the cities destroyed by Aelius Gallus: Negrana, Nestus, Nesca, Magusus, Caminacus, Labaetia, Mariba and Caripeta – the farthest point he is said to have reached (6.160). Pliny records certain details of the life of the Arabians that were reported back by Gallus: the nomads live on milk and the meat of wild animals; the rest of the population extracts wine from palm trees, and procures oil from sesame; the Minaeans are rich in flocks, and have land fertile in palm groves and timber; the Cerbani, Agraei and especially the Chatramotitae have the best warriors; the Carrei have the most territory, and the most fertile; the Sabaeans are the wealthiest of all the peoples of the region, given the forested land they possess, as well as gold mines and the production of honey and wax (6.161). The forests of Arabia are also cited by the poet Manilius (*Astronomica* 4.754), whose date may straddle the reigns of Augustus and his successor Tiberius. Manilius also references how the Arabians are effeminate (*Astronomica* 4.654, 4.754). The report of Aelius Gallus likely emphasized how they were inefficient and ineffectual fighters (enervated, one might think, from the hot climate). The palm trees of Arabia are cited by the Augustan poet Ovid (*Metamorphoses* 10.478), who also notes the rich scents of Arabia (*Heroides* 15.76).

Pliny the Elder was not writing history, and so any details he provides on either the Gallus or Gaius Caesar expeditions to Arabia are incidental to his encyclopedia subjects (and of course his readership had access to far more sources than survive for us, and were thus better able to be knowledgeable about the historical events). Augustus, at any rate, might have been pleased to know that whatever the actual results of his Arabian enterprises, there would be no Roman efforts at conquest or even much in the way of exploration of that region for decades after his reign. None of his immediate successors would be able to claim that they had done anything in Arabia; the name of the great Augustus is at the head of the list of Roman emperors, and at the start of the list of Roman emperors under whose auspices Arabian expeditions were conducted. Augustus' adoptive father Julius Caesar had led the first Roman expedition into Britain (an island that Augustus had decided not to attempt to conquer during his long reign); his adopted son Augustus would be credited with ordering an expedition on the other side of the Roman world.

Of Aelius Gallus' expedition to Arabia Felix, then, besides a few possible poetic allusions in contemporary poets, the historical record has left us a brief note in Augustus' *Res Gestae*, a brisk narrative in the history of Dio, a longer account by the contemporary Strabo and a short vignette in Pliny's vast work. Little else can be added to the scanty record. The poet Virgil lived from 70–19 BC, and the references to Arabia in his *Aeneid* (and elsewhere in his poetic works) may well be infused with a personal knowledge of the military adventure of 25–24 BC. For Virgil, Arabia is a distant land noted for its exotic incense and other products. The Arabians are allied with Mark Antony in the forces depicted as being arrayed against Octavian and Agrippa at the Battle of Actium (*Aeneid* 8.704–706). In historical reality, we have no evidence whatsoever outside of Virgil that Antony had Arabian forces in his military retinue; the depiction of the Arabians on the celebrated Shield of Aeneas in Book 8 of the *Aeneid* allows for another example of propaganda and attestation of a victory that arguably never happened. Virgil explicitly identifies the Arabian allies of Antony as the Sabaeans; again, there was quite likely an intended reference in all this to the expedition of Aelius Gallus. We cannot be sure of the exact import of Virgil's mention of Antony's Sabaean allies. There may have been Sabaeans living across the Red Sea in modern Eritrea and Ethiopia, but we cannot be sure that any of these contingents would have been in Cleopatra's employ at Actium. What may have mattered most for Augustus was that a Roman force successfully made it far into Arabian territory, with the successful sacking and destruction of several cities. The losses due to the desert and the hardships of both climate and locale would only make the achievements all the more splendid, and the betrayal of the Romans by the treacherous Syllaeus would only serve to illustrate all the more clearly the contrast with the nobility of Gallus' Roman force. In other words, enough had been done in Arabia to satisfy the demands of an Augustan propaganda ministry; nobody would have complained that the Romans were not in permanent occupation of a remote, largely desert kingdom. Aelius Gallus would eventually be recalled from office for his failures in fighting the Kushites to the south of Egypt. As for his conduct in Arabia Felix, one might imagine that he could neither be seriously criticized nor lavishly praised (except, perhaps, in his fantasy that a naval war could be expected against the Arabians – and certainly in his trust in Syllaeus. Modern scholars have not been particularly forgiving of Gallus for either fault. The consensus has been that Gallus was incompetent and unprepared, and that the decisions he made reflected both his lack of understanding of the demands of the situation and his less than stellar grasp of military strategy and tactics). It does well to remember that his assignment was also exceedingly difficult, and he and his men were true explorers, venturing into regions no Roman before them had likely seen.

The expedition of Aelius Gallus is also probably referenced in another Augustan poet, the famous composer of love elegies Sextus Propertius (*c.* 50–15 BC). Propertius speaks of how '*et domus intactae te tremit Arabiae*' (*c.* 2.10.16): 'the house of virgin Arabia trembles before you'. 'Virgin' here refers to the novelty of the expedition – no Roman army before had ever attempted it. As in Virgil, so in Propertius we see what may be labelled poetic propaganda in support of the political regime. The language is vague and unspecific, but the import is clear: Augustus is the victor over Arabia.

Some scholars have sought to analyze exactly what was afoot in Augustus' orders regarding the Arabian campaign of Gallus (beyond the desire for economic riches and military glory). The obvious connection is to Rome's dealings with its constant 'Cold (occasionally hot) War' bugbear Parthia. Speculation is ultimately all we have here – especially since Aelius Gallus did not enjoy a rousing success in his desert campaign.

We might well conclude that the Augustan dream of the conquest of Arabia – or at least its subjugation – was largely the stuff of the fancy of poets. It would be left to another emperor to carry out operations in that theatre of the Roman world, and to establish a more lasting presence. He would know successes and great triumphs alongside setbacks and reversals. But in the final assessment, his laudable achievements would prove all too fleeting in their import. For now, a Roman army of respectable size had indeed invaded Arabia, and some men would live to return home to tell the tale of the fabled East.

For further reading on the expedition of Gallus, there is a valuable study by Shelagh Jameson, 'Chronology of the Campaigns of Aelius Gallus and C. Petronius' in *The Journal of Roman Studies*, Volume 58, Part 1 and 2 (1968), pages 71–84. For Jameson, even the friendship of Strabo with Aelius Gallus could not conceal the incompetence of the prefect. She considers the relative length of Strabo's account to be possible evidence for the significance of the campaign. Jameson ultimately concludes that the expedition must have ended when Gallus was recalled on account of the inordinate length of the operation – in other words, it was not the hardship of the locale that spelled the end for the mission. Jameson also considers the question of the date of the prefecture of Gallus and the expedition (which is disputed; she analyzes in detail the problem of whether the whole affair commenced earlier than 25–24 BC). There is a lengthy older article by Sprenger, 'The Campaign of Aelius Gallus in Arabia' (*The Journal of the Royal Asiatic Society of*

Great Britain and Ireland, New Series, Volume 6, Number 1, 1873, pages 121–41), with detailed analysis and a generally unfavourable view of the competence of Gallus. For those with German, note Christian Marek's 'Die Expedition des Aelius Gallus nach Arabien im Jahre 25 v. Chr.' in *Chiron* 23 (1993), pages 121–56. Marek is the main source for the argument that the expedition had a strategic purpose relative to Rome's dealings with Parthia – namely that the Roman operation was meant both as a distraction and diversionary manoeuvre to cover the actions of the client king Tiridates in Armenia, and also to provide a base for a second front to threaten Parthia. In any case, after the Gallus expedition there would be no further military engagement in Arabia during the reign of Augustus, and indeed during the subsequent principates of Tiberius (AD 14–37), Caligula (37–41) and Claudius (41–54), Arabia would fail to figure in Roman military policy. One need not ascribe that failure to commentary on the Gallus expedition. There were more pressing concerns in the empire than Yemen – and, in any case, Tiberius does not seem to have been driven by the same romantic dreams that characterized the happiest times of the Augustan principate.

Lindsay Powell conveniently summarizes the ancient evidence and provides an overview of the campaign in his 2018 Pen & Sword monograph *Augustus at War: The Struggle for the Pax Augusta*, pages 49–51, a valuable work that is extremely detailed in its consideration of the many military operations conducted under Augustus' long tenure. Bowersock's *Roman Arabia* also provides a convenient appraisal of our surviving sources, with his customary learned and reliable analysis. There is useful information too in the 2005 Harvard University Press edition of the translated work of Maurice Sartre, *The Middle East under Rome* (translation by Catherine Porter and Elizabeth Rawlings, with Jennifer Routier-Pucci), with extensive annotation and bibliography. The Harvard English edition of Sartre's work provides the complete 'Roman' material from the author's mammoth history '*D'Alexandre à Zénobie*', with some corrections and updates subsequent to the French 2001 original and 2003 revised editions. Sartre's book is especially noteworthy for its holistic approach to Roman involvement in the Middle East and Arabia; within the confines of the present series, each volume on 'Roman Conquests' focuses on a particular geographic region, but matters often demand consideration of the interconnected reality of Roman military and political adventurism.

In an interesting side note, Aelius Gallus is also cited by the famous Greek medical writer Galen (AD 129–*c*.200/216) for the antidote against viper and snake bites that Gallus is said to have taken with him out of Arabia, an antidote that Gallus used to save the life of Augustus (cf. Galen, *De Antidotis* 2.14, 2.17; 14.189–190 and 203 in the edition of Kühn of the complete extant medical writings – the recipe exists in Galen in two versions). If the expedition to Arabia Felix failed, Augustus would thereby perhaps prove to be 'Felix' (Latin for 'fortunate' or 'lucky') in having commissioned the whole ill-starred venture, and Rome would have received some medical benefit, at least, from having embarked on the fantastic enterprise.

Close study of the surviving historical sources, however, provides the best source of information about ancient Roman military history. Augustus' *Res Gestae* was not intended to be a historical work *per se*, and whatever details it offers are, as we have seen, frustratingly brief. Both Dio and Strabo, we have noted, are available in the Loeb Classical Library, with the original Greek text and facing English translation; together they provide the bulk of our knowledge of the Gallus enterprise. Also as aforementioned, Strabo has been served well by the work of Duane Roller: *The Geography of Strabo: An English translation, with Introduction and Notes* (Cambridge University Press, 2014) and *A Historical and Topographical Guide to the Geography of Strabo* (Cambridge University Press, 2018) provide the best available access to the work for the Anglophone reader. The *Res Gestae* of Augustus is available in the Loeb collection (paired with Velleius Paterculus' Roman history), while there are Oxford as well as Cambridge editions by Brunt and Moore (*Res Gestae Divi Augusti: The Achievements of the Divine Augustus*, Oxford, 1967) and Cooley (*Res Gestae Divi Augusti: Text, Translation, and Commentary*, Cambridge, 2009) respectively that provide commentary. The Loeb Library has a complete edition of the encyclopedia of Pliny the Elder in ten volumes, and it should be noted that the Budé series (with French translation facing a critical Latin text) contains excellent commentaries in lavish editions. Diodorus Siculus is available in the Loeb Library as well, with the complete history in a dozen volumes. The poet Manilius is most easily accessible via the Loeb edition by George Goold (the same editor prepared the standard critical edition of the *Astronomica* for the Teubner series). Propertius is vexed by a notoriously difficult textual tradition, and it is difficult to recommend one translation over another, although the Oxford World's Classics edition of Guy Lee may be suggested. For Virgil, there is a dizzying array of bibliography materials: the Oxford World's Classics translation of Frederick Ahl is reliable for the general reader, whereas the aforementioned Wiley-Blackwell

Virgil Encyclopedia provides a good overview for a wide range of topics relevant to the poet, including his treatment of Arabia.

The expedition of Aelius Gallus ended in disaster – it was a fiasco on any number of levels – but it would not be the last engagement of Roman military units in the remote deserts of Arabia.

Chapter 2

Roman Naval and other Military Operations in the Red Sea under the Early Principate

Rome did not secure new territory in Arabia as a result of the failed military adventurism of Aelius Gallus. We know precious little about what happened in the region in the immediate aftermath of the expedition, as surviving sources provide little information. We have meagre information as to what else (if anything) may have happened militarily in Arabia under Augustus, let alone under his immediate successors Tiberius, Caligula and the rest. However, one curious surviving reference has served to engender more questions than answers.

The so-called *Periplus Maris Erythraei* – to give it its Latin name – is a somewhat mysterious text written in Greek and sometimes attributed (for no good reason) to the historian Arrian (who himself authored a *Periplus Ponti Euxini*). A '*periplus*' was a guide to coastal installations and harbours of a particular body of water; the text in question surveyed the Red Sea (as Arrian's work would do for the Black). We do not know who wrote the *Periplus*, or when it was composed. It is written in a clumsy style, by someone who was evidently not entirely at ease with grammatical constructions. It may date to the middle of the first century AD, but certainty is impossible given the state of the extant evidence.

It is a tantalizing text, and an especially tantalizing piece of evidence is to be gleaned from its brief paragraphs. The author indicates (paragraph 26) that not long before his own time, 'Caesar' (if that is the correct reading of a vexed text) subjugated a city of 'Arabia Felix', probably – though by no means certainly – the modern Aden in Yemen. Aden is a location of tremendous strategic value, which explains its place in British colonial history as well as in the wars of the Middle East and the Horn of Africa; control of Aden helps to secure trade routes between India and the Mediterranen. Arabia Felix was the southerly realm of the Sabaean Arabs, the object of the failed Gallus expedition under Augustus.

If the *Periplus* does indeed date to the middle of the first century, then the reference is to some operation or other in the early principate. We have no further evidence for such military actions, and it is not clear that the enigmatic detail in the *Periplus* refers to anything connected to the expedition of Aelius Gallus.

To add to the confusion, it is not entirely certain what exactly is meant geographically by 'Arabia Felix' (the Greek 'Arabia Eudaimon'). The traditional understanding has been that the name refers to the modern realm of Yemen. The scholar Jan Retsö has argued that the term referred originally to the coast of the Arabian Peninsula opposite the island of Bahrain, and that it derived its optimistic label of 'Happy' from a belief that the area was a home of the gods. The geographical descriptor was then extended to refer to the entire peninsula – including, of course, the far southern region that today constitutes Yemen. 'Felix' or 'Eudaimon' might well have originated as a mark of how the area was blessed because it hosted a home of the gods – and, by extension, it was happy because of the rich spices and treasures of the region, sure signs of the favour of the immortals.

The text of the *Periplus* thus presents an array of vexing and troublesome problems. We do not know for sure what 'Arabia Felix' refers to, we do not know exactly when the *Periplus* was composed and we are ignorant as to its author. We do not know if the military action referenced in it refers to the campaign of Aelius Gallus or to some later action. The entry in the second edition of the *Oxford Classical Dictionary* draws conclusions from the slight evidence: 'Roman naval predominance in the Red Sea was secured and the reduction of Aden (Arabia Eudaemon) early in the Principate facilitated the movement of Greek merchant convoys on their passage from Egypt to India and back (Anon. *Peripl. Mar. Erythr.* 26).' A number of unverifiable assumptions are made in this summary, though it is clear enough that Roman interest in the region was certainly economic (though not to the exclusion of considerations of military defence): control of the trade routes to India was of inestimable financial value to the Augustan and later regimes.

To sum up, then: the *Periplus* reference to Roman military operations in Arabia Felix either refers to the Aelius Gallus expedition under Augustus or to some otherwise unknown campaign. It is conceivable that the account is a reflection of the activities of Gaius Caesar in Arabia, an expedition that is notoriously poorly documented. Yet it is exceedingly difficult to reconcile the narrative of the *Periplus* with other surviving sources on the Gallus expedition, let alone the travels of Gaius Caesar in the region. The author of the *Periplus* may have had incorrect information; conversely, he may have altered history, we might say, to flatter the Romans – they had, after all, managed to send a military force into one of the most remote regions of the known world, and fiasco notwithstanding, perhaps the ill-fated Aelius Gallus was thought to have deserved some credit, after all, for his desert adventures.

If the evidence of the *Periplus* is mysterious, so too is the general history of Roman involvement in Arabia in the early principate. Glen Bowersock (*Roman Arabia*, page 54) highlights a passage of Strabo (16.4.21) that speaks of the Nabataean Arabs as being subject to Rome – that is, that they constituted a Roman province. Strabo notes that the Nabataeans were given to incursions into Syria before they were subdued; now both they and the Syrians are subjects of Rome. Bowersock raises the possibility that the Nabataean Arabs may have been briefly annexed by Rome and then restored to client kingdom status. We cannot be certain in the absence of further evidence, but the alternative is to conclude that Strabo was simply mistaken. It is clear evidence of the relative paucity of our sources that we cannot even be certain of the exact political or provincial status of 'Nabataea' in this otherwise fairly well documented period of Roman history. We have considered the problem of the exact status of Augustan Age Nabataean Arabia in our examination of the poorly documented expeditions of Gaius Caesar in the region. What is certain is that we have no real evidence of any interest in Arabian military conquests or expansion in the reign of Augustus' successor Tiberius. The same dearth of sources attends the status of Arabia during the reigns of his successors Caligula (AD 37–41), Claudius (41–54), Nero (54–68) and the emperors of the so-called 'Long Year', AD 69 (Galba, Otho and Vitellius). There were no known military expeditions in Arabia during this long period, and the sources on the reigns of these emperors are devoid of anything in the way of helpful information on the status of Roman Arabia. The same is true for our documentation on the Flavian emperors Vespasian (AD 69–79), Titus (79–81) and Domitian (81–96). What evidence we possess – for example, that the Nabataeans sent 1,000 cavalry and 5,000 infantry to Titus in his campaigns against the Jews in AD 67 (Josephus, *Jewish War* 3.68) – offers no significant supplement to the story of Roman military history in Arabia. There is admittedly some evidence that Domitian expanded the borders of Roman Syria into areas that may have been in the Nabataean sphere of influence, but this was done without anything in the way of armed conflict (at least that we know of), and the famous volcanic district of Lajat (the ancient Trachonitis) in southern Syria was probably not a source of significant contention during his principate.

It is as if Arabia fell off the Roman radar, if not the Roman map. There were more pressing Roman concerns, to be sure, in Germany, Gaul, Britain and elsewhere. Whatever economic routes for trade and commerce existed via Arabia, there was apparently no interest in military adventurism in that distant realm. The dreams of Alexander and Augustus had faded from the Roman imperial consciousness. They would be revived in the reign of the man who would come to be known as the *optimus princeps* – the emperor Trajan, under whose auspices the Roman Empire would attain its greatest territorial extent, and under whose reign Arabia would definitively be reduced to provincial status.

Further information of relevance to the topic of the enigmatic reference to a Roman expedition to Arabia in the *Periplus* can be found in the papers of the aforementioned scholar Jan Retsö: his 'When did Arabia become Arabia Felix?' in *Proceedings of the Seminar for Arabian Studies* 33 (2003), pages 229–35, and also 'Where and What was Arabia Felix?' in the same journal (Volume 30, 2000, pages 189–92). The *Periplus* may be found in the classic two-volume edition of the minor Greek geographers, Karl Müller's *Geographi Graeci Minores* (with Greek text and Latin translation), while more useful to the general reader is the exemplary edition of Lionel Casson, *The Periplus Maris Erythraei: Text with Introduction, Translation, and Commentary* (Princeton, 1989).

Chapter 3

Trajan and Arabia Petraea

D omitian, the last of the Flavian emperors of Rome, was assassinated in a palace coup in September AD 96. His caretaker replacement – the aged Nerva – enjoyed a brief reign until 98. In that year, one of the undisputed finest of Roman emperors commenced his happy rule. Trajan reigned from 98–117, one of the so-called 'Good Emperors' under whose administration Rome arguably reached the height of its prosperity and power.

The Nabataean Arabs certainly constituted a client kingdom of Rome at the outset of Trajan's principate. Whether Arabia had been a province at some earlier point cannot be definitively stated; what is known for certain is that Trajan established an Arabian province in AD 106–107.

We know that the last ruler of the independent Kingdom of Nabataean Arabia enjoyed a long tenure, his monarchy lasting from AD 70–106. His death was the occasion for the annexation of the kingdom and its reduction to provincial status. Frustratingly and regrettably, we have no clear evidence of why and how the annexation took place. The surviving epitome of Book 68 of Dio's Roman history speaks laconically of how Aulus Cornelius Palma, the Roman governor of Syria, subdued the region of Arabia around Petra (in modern southern Jordan) – in other words, the establishment of the province of Arabia Petraea (68.14). The epitomes of Dio are of uncertain content – we simply have no idea what actual vocabulary the epitomizer may have copied from the original source, or when. The epitomes are of great value in the absence of the actual text of Dio – but they must be used with caution.

Was there a military expedition involved in the reduction of Nabataean Arabia to provincial status in AD 106? It is certainly possible, perhaps likely – but we cannot be certain. The fourth-century Roman historian Ammianus Marcellinus makes reference to this provincial event in his great history (14.8.3). His exceedingly brief, *en passant* reference could be taken to refer to armed invasion, but there is no way to be certain. The fact that a Roman governor from a neighbouring province was involved in the matter might well be circumstantial evidence of military action, but it could also be explained as a simple administrative measure, even if one in which the threat of military force was all too present. Another fourth-century writer of Roman history – Eutropius – simply notes *Arabiam postea in provinciae formam redegit*, 'Arabia is then reduced to a province' (8.3.2; cf. 8.6.2).

A grand military operation in Arabia, however, can be ruled out. Such a conquest would be recorded in even the scanty annals of what survives to document this period. Certainly as soon as Arabia Petraea was constituted as a province, Roman military forces moved in to occupy the region. Any armed resistance to the Roman occupation would have been minor. Trajan had already attained military credibility elsewhere in the empire, not least in his impressive work in Dacia – there was no need to exaggerate the operations, whatever they may have been, in Arabia. It has been noted by multiple scholars of the reign of Trajan that he never adopted the grandiose title *Arabicus* to commemorate his exploits. We can be reasonably certain that whatever fighting took place in Arabia – if any – was not particularly significant, at least not in light of the other military victories of the age. 'On balance the evidence for the annexation of Arabia implies a military presence and perhaps even some military skirmishes, but no major conflict,' says Bowersock (*Roman Arabia*, page 81).

We have observed that there is no definitive evidence of a Roman province of Arabia prior to Trajan. It is possible, however, to speak of the borders of what constituted Trajan's Arabia Petraea. Its name was taken from its celebrated city of Petra. It extended to include the Sinai Peninsula of modern Egypt as well as portions of north-western Saudi Arabia. Petra was certainly one of the few major settlements in the province; Bostra in what is today south-western Syria was another. Bostra would be renamed Nova Traiana Bostra, and the Via Traiana Nova would be the new road that connected Damascus, Bostra and other locales to the Red Sea. Inscriptional evidence survives that attests to the new province and its storied road. Besides inscriptions, there is also the numismatic record of ancient coinage. Julian Bennett (see below) says of the great new road of Trajan in Arabia that 'it is the single most conspicuous monument in the region to the manifest destiny of Rome' (page 177).

The Kingdom of Nabataean Arabia had a small foothold on the Mediterranean Sea, and so the annexation of the new province was in fact the final step in definitively turning the Mediterranean into a Roman sea across every inch of its coastline. Client kingdoms may have been subject in some sense to Rome, but a province was a vastly different entity – and Trajan had established his Roman Arabia.

Trajan's new province did not come anywhere close to occupying the entirety of the Arabian Peninsula, and it certainly did not encompass the territory of the Sabaean Arabs where Aelius Gallus had conducted his ill-fated expedition so many years earlier. But it was a step – and a significant one – toward the equation of Trajan with Alexander the Great, and toward the refinement of Roman rule in 'Arabia'. It was a stable political and military entity, an achievement that may not have merited a panegyric *agnomen* or special name for the emperor, but which certainly deserved the tributes that were inaugurated by civil and military officials – not least the Legio III Cyrenaica that moved from Egypt into the new territory as an occupying force. There is an article by D.L. Kennedy, '*Legio VI Ferrata*: the Annexation and Early Garrison of Arabia' (*Harvard Studies in Classical Philology* 84, 1980, pages 283–309), which considers the problem of the legionary movements in this period. It seems that the Third Cyrenaican was the original garrison force, and that other forces stationed in Syria were possibly part of the early occupation – it is likely, after all, that there would have been an increased military presence in the new province to mark its initial annexation and to maintain order in the wake of the Roman occupation. We also have evidence that Nabataean Arab forces provided auxiliary units to supplement the Roman legionary forces. A useful study of the local problems confronted by the Roman army in this region is that of Benjamin Isaac, 'Bandits in Judaea and Arabia', in *Harvard Studies in Classical Philology* 88 (1984), pages 171–203, with consideration of the police duties of Roman military units in Arabia and the threat of nomadic invasion and plunder.

Legio III Cyrenaica is studied in brief in Stephen Dando-Collins' useful *Legions of Rome: The Definitive History of Every Imperial Roman Legion* (London, Quercus, 2010, cf. pages 120–21). The legion had fought for Mark Antony, and eventually surrendered to the future Augustus; it was stationed in Egypt for a long time indeed before it became an Arabian occupation force. The new legionary outpost at Bostra would be its Arabian home – and the Third Cyrenaican would never be recalled permanently from Arabia. Dando-Collins speculates that the emblem of this sole Roman Arabian legion may have been a depiction of the horned god Jupiter-Ammon. The historical record of the legion ends sometime in the tumultuous fourth century.

We cannot be sure what this legion had to do in the early days of its transfer from Egypt to Arabia. It is easy to indulge in wonder about the thoughts of the legionaries and their officers who travelled into the distant Nabataean realm. Those interested in fighting and military reduction of a new province would be disappointed: masonry and quarry work awaited them more than swordsmanship and conquest.

For what seems clear from the surviving archaeological record, at any rate, is that the efforts of Trajan's forces in Arabia were not so much acts of overt military invasion as refinement of the infrastructure and indeed what we might call Romanization – turning a desert into a functioning, efficient Roman territory. The governor was Gaius Claudius Severus, who may well have directly replaced Aulus Cornelius Palma in local control once Arabia was annexed as a discrete province. Inscriptional and numismatic evidence for the Roman occupation of Arabia seems to indicate that the new province was not 'advertised', as it were, until AD 111 – some five years after the Roman takeover. It can be speculated that Trajan wished to make sure that the Roman invasion was absolute – roads needed to be built, the apparatus of provincial government needed to be established, the military presence needed to be garrisoned and properly dispersed. Arabia Petraea was a frontier province, an extreme outpost for the eagles of Roman legions and for Roman civilization and culture. Anyone who was remotely versed in the history of the region knew that there were many problems that could be expected to befall the new Roman overlords. Trajan was clearly careful and methodical in his efforts to establish his showcase new province. Arabia Petraea may have represented the very border of the empire, but it was not to be deprived of infrastructure and evidence of Roman amenities. Arabia Petraea would have been an enormous province, one in which Roman occupation could not have involved anywhere approaching saturation levels of coverage. One need only consider the vast expanses of the Sinai desert, a region where even the modern nation state of Egypt has difficulty in exercising effective control over the inhospitable territory. Rome controlled the Sinai and it was part of Trajan's province – but what that meant in practical terms is unknown.

To give one indication of the distant expanse of this new province, archaeological remains from Mada'in Saleh (the ancient Hegra) in the Hejaz region of Saudi Arabia constitute the first World Heritage Site in that country. The remains mark one of the most distant and remote certain outposts of Roman military might thus far identified. Hegra would have been an ideal showpiece in the Trajanic crown of conquests: arguably a valuable place in terms of protecting trade routes, but also a sign of Roman domination in a region that had long captured the fascination of would-be conquerors from Alexander to Augustus. Most of the archaeological remains from the locale speak to Nabataean development of the site; the Romans simply occupied an existing settlement and turned it into a fortified base for the army. Life in the province under Trajan seems to have been relatively peaceful and without significant, memorable disturbance. Arabia had been a quiet corner of the empire before Trajan's annexation, as it enjoyed the last years of the long rule of its Nabataean monarch Rabbel. The transition to a status as yet another frontier province in Trajan's ongoing efforts to re-establish and fortify a new *Pax Romana* seems to have been remarkably successful. If there was any chaos or conflict in the region under Trajan, no appreciable record survives to tell of the calamity. The establishment of the province of Dacia had come about only at the cost of exceptionally sanguinary strife – Arabia would be a markedly different tale for Trajan. Rabbel may have had a son at the time of his death (one Obodas). It would be intriguing to know more about the exact course of events in the wake of the monarch's demise and Trajan's annexation. But if the Nabataeans had any appetite for war or armed resistance to Roman occupation, it was short-lived and by no means ravenous. The Legio III Cyrenaica moved in largely without effective opposition.

Arabia did have a coast, of course, and there were naval considerations alongside the ground forces needed to hold the new territory. We are woefully ignorant of what exactly was done in this period to secure the Red Sea coast.

Eutropius' Roman history (8.3.2) does contain the interesting (albeit frustratingly laconic) detail that '*in mari Rubro classem instituit ut per eam fines Indiae vastaret*': Trajan established a fleet on the Red Sea so that he could have a naval force with which to assail the borders of India. A grandiose operation indeed, and one which is quite poorly attested. The fourth-century Roman historian Festus (20) – the author of the *Breviarium rerum gestarum populi Romani*, or 'Abridgment of the History of the Roman People', – writes '*in mari Rubro classem instituit*' (i.e., language identical with that of Eutropius). For Festus, Trajan was a new Alexander who drew near to the very borders of India. It is unlikely, we might conclude, that Trajan established a *de facto* Indian invasion or even assault fleet on the shores of the Red Sea. It is more probable that any naval presence in Arabian waters was designed to defend against the piracy threat that imperilled Roman trade routes and commerce. Certainly no such military operations against India are attested in any surviving source, and we are left with the obscure record found in our two late Roman historians. A Roman naval base at Leucê Comê would have been helpful in assuaging any bad memories of the fiasco of Aelius Gallus' attempted invasion of Sabaean Arabia. We should also remember Cleopatra's dream of escaping Octavian by outfitting a naval force to sail away from the Red Sea to India. There is every reason to believe that Roman naval forces did patrol the Red Sea in Trajan's time, even if their duties were less glorious than the abridged accounts of the fourth century suggest.

One intriguing source of information about Trajan's province of Arabia comes from the remarkable archaeological find known as the 'Babatha Archive', a record that must rank among the most important sources of surviving information about life in this region in these times of change. Babatha was a Jewish woman of the early second century AD who left personal documents in a leather pouch in a cave that has come to be known as the 'Cave of Letters' because of the outstanding discoveries found there. Babatha would seem to have been born around AD 104; she may have died during the Bar Kokhba revolt of 132–136, the last of the great Roman–Jewish Wars. The documents in the pouch concern civic affairs, both public and private; they are written in Aramaic, Nabataean and Greek. The documents are valuable for a study of Roman Arabia in that they illustrate the adoption of Roman legal practices in the region from the time of Trajan's annexation of the province. Conveniently for students of Arabia Petraea, Babatha's life almost exactly corresponds to the establishment of the province and the years of its early development. It is a dramatic story: Babatha appears to have retreated to the cave with her documents to seek refuge during the horrors of the rebellion and war; the cave was intended to safeguard both woman and papers. Babatha did not survive, but the record of her legal dealings did in the form of the thirty-five documents of the archive. The Babatha Archive constitutes a precious source for glimpsing something of the coexistence of Arabs and Jews in a time of remarkable transition and transformation in the Roman Near East. One document refers to the new province of Arabia as 'new' even as late as AD 132, when it had existed for a quarter of a century already. The Babatha records provide a window into legal affairs in a fraught period in Roman history, in an intersectional venue where Greek, Roman, Arab and Jewish culture all more or less overlapped. The archive does not shed any light on the military or political realities behind the annexation of Roman Arabia (with one possible, tantalizing incidental note that we shall consider as part of our examination of the history of Roman Arabia under Hadrian), but it does provide precious evidence of the mechanisms of Roman law and provincial government at work in a distant corner of the empire. Babatha's records provide proof of the truth of the statement of Ammianus Marcellinus that the people of Arabia had to follow Roman laws. The Bar Kokhba revolt was not far enough away from Babatha; a wealthy Jewish woman in Roman Arabia was apparently obliged to seek refuge in a cave because of the unrest in a neighbouring province. Babatha was compelled, we must conclude, to abandon her life in Arabia and return to Judaea. Glen Bowersock somberly notes (page 89), 'As of now there is no sign that they ever returned to the palm groves of Arabia. Babatha cannot have been the only refugee who died in the caves of the Judaean desert.' It is a vivid story, of timeless interest.

Another papyrus survival from this period offers a bit more information. A soldier named Gaius Julius Apollinaris of the Legio III Cyrenaica stationed in Bostra wrote a letter to his father in Egypt in March AD 107; another letter survives from February 108. The February letter speaks of how Julius has been promoted and is thus now spared from the stone-cutting activities of his fellows (possible evidence of the public works duties the legionaries were tasked with in the absence of military action).

On every aspect of Trajan's reign, Julian Bennett's monograph *Trajan: Optimus Princeps* (London–New York: Routledge, 1997) can be recommended without reserve. The Roman historian Antony Birley prepared the Penguin Classics edition of the lives of the so-called *Augustan History*, to which he contributed a valuable modern rendition of the life of Trajan that offers a convenient prospectus of the surviving ancient sources (*Lives of the Later Caesars: The first part of the Augustan History, with newly compiled lives of Nerva and Trajan*, London: Penguin Books, 1976). Sources are perhaps surprisingly somewhat limited for Trajan's reign. The very fact of Birley's decision to compose a new life of the famous emperor attests to the basic problem: there is no complete surviving account of his reign. Trajan himself seems to have composed an account of his Dacian Wars modelled on Caesar's celebrated commentaries on his conquest of Gaul, and the famous historian Arrian wrote a lengthy account of Parthian history that covered Trajan's military activities there – but all of this has survived only in the most meagre of fragments or in summary form (the commentaries on the Dacian Wars survive literally in a single sentence cited by the grammarian Priscian to illustrate a point about Latin grammar; for Arrian's original seventeen books on Parthia we are dependent on Byzantine summaries). We possess the tenth and last book of the letters of Pliny the Younger, which is devoted to his correspondence with the emperor; there is also Pliny's so-called *Panegyricus* of Trajan. None of these sources offers much in the way of evidence about Trajan's military and other actions in Arabia. The aforementioned Book 68 of Dio's history of Rome is probably the most valuable surviving ancient source for his reign, and as we have seen, most of that book survives only in later (Byzantine) epitomes. Pliny the Younger's works are collected in a two-volume Loeb edition, while on Pliny's *Panegyricus* of Trajan there is valuable material in Roger Rees' edited volume in the *Oxford Readings in Classical Studies* series devoted to *Latin Panegyric* (Oxford, 2012).

There is a convenient overview of the history of the formation of Trajan's province of Arabia in Fergus Millar's *The Roman Near East, 31 BC – AD 337* (Cambridge, Massachusetts: Harvard University Press, 1993), pages 92–97. Millar provides a learned, succinct account of what we know and how we know it. He offers the usual reminder (page 93) that 'All that we know of the moment of conquest, or acquisition, is a single sentence of Cassius Dio.' Millar argues that the events of AD 106–107 are of little significance in explicating the reasons for the continued Roman expansion in the Near East that we find during Trajan's reign.

Invaluable is the work of E. Mary Smallwood, *Documents Illustrating the Principates of Nerva, Trajan, and Hadrian* (Cambridge, 1966). This collection provides an overview of surviving citations of historical and other events from a variety of sources. Coinage celebrating the acquisition of Arabia as a province (complete with a figure of Arabia standing in front of a camel) are cited (page 37). The coinage refers to Arabia as having been 'acquired' (in Latin, *adquisita*) rather than conquered – circumstantial evidence, we might think, of the nature of the annexation. For an example of a milestone that refers to the provincial organization of Arabia, see page 136 of the same work. There is an extensive bibliography available on specific documents from the Babatha records; for a good start on a vast subject, note Philip F. Esler's *Babatha's Orchard: The Yadin Papyri and an Ancient Jewish Family Tale Retold* (Oxford, 2017), Kimberly Czajkowski's *Localized Law: The Babatha and Salome Komaise Archives* (Oxford, 2017); and Jacobine G. Oudshoorn, *The Relationship between Roman and Local Law in the Babatha and Salome Komaise Archives: General Analysis and*

Three Case Studies on Law of Succession, Guardianship and Marriage (Leiden–Boston: Brill, 2007).

There has been a considerable amount of archaeological work done on the problem of the Roman military forts and garrisons in Arabia. A good study on this topic is David F. Graf's article 'The *Via Militaris* in Arabia', in *Dumbarton Oaks Papers* 51 (1997), pages 271–81.

Chapter 4

Roman Arabia during the High Empire

T
rajan was followed by a group of emperors who continued the line of the so-called 'Good' overseers of Rome, men who presided over what can be considered the high point of the Roman Empire. The reigns of Hadrian (AD 117–138), Antoninus Pius (138–161) and Marcus Aurelius (161–180; co-emperor with Lucius Verus from 161–169 and with his son Commodus from 177–180) saw a flowering of Roman culture and an expansion of peaceful culture throughout the borders of the empire. It is not without reason that the celebrated Roman historian Edward Gibbon commenced his mammoth history of the decline and fall of the empire by stating that, 'In the second century of the Christian era, the empire of Rome comprehended the fairest part of the earth, and the most civilised portion of mankind … During a higher period (AD 98–180) of more than fourscore years, the public administration was conducted by the virtue and abilities of Nerva, Trajan, Hadrian, and the two Antonines.'

Arabia figures little in the history of the reign of Trajan's successor Hadrian, although the events of the aforementioned Bar Kokhba revolt in Judaea certainly had an impact on Roman Arabia. Glen Bowersock has speculated (page 108) that there may have been a more or less systematic persecution of Jews in Arabia during the time of the revolt. The evidence behind the speculation is that the provincial governor Haterius Nepos seems to have suffered disgrace and what the Romans referred to as *damnatio memoriae*, or the 'damnation of memory' – his name was literally erased from inscriptions. Haterius was governor under Hadrian in AD 130; the exact date of his fall from grace is unknown. Bowersock wonders if the departure of Babatha from Arabia was occasioned by some pogrom launched by Haterius for which the governor was later censured.

Haterius was probably appointed as governor in Arabia Petraea on the occasion of the emperor Hadrian's likely visit to the province in AD 130. Hadrian was an inveterate traveller, and there is good reason to believe that he visited Arabia between journeys to Syria and Judaea that year.

Haterius' predecessor as governor was one Aninius Sextius Florentinus, who had died in office and was buried in Petra. Petra now took on the name 'Hadriane', in probable honour of the occasion of the visit of the new emperor. Coins survive that show Hadrian with the allegorical figure of Arabia and a camel, and there is also numismatic celebration of the arrival of the emperor in Arabia. Arabia Petraea was no doubt a quite peaceful place when Hadrian was within its borders, a likely somewhat sleepy, exotically distant outpost of empire – yet one that was also busy with the regular visits of merchants and tradesmen, and the ongoing work of improving infrastructure and urban development projects. The soldiers stationed in Bostra were more akin to an army corps of engineers than anything else – they certainly had no need to engage in military operations, and whatever threats to security there may have been, they were likely low level in intensity.

Not so low level was the great Jewish Bar Kokhba revolt, which eventually saw the personal presence of Hadrian in response to the crisis. The war began in the spring of AD 132 and appears to have lasted for at least three years. The Legio III Cyrenaica was eventually involved in the fighting, transferred from Bostra to deal with the uprising. The Roman military reinforcements from Arabia joined those from Syria and Egypt in a testament to the severity of the uprising and the serious risk to Roman control over Judaea. Sources for the revolt are regrettably meagre.

Book 69 of Dio's Roman history survives in epitome. Dio's account blames Hadrian for the revolt, namely because of the establishment of a new shrine to Jupiter in Jerusalem on the site of the Jewish temple. Hadrian's presence in the Near East quelled any open outbreak of rebellion, though weapons were quietly forged and preparations were made for armed resistance. Dio notes that not only the Jews in Judaea, but the Jews everywhere were stirred up by the eventual revolt. This slender reference has been taken as possible evidence of a Jewish uprising even in, for example, Arabia, that would have accounted for the departure of Babatha from the province – though there is of course every reason to believe that the outbreak of armed rebellion in Judaea was the impetus for Roman persecution of Jews in neighbouring provinces; we might recall the aforementioned mysterious apparent disgrace of Haterius. The Cave of Letters where the Babatha Archive was discovered also contained actual correspondence between Bar Kokhba and his officers. The last fortress of Bar Kokhba's revolt was that of Betar, in the contemporary West Bank south-west of Jerusalem; there were pockets of resistance that survived into AD 136, but for all intent and purpose the revolt ended with the capture of Betar and the death of all the defenders save one youth (Shimon ben Gamliel II), who survived to become president of the Great Sanhedrin.

The Bar Kokhba revolt was a neighbouring threat to Roman Arabia, and the principal apparent consequence of the revolt on life in Arabia was the likely threat to the Jewish population in the region (a threat about which we would know next to nothing were it not for the Babatha and Salome archives). The use of military forces from Bostra to respond to the crisis made perfect sense – they were near at hand. Apart from these effects of the Jewish rebellion, Arabia itself seems to have remained largely peaceful during Hadrian's reign, as the territory of the province does not seem to have been involved in the fighting.

Bostra had taken on the name of Trajan and became known as Nea Traiane Bostra, and Petra took on the name of 'Hadriane' in honour of his successor Hadrian. Preoccupied no doubt by the Jewish crisis, Hadrian's Arabian policy would seem to have been one of continuity with his predecessor. The names of Trajan and Hadrian were fondly remembered in Roman Arabia for some time; the crisis in Judaea and Jerusalem does not seem to have had any appreciable consequence on the continuing relative tranquillity in Arabia Petraea. The city of Gerasa – the modern Jerash in northern Jordan – was greatly developed. The great Arch of Hadrian had been erected there in the winter of AD 129–130 to mark the visit of the emperor there. Gerasa today is one of the best-preserved examples of Roman architecture that survives outside of Italy. A great temple of the huntress goddess Artemis was constructed here, which was converted in the twelfth century into a fortress and ultimately destroyed during the First Crusade. The so-called Pompeii of the East is in itself a lasting testament to the impressive achievements of both Trajan and Hadrian in this frontier realm of the empire. Hadrian was not the expansionist emperor that his predecessor was, but he did not surrender the new province of Arabia Petraea. There was arguably no need to consider such a retreat, as the region was peaceful and exceptionally prosperous.

Arabia does not figure in the long and peaceful rule of Hadrian's successor Antoninus Pius. Indeed, for something like a quarter of a century after the death of Hadrian, life in Roman Arabia was quiet. The surviving biography of Antoninus Pius in the notoriously unreliable collection known as the *Augustan History* speaks of a crested serpent of unusual size that appeared in Arabia during his reign, which ate itself from tail to midsection, while four lions in Arabia became tame and allowed themselves to be captured.

There was an outbreak of some sort of pestilence in Arabia as well. Apart from prodigies and omens of this sort that are recorded in passing, there is no surviving account of any significant happenings in Arabia under Antoninus Pius.

Antoninus took great care in the education of his destined heir, the celebrated philosopher emperor Marcus Aurelius. One of Marcus' tutors was none other than the son of Severus, the first Roman governor in Arabia. Claudius Severus Arabianus received his name from the fact of his birth in the new province. On the occasion of the ascent of Marcus Aurelius to the purple, Arabia remained a stable, imperial praetorian province that was allocated one legion for its defence and security.

In some ways, the reign of Marcus Aurelius (and his co-emperors Lucius Verus and Commodus) continued the pattern of peace in Arabia. This is more remarkable given the outbreak of renewed war in the East: the great Parthian War that was managed by Lucius Verus. It is no exaggeration to say that this war had essentially no effect on Arabia. There is not even any compelling evidence to support the idea that soldiers from Arabia were called in as reinforcements for the crisis in the manner of the Hadrianic reaction to the admittedly much closer Bar Kokhba revolt.

The Arabian peace under Marcus Aurelius does not even seem to have been much affected by the dramatic uprising of the usurper Avidius Cassius. Gaius Avidius Cassius declared himself emperor in AD 175 on the receipt of news that Marcus Aurelius was soon to die. At the time of his usurpation he had enjoyed the special (indeed extraordinary title) of 'Rector Orientis', or 'Ruler of the East' – he was given command, or *imperium*, over all of the eastern provinces in the wake of a rebellion in Egypt that had been occasioned by rising grain prices. Commodus was only 13 years of age in 175; Dio Cassius thought that Marcus Aurelius' own wife Faustina had encouraged Avidius Cassius to take power (so too the author of the *Augustan History* 'life'). Avidius' revolt would in fact last all of about three months; upon receiving word that Marcus Aurelius planned to invade in order to depose the usurper, a centurion murdered Avidius. Avidius may have received the support of Arabia Petraea in his rebellion, and might have been able to count on the support of its single legion – but there was no fighting, and certainly no retribution inflicted on Arabia (or any of the eastern provinces) by Marcus Aurelius. The 'life' of Avidius Cassius in the *Augustan History* speaks of campaigns of Avidius during the Parthian War in 'Arabia', but there is no evidence that the general and would-be emperor ever fought in the territory of the province.

Glen Bowersock (page 112) raises the possibility that Avidius failed to receive support in Arabia for his uprising because there was a 'natural suspicion between the inhabitants of Transjordan and the more Hellenized and ambitious Syrians'. Avidius was declared an enemy of the state by the Senate as soon as word reached Rome of his attempted usurpation. His position was difficult from the outset – indeed quite perilous – but he did have significant support in the East, especially in his native Syria. Syria at the time possessed three legions, with one in Egypt and two in Palestine – as well as that single Arabian army. But what Arabian 'support' exactly meant during the three months and six days of Avidius' 'reign' is unknown. There is no real evidence whatsoever that Avidius had Arabian support, and in any case whatever support he might have hoped to count on in his hour of need was never utilized. The whole enigmatic affair was over almost before it had started.

Marcus Aurelius would ultimately be succeeded by his son Commodus, whose character and ability as emperor paled dramatically in comparison to his noble father. Arabia was quiet during the the reign of Commodus (AD 180–192), but his assassination on New Year's Eve ushered in the crisis of empire of the year 193 and the so-called Year of the Five Emperors. That crisis would ultimately be resolved in favour of the great African emperor Septimius Severus – but the events of that dramatic period of civil war would open a new chapter on the history of Rome's eastern desert frontier province.

For the reign of Hadrian, Antony Birley's monograph *Hadrian: The Restless Emperor* (London–New York: Routledge, 1997) is a standard guide. Birley has also authored an important study of Marcus Aurelius, *Marcus Aurelius: A Biography*, first published in 1966 and then issued in a revised 1987 edition that appeared jointly from Batsford in Great Britain and Yale University Press in the United States. Frank McLynn's mammoth *Marcus Aurelius: A Life* (Cambridge, Massachusetts: Da Capo Press, 2009) is a goldmine of useful information. M.C. Bishop is the author of *Lucius Verus and the Roman Defence of the East* (Barnsley, South Yorkshire: Pen & Sword Military, 2018), which provides an account of the Parthian Wars.

Chapter 5

Roman Mesopotamia

An Introduction to Trajan's short-lived Province

We have considered the origins of Roman involvement in Arabia, an involvement that in some sense reached its climax with the establishment of a province under Trajan in AD 106. That province was enhanced and strengthened under his immediate successors, though apart from the spillover effects of the Bar Kokhba revolt under Hadrian, there were no major events in Roman Arabian history until the reorganization of the province under Septimius Severus – the subject of our next chapter.

Septimius Severus was not only a reorganizer of Arabia. He was also a conqueror in that equally vast region of the Roman Near East known as Mesopotamia.

'Mesopotamia' is a Greek name that offers a convenient geographic label for the territory – the appellation literally means 'the area between the rivers'. The rivers in this case are the great Tigris and Euphrates, and the land between those rivers is among the most ancient and famous locales of civilization in the world. Mesopotamia is roughly contiguous, then, with contemporary Iraq, Kuwait, portions of Syria and Turkey – the land of the so-called Fertile Crescent, the home of the great cultures and civilizations of the Sumerians, the Akkadians, the Assyrians, the Babylonians, the Persians, the Greek empire of Alexander and his successor Seleucid Empire, and the mighty Parthian kingdom that was destined to be Rome's 'Cold (and sometimes quite 'hot') War' rival.

Mesopotamia was, like Arabia, in large part a desert region, with a harsh and unforgiving climate. From the Taurus Mountains of contemporary southern Turkey, down to where the Tigris and the Euphrates empty into the vast Persian Gulf, Mesopotamia is a land of striking contrasts in both climate and culture.

Mesopotamia was a natural battleground between Rome and Parthia, existing like Armenia as a buffer between the two great empires. 'Mesopotamia' was also destined to be the label for not one but two Roman provinces, one established by Trajan and the other by Septimius Severus. Trajan had established the province of Arabia, and Septimus would reorganize and indeed expand it; the two emperors would also establish Mesopotamian provinces for Rome, though with ultimately far less success than their Arabian counterparts.

In his busy year of AD 116, Trajan established both Mesopotamia and Armenia as new Roman provinces. His successor Hadrian would abandon Roman conquests east of the Euphrates almost immediately after Trajan's death; the expansionist policies of the *optimus princeps* would not be maintained. Trajan's formation of these two provinces was the tangible result of his successful prosecution of a war with Parthia that he had contemplated since at least 112. Armenia had been a nominally independent kingdom that, like Mesopotamia, was a buffer zone between the two great empires; depending on who the current monarch there was, the kingdom was more or less pro-Roman or pro-Parthian. The two powers used Armenia as a playground for their own rivalries, and interfered more or less regularly in the rule of that kingdom. Dio Cassius, as we have seen, survives for this period only in epitome. What survives of Dio's account is not particularly flattering to Trajan. For Dio, there was no real reason for Trajan to go to war against Parthia other than the pursuit of glory. Alexander the Great, after all, had conquered the East to the gates of India; Trajan was no doubt tempted by the possibility of his becoming a Roman Alexander, indeed a new Pompey the Great who could go far beyond the achievements of his Roman Republican predecessor in settling affairs in that distant region.

The Legio III Cyrenaica from Bostra in Roman Arabia is, not surprisingly, known to have been among the military forces that Trajan was able to assemble for his war on Parthia. Trajan was both soldier and diplomat; there were border kingdoms that entered into negotiations with Rome in the early stages of his personal involvement in Mesopotamia. Trajan's eventual successor Hadrian saw to the massing of Rome's military forces in Antioch, the Syrian city which would also serve as the place where Trajan would meet with the ambassadors and representatives of the minor kingdoms that came to negotiate and parley with the emperor. Hadrian had first-hand knowledge of and involvement in Trajan's Parthian War. Whatever his participation at this stage in Roman military history, when he would eventually abandon much of what Trajan had conquered, nobody could accuse him of lack of awareness of the situation on the ground.

We may trace the history of the war via the surviving epitome of Book 68 of Dio – not the best of sources, but the only essentially continuous record of the war that we possess. Already when he was in Athens, Trajan was contacted by the Parthians, who were interested in negotiation and knew of Trajan's reputation as a man of deeds as well as words. Trajan was not interested in negotiation; he refused to accept the gifts the Parthian emissaries offered, and indicated that he would proceed from Greece to Syria – where he would do what was right and proper. At Antioch, King Abgarus of the border realm of Osroene – a monarch of a dynasty of Arab origin in Upper Mesopotamia – sent presents and offered friendship with Trajan. Abgarus refrained from coming in person, Dio's epitomizer observes, because he was worried that he would offend the Parthians.

Trajan prosecuted his war, conquering Armenia by AD 114 and receiving the title of *Optimus* from the Roman Senate when word arrived in Italy of the emperor's great victory. Trajan is reputed to have marched on foot with his army, crossing every river alongside his men, a true soldier emperor sharing in the hardships occasioned by the pursuit of glory. If Dio's Trajan is presented as someone who had no real pretext for war, at the very least he is also depicted as being the consummate soldier, ready to perform the basest of tasks alongside his men.

Trajan proceeded to Edessa (the modern Urfa) in what is today south-eastern Turkey. There he met Abgarus. Dio's epitomizer reminds his readership that Abgarus had hitherto failed to see Trajan in person, a cautious tactic exercised also by Mannus, who is identified as another Arabian monarch, and Sporaces of Anthemusia. Abgarus now solidified his friendship with Trajan. Allegedly a major factor in the establishment of amicable ties was the handsome son of the king, a youth named Arbandes who was the apparent recipient of significant attention from Trajan, and who performed some sort of barbaric dance at a banquet for the emperor.

By AD 115, Trajan was also meeting with heralds from other Mesopotamian minor kingdoms that were seeking peaceful terms. Mannus and Manisarus sent emissaries. Mannus was held in distrust by Trajan, and so he did not wait for them to approach him, but rather he anticipated them by proceeding to Adiabene and thus securing his position.

AD 115 was also the year of a massive earthquake in Antioch that nearly took the life of Rome's great emperor. Trajan is said to have escaped disaster by climbing through a window, assisted by a being of superhuman size, some quasi-divine figure sent from heaven to save Rome's anointed one. Epitomes are by nature selective; historians would gladly sacrifice the Dionic account of the horrors of the earthquake at Antioch in favour of more details on the prosecution of Trajan's war.

Earthquakes and natural disasters notwithstanding, by the spring of AD 116 Trajan was ready to launch a full-scale invasion of Mesopotamia. The Romans managed to seize all of Adiabene; Dio's epitomizer notes that Trajan was now not far from where Alexander the Great had won his victory over the Persian king Darius at Gaugamela. Trajan was able to proceed largely unopposed to Babylon, Parthian strength having been sapped by constant civil turmoil (a major factor in the eventual decline and fall of that empire). The Tigris was crossed and Ctesiphon captured; the Romans were now some 22 miles south-east of contemporary Baghdad in Iraq, deep in Parthian territory. The Romans were in control of this great city, but only for a short time – Hadrian would return Ctesiphon to the Parthians the very next year. Adiabene would be the site of a third province that resulted from Trajan's lightning war against Parthia, namely the equally short-lived province of Roman Assyria. Some scholars have questioned whether or not there ever was such an 'official' province; coinage attests to the new provinces of Mesopotamia and Armenia, but nothing similar exists for Roman Assyria. We are not even sure exactly where Roman Assyria was located. It may have been east of the River Tigris, or in central Iraq between the Euphrates and the Tigris. Eutropius (8.3) says simply that Trajan established the three provinces of Armenia, Assyria and Mesopotamia, with no delineation of their boundaries. Festus (20.2) mentions the same three provinces, and locates Assyria in that fertile region of modern Iraq between the two rivers (indeed, he compares its fertility to that of Egypt).

After having captured such a major city, Trajan is said to have desired to travel down to the Erythraean Sea, that is, the Persian Gulf. Dio's epitomizer records the poignant, haunting tale that Trajan succeeded in making his way to the Persian Gulf, where he saw a vessel that was departing for India. Ruefully, the aging emperor commented that he, too, would have wished to travel east to India, were he younger – no doubt that day on the shores of the Persian Gulf was one deeply imbued with the spirit and dashed dreams of a would-be Alexander. And yet the epitomizer accuses Trajan of a certain arrogance, noting that he wrote dispatches to the Senate in which he boasted that he had proceeded a greater distance than Alexander – even if, in point of fact, his conquests would be exceedingly fleeting. Interestingly, we are told that the Senate could not even keep track of all that Trajan was doing in this period – contemporary historians may take some pleasure in that detail – and he was awarded blanket triumphs for all the peoples he conquered, since the names and places were too many to keep in correct order and proper place.

Trajan was destined never to see Rome again, the epitomizer recalls – and, in a case not dissimilar to Alexander's, many of the areas he had pacified began to rebel almost as soon as he had departed. This was a lightning-fast operation, with little in the way of time or effort spent on consolidation. We are left throughout with no doubts whatsoever as to why Hadrian abandoned so much of this territory on his accession. Arabia Petraea was comparatively quite peaceful indeed.

Trajan, hauntingly, would visit Babylon and the very room where Alexander had breathed his last, offering sacrifice to his storied predecessor in dreams of eastern glory. He established one Parthamaspates at Ctesiphon as king over the Parthians, and proceeded on to Hatra, a city in what is today the Nineveh governorate of Iraq. This was the capital of the small Kingdom of Araba, one of the many buffers between Rome and Parthia; Dio's epitomizer refers to it ambiguously as 'Arabia'. Hatra, he notes, was small and not particularly prosperous, a desert realm with little water and no timber or fodder for animals. A siege, we are told, was impossible by any vast multitude precisely because it was impossible to supply a large army in the vicinity, and neither Trajan nor later Septimius Severus was able to capture this seemingly godforsaken place. Trajan launched a cavalry attack, which was repulsed; the emperor himself was nearly wounded in the fighting. His gray hair was seen by the defenders of Hatra, who managed to kill one of his cavalry companions in their attempted assassination of the emperor. Dio's epitomizer credits natural phenomena such as lightning, hail and peals of thunder as marking the dire omens that accompanied the doomed Roman attack. Trajan eventually gave up the assault, and soon thereafter his health began to fail – his inability to capture Hatra was his first real failure in the Parthian War, and it marked the beginning of his decline.

Troubles were brewing for Trajan elsewhere in the empire. A gory summary follows of a Jewish revolt at Cyrene that was marked by cannibalism against Greeks and Romans, with belts made from the entrails of victims and men fed to wild beasts and forced to fight as gladiators. The unbelievable number of 220,000 are said to have perished in the strife. The revolt spread to Egypt, and even to the island of Cyprus, where 240,000 are said to have died, in consequence of which no Jew was allowed to go to the island thenceforth, with the penalty of death imposed even if a storm drove someone there involuntarily. We do not have much in the way of information about this Jewish revolt, but it was apparently serious enough to warrant Trajan's immediate attention. It was also a harbinger of the Bar Kokhba revolt that lay in the not too distant future.

By early in AD 117, Trajan was planning to commence new operations in Mesopotamia, but his health continued to fail. He left Hadrian with the armies in Syria, and proceeded on his way to a home he would never again see. He died at Selinus in Cicilia, suspicious that he had been poisoned – but he had also suffered a stroke and had dropsy, alongside other medical maladies that included bloody diarrhoea. He was 60 years old by this point, and had maintained an astonishing, indeed dizzying pace in his eastern campaigns. His death from natural causes cannot be considered a surprise by any means. Eerily like the Alexander he evidently sought to emulate, Trajan had made no careful plans for the maintenance of the empire he had captured. Nabataean Arabia was easy in comparison. It had been a client kingdom under the stable reign of Rabbel for over thirty years, and may have been a province at some previous time in Roman history. Its present provincial borders were identical to those of the client kingdom it had replaced. It was largely pacified, with greater interest in economic concerns than military, and it was sufficiently far away from the Parthian sphere of influence.

Mesopotamia was different. Roman commanders such as Lucullus and Pompey had dreamed of Alexandrian glory in its vast expanses. The Parthians were directly on the border, and in control of major swathes of land. The region was not nearly as wealthy as Arabia, and it was an unforgiving climate for resident and invader alike in ways that rivalled even the brutal deserts of Arabia. It was, in short, a graveyard of empires. Hadrian could not be seriously criticized for trying to come to terms with the Parthians on reasonably amicable terms once his predecessor was dead. Hadrian even considered abandoning Trajan's newly conquered province of Dacia in Eastern Europe; the only real difference in that region was that Roman colonists had already started to settle in the new province – the same could hardly be said for the provinces of Roman Armenia and Roman Mesopotamia. Both Eutropius and Festus report that Hadrian was jealous of Trajan's conquests and thereby sought to lessen them by returning territory to Parthia – but this is an unfair and unjust criticism of the new emperor. Trajan's conquests were untenable without a massive investment in men and material, and there were other pressing concerns in the empire. Armenia, Assyria and Mesopotamia would be reduced to footnotes in

Roman history, short-lived provinces that never really had any time to be constituted as normal, functioning *provinciae*. It is all too easy with the benefit of hindsight to argue that the territories could have been managed and maintained. It is also not easy to appreciate the criticisms of those Roman officials who were disappointed by the reduction in the number of potential new provincial appointments occasioned by the deletion of three provinces at a single stroke.

Still, whatever the reasonableness of Hadrian's decisions, he could not realistically escape the charge that he was besmirching the memory of his glorious predecessor, and he was, after all, directly instituting a new Roman strategy of retrenchment and defensive reaction in lieu of martial conquest and expansionist policy. He could not have known that the empire would reach its greatest extent under Trajan; there would never be another emperor who would rule over so vast an expanse of territory, even if 'rule' was itself an ambiguous term. Trajan's memory was held in the highest regard, but his foreign policy in the East was abandoned in favour of a more conservative policy, and it would be for later emperors of Rome to venture forth again in pursuit of martial glory in Mesopotamia against the Parthian foe.

Dio's epitomizer credits Trajan with the Roman conquest of Armenia and most of Mesopotamia, but also notes that all of it was for nothing. Even Trajan's would-be Parthian king Parthamaspates was rejected, and the Parthians essentially went back to their own business. The epitome of Book 69 of Dio even adds the detail that the so-called Parthian Games that had been instituted in honour of Trajan's victories were soon to be discontinued. The case of Dura-Europos is an interesting one to study in the Trajan–Hadrian transition period. This famous city was located near what is today the village of Salhiyé in far eastern Syria. It was a Seleucid site that dated back to 303 BC, in the confused and violent years following the death of Alexander. It was eventually captured by the Parthians, who remained in control until Trajan's arrival in AD 114. The Legio III Cyrenaica erected a triumphal arch at Dura-Europos to commemorate the achievements of the emperor there. And yet before the end of 117, Hadrian had ceded it back to Parthia as part of his hasty settlement. Major archaeological excavations would be carried out at the site in the 1920s and 1930s, including work done by the famous Roman historian Michael Rostovtzeff, then at Yale University. One of his graduate students was a participant in the work done there – Roland Boecklin, my predecessor as Professor of Classics at Ohio Wesleyan University.

Chapter 6

Roman Mesopotamia from
Hadrian to Septimius Severus

adrian's immediate abandonment of Trajan's policy of conquest in Mesopotamia has been both praised as sound foreign policy and criticized as jealous petulance in the wake of the achievements of his venerable predecessor. Mesopotamia would not really capture the Roman imagination or interest during the rest of the long years of Hadrian's imperial tenure, or during the even longer reign of his successor Antoninus Pius. It would, however, re-enter the Roman consciousness during the subsequent joint rulership of Marcus Aurelius and Lucius Verus.

Rome would once again become involved in a 'hot war' in the East. Students of the relationship between the United States of America and the Union of Soviet Socialist Republics might find much of interest in a careful appraisal of Rome's association with Parthia over the centuries. Neither Rome nor Parthia was ever, it would seem, intent on the absolute destruction of a neighbour whose very existence contributed to the stability of the Mediterranean world. On the day that Gaius Julius Caesar had been assassinated (the Ides of March in 44 BC), Rome was planning a great campaign against Parthia at least in part to avenge the infamous defeat of Caesar's one-time colleague in power, Marcus Licinus Crassus. Mark Antony would himself seek to do what Caesar had not lived to accomplish, but Antony's invasion of Parthia was a fiasco that left him without much in the way of military glory and with an increasing indebtedness to his lover Cleopatra. It was a major theme of Augustan propaganda that he had secured the return of the standards that had been lost by Crassus' legions. This was seen as the *de facto* establishment of peace with Rome's fearsome neighbour, and could easily be construed by the work of clever, talented poets into a victory – for why would anyone have returned the standards if they thought they could have retained them by force of arms? By the last years of Augustus' long rule, troubles in Germany were the dominant foreign policy issue of the empire; Tiberius and Caligula would be interested in the same region, the latter emperor also with the Britain that his successor Claudius would finally see added to the empire – the conclusion of the dreams of Julius Caesar from so long before. But none of these men were overly preoccupied with Parthia, except in the matter of the seemingly endless squabbles over affairs in Armenia with which the pages of Tacitus are replete. It is true that under Nero there was a war with Parthia over Armenia, which was fought from AD 58–63. Famous for being the only major foreign war of Nero's long reign, it was essentially a draw. The Treaty of Rhandeia that ended the war was something of a compromise, and there was criticism of Nero that he had in effect ceded Armenia to the Parthians – but that treaty would more or less remain in effect until Trajan's campaigns in 114.

War between Rome and Parthia was, both sides realized, a hazardous and draining enterprise. Both sides had worries on other fronts, as well as occasional civil unrest and internal power struggles. The maintenance of adequate defences on both sides of the border was a major drain on imperial coffers for both parties. If empires do better with the presence of a rival, then there was significant advantage in maintaining a balance of power, or at least an uneasy peace. It is in some ways no surprise that there was no significant war between Rome and Parthia for the entirety of the dramatic first century AD, save the Armenian conflict under Nero (which does not much concern the history of Mesopotamia, let alone Arabia). Parthia was useful to Rome, as Rome was to Parthia – and it seems that many a ruler of both empires realized this salient fact of the competitive relationship.

Trajan himself had not sought the utter ruin of Parthia. Territorial ambitions and an upper hand in the affairs of such regions as Armenia were more than enough to satisfy even the most ambitious of Roman emperors, it would seem. And the troubles that emerged in the Roman–Parthian relationship at the outset of the joint reign of Marcus Aurelius and Lucius Verus were once again a case of those recurring pesky problems in Armenia. The story can probably be guessed: the Parthians had entered Armenia and deposed a pro-Roman king; the Romans in Cappadocia responded to the Parthian incursion into Armenia, and seem to have blundered their way into losing a legion in the process – a legion that may well have been the famous 'Ninth Legion' (Legio IX Hispana) that some scholars think was lost in the north of Britain, a unit that has been the subject of much fiction (both written and cinematic) in speculation on its mysterious fate.

Whatever the identity of the lost legion, the reaction in Rome was the same: Lucius Verus – Marcus Aurelius' imperial colleague – was assigned to respond to the new eastern crisis, and he set out at once. The surviving epitome of Book 71 of Dio tells something of the dramatic tale, commencing with the aforementioned loss of the legion. We are not fortunate, however, in that by the time of the Byzantine epitomizer it seems that relevant portions of Dio's history were already lost. What passes for an epitome of Dio, then, is not really even that – Xiphilinus says he relied on other books, works that he does not name. Along with what remains of 'Dio', we are also dependent on the notoriously unreliable 'life' in the *Augustan History*, which paints a consistently negative portrait of Lucius Verus as a decadent lover of luxury and incompetent wastrel. One of the most disreputable emperors to emerge from our surviving ancient sources was thus involved in one of the most important campaigns of the age – a dramatic return of Roman might to the far-flung eastern corners of the empire.

The Parthian king Vologaesus had managed to surround the legion on all sides at Elegeia in Armenia, and after destroying the unit he was advancing toward Roman Syria. Lucius Verus – like Trajan before him – proceeded to the great city of Antioch, where he began to gather an enormous Roman force to respond to the resurgent Parthian threat. Besides the bad news regarding the loss of the Roman legion in Armenia, there was also a major defeat inflicted by the Parthians on a Roman force under Lucius Attidius Cornelianus, the governor of Syria (this is reported in the *Augustan History* 'life' of Marcus Aurelius, 8.6). We are also told (cf. the same 'life', 12.13) that northern commanders were told to avoid conflict in the wake of the needed transfer of large numbers of troops relatively quickly to the Parthian front. Lucius Verus had been thought to be healthier than Marcus when he set out for the eastern wars, but he seems to have suffered what may have been a stroke at some point on his journey. He would be dead by AD 169, and his health was a significant factor moving forward in these years of conflict and martial strife. Lucius' time in Antioch is famous for his canal construction to allow for the easier transport of supplies on the River Orontes. When the riverbed dried up, huge bones were found that were interpreted to be those of some giant – perhaps of the river's tutelary spirit.

Armenia would be the scene of great Roman victories, including the capture of its capital Artaxata in AD 163. Lucius Verus would be hailed as *Armeniacus* for this victory, though it was achieved without his ever having glimpsed combat there. A new king was installed in Armenia – pro-Roman, to be sure – but nothing of the order of Trajan's establishment of an Armenian province was contemplated.

The Parthians had suffered a setback in Armenia, but they were still active across the long border with the Roman world. There was apparently Parthian interference in the affairs of Osroene, that client kingdom in Mesopotamia that was centred on Edessa. The Romans knew that they needed to respond to the Parthian threats to Syria and elsewhere, so AD 164 was spent in preparation for a major campaign.

Avidius Cassius – the future Syrian governor who would one day cast his own hat into the imperial ring – was the man of the hour alongside the young co-emperor Verus. He would engage Vologaesus' Parthian force, and by AD 165 he would be celebrating the burning to the ground of the palace of the king at Ctesiphon. The city that Hadrian had returned to the Parthians decades before had been reconquered by Roman steel. Indeed, the prominence of Avidius Cassius in this period was quickly attained, forged in the Parthian conflict. Dio's epitomizer says that Cassius lost a significant portion of his force to famine and hardship as he made his way back from Ctesiphon – indeed, the second Roman conquest of that storied city was not destined to last much longer than the first. The Parthian city of Seleucia was also captured in the same campaign that saw the fall of Ctesiphon. The Parthians had now suffered major losses on both banks of the River Tigris. Lucius Verus would add the title *Parthicus Maximus* to his array of appellations. In 166, he would receive a third and final honorific title – *Medicus* – on the occasion of the crossing of Cassius' army across the Tigris and into Media. It is no surprise that Cassius would be one of the consuls of 166; he was clearly the one general who deserved the bulk of the credit for the successful operations against Parthia in this period. When the day came that he would aspire to take over the empire, no doubt the extent of his history of military victories against Rome's inveterate enemy was a factor in his imperial ambitions.

These titles in praise of Lucius Verus stand in marked variance to the aforementioned picture of the young emperor as presented in the Augustan biography. This tells us that on his way to the Parthian War, Lucius Verus was accompanied for part of the journey by Marcus Aurelius. But after parting ways in Capua, Lucius started a habit of gorging himself sick at everyone's villas, so that before long he was too ill to proceed from Canusium in Apulia, and Marcus had to hurry to his co-emperor's side. The ancient biographer asserts that while the entire eastern world was in disarray, with legions having been slaughtered, Lucius Verus was indulging in the life of luxury and repose. That same decadent lifestyle is imputed to the emperor upon his arrival in Antioch, where the four-year positive progress of the war is credited to his generals, while their leader pursued his passions with abandon. Indeed, it has been argued that one of the best military qualities of Lucius Verus was that he was perfectly willing to delegate the control of the eastern wars to men who were far more competent than he in prosecuting campaigns. Lucius Verus may well have been given over to the pursuit of luxury, but he seems to have known better than to second-guess the decisions of his commanders, and the result was a significant set of Roman victories.

The author of the Augustan biography of Marcus Aurelius notes that while Lucius Verus was living a life of ease in Antioch, his more conscientious imperial colleague was seeing to all of the affairs of empire (both in peace and in war) from Rome, and was tolerating the inexcusable lifestyle of Verus. The various titles that were awarded to Verus were also accorded to Marcus Aurelius, though out of modesty he at first refused them. The reason why Verus returned to Rome when he did is given as the fact that he had been warned that his colleague would seek sole credit for the prosecution of the war – another of the many slurs against Verus in the ancient biographical tradition.

Nisibis – the modern Nusaybin in the Kurdish-dominated region of south-eastern Turkey (Mardin Province, very close to the Syrian border) – was held in Roman hands for some time after this war. It had been captured by the great republican commander Lucullus – another would-be Alexander in some regards – and also by Trajan. Ctesiphon was returned to Parthia yet again. No new provinces were created as a result of this new Parthian War, which if anything was a dramatic reinstatement of something, at least, of the *status quo ante bellum*. Marcus Aurelius and Lucius Verus did not harbour any apparent dreams on a par with those of Trajan. We may surmise that the busy Legio III Cyrenaica returned to Bostra in Roman Arabia, ready to resume its defence of that quiet corner of the empire, and perhaps to engage once again in public works and deferred maintenance.

We must mention at this juncture one of the most amazing events in the diplomatic history of Rome. The year AD 166 is famous in the annals of Roman foreign policy for the record in the *Hou Hanshu* of a Roman embassy to the court of the Chinese emperor Huan. A Roman delegation thus reached ancient China in 166, at the climax of the Parthian War. It is an extraordinary footnote in the history of an extraordinary age of foreign conquest, one where the achievements of Roman commanders would have earned the commendation, we might think, of a Trajan. It is also a reminder of the fundamentally economic nature of Roman involvement in the East: the region was valuable for securing trade and commercial routes to India and the Far East. Parthia was a competitor power in the economic conflict that ran parallel to any military considerations, and as the taste for luxury items in Rome grew, the need to secure eastern trade grew ever more important a desideratum.

Avidius Cassius, as we have seen, was to be awarded an extraordinary command over Roman forces in the East – a natural enough consequence of his performance in the war, and perhaps inevitable given that Lucius Verus intended to return home to Rome. He would remain more or less secure until the dramatic events of AD 175, when he would respond to the false news of the death of Marcus Aurelius with his fatal bid for power. Lucius Verus, for his part, would be back in Rome certainly by the end of summer in 166, his Parthian War having ended on favourable terms for Rome.

Marcus Claudius Fronto was another Roman general on Verus' eastern staff; to him is credited the Roman assault on Osroene. Publius Martius Verus would survive the war and live to help to suppress the Cassian revolt of his one-time colleague in arms.

Mesopotamia returns as a focal point of Roman military attention in the Severan Age. The revolt of the Syrian governor Pescennius Niger had created Mesopotamian problems principally because of the support that had been accorded to Niger's adherents by various players in the region – notably such buffer parties between Rome and Parthia as Osroene, Adiabene and the Scenite Arabs. The defeat of Niger in AD 194 did not spell the end of the problem in Septimius' eyes; he sought to strengthen his position in the East by a determined march against those who had sided with his rival claimant for the throne. In 195, Septimius Severus would do what Trajan before him had inaugurated: he would launch a campaign into Mesopotamia, seeking, some ancient sources would assert, the same sort of glory as his predecessor.

Once again we are indebted to the epitomes of Dio, whatever the problems inherent to that source material. Book 75's summary reports that Osroene and Adiabene had revolted against Rome and laid siege to Nisibis, but Septimius defeated them. However, after Niger's death they are said to have sent emissaries to Septimius, asking for credit for what they had done, asserting that their actions had been aimed at those who supported Septimius' rival. In addition to their demands for favours, they were not willing to abandon fortified positions that they had captured – a *casus belli* was thus established, and Septimius was resolved to make war on his Mesopotamian enemies yet again.

Septimius crossed the Euphrates in AD 195 and nearly lost much of his army because of the harsh desert conditions and lack of water. A dust storm added to the hardships. Water is said to have been found at last, and because they had been so thirsty, they were apparently helpless as to what to do with nature's boon – until Septimius drained a cup of water in their presence and showed them how to drink. Septimius finally arrived at Nisibis, which he used as a base whence he sent out numerous commanders (Lateranus, Candidus and Laetus are named by Dio's epitomizer) to launch attacks in three directions against his foes. This was the occasion for the aforementioned episode where the (Scenite) Arabs sent emissaries with peace offers, all of which were rejected because they had offended Septimius by failing to come to him in person.

Septimius was like some divinely sent presence in the region: the Scythians, we are told, contemplated attacking the Roman position, but while they were planning their assault, thunder and lightning struck and killed three of their leaders, thereby ending what might have been a Scythian War.

Further tripartite attacks were sent out from Nisibis, with appreciable success. Septimius is said to have boasted that he conquered a vast territory that aided the defence of Syria – an assessment that Dio's epitomizer contradicts, noting that Septimius' conquests in the region were nothing but a source of constant war and incredible expense to Rome. In an amazingly prescient analysis, we read that the capture of these immense lands yields very little in benefits, at great expenditure – and that now the Romans are compelled to fight the battles of the neighbours of the Medes and the Parthians, rather than their own.

The appraisal is harsh. Septimius Severus had set out for war simply in pursuit of glory, and while significant victories were achieved under his auspices, the result in Mesopotamia was, in the end, perhaps not very much. To be sure, Septimius had defeated a serious uprising in the Niger campaign. He had intelligently reorganized the Roman province of Syria by his astute and probably long-overdue division of the territory, and he had enriched Roman Arabia – an appropriate gesture given the loyalty and long tranquillity of that distant realm. He had punished the supporters of Niger and had demonstrated the power of Roman military might in distant corners of Mesopotamia. And unlike Marcus Aurelius and Lucius Verus before him, he had further plans for the reorganization of the Roman East that were reminiscent of what Trajan had once set in motion.

The usurper Clodius Albinus was a more pressing concern for Septimius at this juncture, however. In the autumn of AD 196, Albinus prepared for his short-lived gamble for empire. That gamble would end at the Battle of Lugdunum on 19 February 197. Septimius Severus was certainly arrogant and vaunting in the wake of the victory: he rode his horse over Albinus' dead body, and his family – initially pardoned – soon joined their ill-fated relative in death. The head of Albinus was sent to Rome, together with a letter to the Roman Senate that chastised them for their support of the would-be usurper. Lugdunum was essentially sacked, and those who had in some way or other supported Albinus suffered greatly.

One wonders if Septimius Severus was profoundly irritated that his western rival had forced the interruption of his Mesopotamian campaigns. Certainly the ruthlessness of Septimius in the prosecution of the Albinus affair is a black mark on the emperor's record – though it could be argued that he was interested in shoring up his position against any future internal uprising. The Septimius who is said to have praised the savagery of Sulla, Marius and Augustus in contrast to the clemency of Pompey and Caesar is a chilling figure, though not without humour. In defence of his predecessor Commodus, Septimius is said to have noted that the senators mocked and derided Commodus for slaying beasts in the arena with his own hand, while one of their own number was in the nearby harbour district at Ostia with a prostitute who imitated a leopard. Senators were also accused of buying the golden helmets that Commodus – the imperial gladiator – had worn in his fights. The hypocrisy denounced by Septimius was no doubt valid in its import, even if the severe measures taken by the emperor could be denounced as extreme. Of course it was also an extreme age. Dio's epitomizer further notes that thirty-five senatorial supporters of Albinus were actually pardoned, though twenty-nine others were executed.

We have speculated that perhaps the emperor was displeased at the interruption of his Mesopotamian exploits. Certainly – and not surprisingly – while he was tending to the civil war with Albinus, the Parthians began to run amok again in the East. Dio's epitomizer notes that they launched a full-scale invasion of Mesopotamia, perhaps counting on the fact that Septimius might never return to his old battle haunts. Nisibis was nearly captured. The year was AD 198, and Septimius Severus was soon back in Mesopotamia and at Nisibis. The Parthians retreated upon the news of his advent; they apparently had no interest in a pitched battle against their former conqueror. Seleucia and Babylon were abandoned, and Septimius launched his own lightning attack, capturing both territories. He reached Ctesiphon, and the celebrated city was once again seized by Roman forces.

Septimius is said to have afforded his men free rein to plunder the city. Over 100,000 captives are said to have been taken, with many killed. We are told – perhaps somewhat astonishingly – that once again Ctesiphon was abandoned.

The year AD 198 would be that in which Septimius Severus would achieve the title that had been enjoyed by Trajan: *Parthicus Maximus*. It was, in fact, awarded on 28 January of that year. Anthony Birley (page 130) notes that it was exactly 100 years since Trajan had assumed the purple.

Trajan had failed to capture the fortress of Hatra. Septimius may have been inspired at least in part by that previous debacle, for either in AD 198 or 199 he was prepared to assault it himself. However, his siege engines, we are told, were burned, many Roman soldiers were killed and even more were wounded. What Trajan had failed to accomplish deep in Mesopotamia, Septimius would also fail.

There is an interesting literary detail from this war. A military tribune by the name of Julius Crispus was apparently frustrated at the prosecution of the campaign. He quoted verses 371–73 of Book 11 of Virgil's *Aeneid*, where the orator Drances (some have seen in him an allegory of Cicero against Mark Antony) made a sarcastic comment that the Latins were fighting against Aeneas' Trojans so that the commander Turnus could marry the princess Lavinia. It was a learned quip, spoken by a man well-versed in the poetry of Rome's premiere Augustan poet. It also cost Crispus his life – Septimius had him executed for his recital of Virgil.

By the later months of AD 198, Septimius was determined to finish what he had failed to accomplish in the siege of Hatra. This required the construction of many more siege engines and the preparation of large stores of supplies for the intense desert siege. Once again, at first the emperor succeeded in losing large amounts of expensive equipment, and many more soldiers. One can imagine something of the frustration of an Alexander at Tyre or Gaza – ancient sieges were always supremely annoying to active, great military minds. Enemy cavalry constantly assailed the Romans, providing mosquito-like attacks that hampered Roman progress and whittled down Septimius' force. Archery was employed effectively, even against some of Septimius' own bodyguards. Those Roman soldiers who drew near the walls of Hatra fared the worst, assaulted as they were by bituminous naphtha (we may compare the perils faced in another, more republican age during Lucullus' Mesopotamian campaigns).

Finally, the outer circuit of Hatra's defences were breached. At this juncture, Septimius showed supreme, indeed admirable (some might think) restraint. His men – no doubt as frustrated, if not more so, than he – wanted to rush in to assail the site. He held them back, offering a respite for what he assumed would be voluntarily sought terms for surrender. Hatra was, after all, reputed to be exceedingly wealthy; he expected that the inhabitants would be willing to come to terms to avoid enslavement.

However, during the ensuing night given over to peace, the wall was repaired. The next day, Septimius ordered his men to attack again – it was obvious that the defenders of Hatra were not aware of Septimius' intentions, or that they had no intention of surrendering. Dio's epitomizer describes at this juncture an interesting miniature mutiny in Septimius' army, complete with ethnic slur. He notes that the Europeans in Septimius' army were angry; they would no longer obey the emperor – and, besides, they were the only part of the army that was competent. The Syrians in the army had to make the assault on their own, and given their incompetence, they were slaughtered by the enemy. The epitomizer interprets these events as the judgment of heaven: Septimius could have taken Hatra, but he refused to finish the job at the critical moment. Later, when he wanted to sack the city, his own men refused to support his initiative. Septimius is said to have been told by one of his associates that with 550 of his European soldiers, he would finish the job. The emperor is reported to have asked where he was supposed to find so many men – a clear condemnation of the mutinous men who overheard the remark. If Septimius hoped thereby to goad his men into completing the mission, he would be disappointed yet again.

Hatra (and its king, Barsemius) survived, and Septimius proceeded to Palestine, where he is said to have sacrificed to Pompey's ghost. One wonders if he regretted his earlier criticisms of Pompey in his senatorial communications. He travelled on to Egypt, and would have visited the southern border with Ethiopia, we are told, had there not been an outbreak of pestilence. He also – extraordinarily and tellingly – locked the tomb of Alexander, wishing that no one henceforth would gaze on the body of the man he had sought to emulate. Our sources are not clear on the exact disposition of affairs in Hatra when Septimius left. Reading what survives of Dio, one might well think it was all a total failure. But it is also possible that at least a token Roman force was left behind.

The years AD 198–199 were those spent in the reorganization of the Roman East that we have discussed in connection with the Roman conquest of Arabia. Parts of Syria Phoenice were added to that favoured Arabian province.

Herodian is another source for Septimius' Mesopotamian War, indeed our only other continuous account of the campaigns. At 3.8.9, he notes that one pretext for the whole affair was that Hatra had supported Pescennius Niger. Septimius is said to have contemplated an assault on Armenia, which was forestalled by gifts and lavish presents that were presented to him. Abgar, the king of Osroene, is said to have handed over his children as hostages of his good faith – and he also supplied auxiliary forces. Septimius is said to have crossed Mesopotamia and the territory of Adiabene, and to have hurried on to Arabia Felix – that difficult passage that we have discussed above. The siege of Hatra is described next, including the detail that the defenders filled clay pots with stinging insects that they used against the Roman assailants. The insects are said to have crawled into the eyes of the soldiers (some scholars have argued that the reference must be to arrows, not insects). Most of the army died from extreme heat rather than battle wounds. Herodian notes that Severus retired rather than see the destruction of his entire army. There is thus no report of the mutiny of the Europeans during the second siege of Hatra. Indeed, in Herodian's account there is only one siege of Hatra, not the two recorded in the epitome of Dio. Herodian records that the men under Septimius were upset at the lack of success against Hatra, having been accustomed to achieving victory in all their endeavours. Whittaker wonders in his Loeb annotations to Herodian if Septimius was not actually present for the first siege of Hatra, noting that it is not clear why there would have been two in relatively quick succession. Herodian claims that the Romans did enjoy good fortune, however, since after the failed siege of Hatra they embarked on ships and were not carried to the Roman bank of the river, but to the Parthian – thus affording them the chance to besiege Ctesiphon. Herodian claims that the Parthians were not even aware of the assault on Hatra, when they soon found themselves under attack; the Romans were able to plunder the region successfully and to capture the city. The women and children housed there were captured, while the Parthian king (incorrectly named as Artabanus instead of Vologaeses) narrowly avoided the same fate. In Herodian's estimation, it was purely by 'tyche' – the Greek concept of luck or fortune – that Septimius succeeded in earning his Parthian glory.

Herodian's account is impossible to reconcile with that of Dio's epitomes. Scholars have made some attempt to account for the chronology of events and the exact route followed by Septimius in his eastern campaigns. The Augustan 'life' offers some help here, though not much. The 'life' records that he set out for the campaign (i.e., in AD 197 after the defeat of Albinus), first putting on a gladiatorial show for the populace. Many were executed, however, on charges both false and true (including for making jokes such as mockery of his name – *Severus*, as in the Latin adjective from which the English 'severe' is derived). From Brundisium, Severus is said to have proceeded to Syria without any interruptions. Near the end of summer, he is said to have invaded Parthia, having captured Ctesiphon as winter was drawing on – the biographer notes that wars are better prosecuted in that region in the winter (owing no doubt to the relief from the heat), though the soldiers are compelled then to eat grass roots and thus contract sickness and disease. The Parthians put up stiff resistance, and the soldiers suffered gastric complaints. Ctesiphon was still captured, and the Parthians driven into flight. Upon his return to Syria, he is said to have refused a triumph because his arthritis would not allow him to stand in his chariot. There is word in the 'life' of some action for which he was awarded a triumph over the Jews – this is a matter of mystery. There is also a detail that he banned conversion either to Judaism or to Christianity – scholars have questioned these religious edicts, though there is no good reason to doubt their possibility.

What we can be relatively certain of is that there was essentially no Parthian resistance to Septimius in places such as Seleucia and Babylon, and that even the great city of Ctesiphon was only lightly defended. Avidius Cassius had done significant damage in this region years before, and it is clear that the Parthians had never fully recovered their territory in terms of manpower and perhaps even will. Septimius failed to capture the Parthian king, but he captured immense amounts of wealth and treasure from the sack of Ctesiphon. All told, AD 197 was a year of enormous successes for the emperor. Albinus had been defeated in the spring, and by the end of the year, the Parthians were on the run.

We cannot be certain as to Septimius' intentions in this period, but we do know that there is definite evidence of tensions in the army. We have already mentioned the death of one soldier for quoting lines of Virgil's *Aeneid*. Another soldier who faced execution in this period was Julius Laetus, who had served with distinction both in the East and at Lugdunum in AD 197. Laetus had been responsible for the defence of Nisibis from Parthian attack the same year. The epitomizer of Dio claims that Laetus' fall came after men refused to fight unless Laetus led them, and that Septimius sought to deflect responsibility for the murder onto his men; he was evidently viewed by some (if not Septimius himself) as another would-be rival for supreme power. Certainly others were killed in this period for suspected loyalty to Pescennius Niger. The emperor was busy not only with the Parthian War, but also with providing a more stable base for his own rule over the empire. Septimius allegedly killed Laetus out of mere jealousy, and this may well be true. But he had more than ample justification for paranoia given recent imperial history.

Frustratingly, Herodian is not much interested in the Severan settlement of the East. He simply reports (3.9.10) that the administration of each territory was arranged as was dictated by the circumstances. Severus then proceeded to depart for the last time from Syria, making his way to visit the armies in Moesia and Pannonia before finally returning to Rome. Adventures in Britain still awaited the aging emperor; his campaigning days were by no means at an end.

We are ignorant of the exact date of the reconstituting of Mesopotamia as a Roman province. Trajan had established it, and Hadrian had instantly abandoned it. Severus would again imitate his 'best' predecessor by restoring it. It was probably all accomplished sometime in AD 198 or 199, in the aftermath of the great victories of 197. We know from inscriptional evidence that one Titus Claudius Subatianus Aquila served as the first prefect of Mesopotamia, before being stationed to a similar post in Egypt. We also know from our poor surviving sources that Severus defended his new province with three legions, I Parthica, II Parthica and III Parthica. We know that the Legio II Parthica was stationed at Singara, with which we may compare Mount Sinjar in Iraq, made infamous because of the atrocities of the Islamic State of Iraq and the Levant in 2014. Singara was thus to the south-east of Nisibis, and served as a northern point of defence for Severus' province.

Septimius Severus was also responsible for the fortification of the province of Arabia Petraea as part of his defence and reorganization of the Roman East. The vast desert frontier was ultimately to be guarded by a series of forts along the so-called *Limes Arabicus*, or 'Arab border'. The forts and outposts were not designed so much to withstand the attacks of large-scale powers, but rather the desert brigands and marauding, pillaging desert threats that occasionally emerged to hamper Roman commerce.

Significant work has been done on the question of the border defences of the Roman Empire by ancient historians and archaeologists. The editor of the Loeb Herodian, C.R. Whittaker, authored a work, *Frontiers of the Roman Empire: A Social and Economic Study* (Baltimore–London: The Johns Hopkins University Press, 1994), which can be recommended as a good start to a vast subject. David J. Breeze has authored the Pen

& Sword study *The Frontiers of Imperial Rome* (2011), with extremely detailed coverage of the subject (Chapter Nine is devoted to the desert borders of the empire). Breeze offers coverage of the inscriptions found in modern-day Saudi Arabia that attest to the detachments of the Roman legion in Bostra (in contemporary Syria) that were evidently stationed at outposts along the border; the little bases were apparently spaced about a day's march apart, which allowed for relatively rapid movement in response to crises. Breeze notes that the main legionary base was probably at Bostra so that it could respond as reinforcement to Parthian crises in more northerly regions. While the base there could house the entire legion, it seems there were always units absent on border patrol duty. The Via Nova Traiana was located next to the border defence network, which was thus able to provide ready assistance to protect commercial traffic. It was no doubt a highly organized system that attests to Roman efficiency in developing and guarding Arabia. Septimius Severus was concerned with both the conquest of his enemies and the protection of his empire, and he devoted significant time and resources to the management of the later challenge.

By the time Septimius left the East, it was in a far better position from the Roman point of view than it had been in some time. As was perhaps inevitable – certainly as had been seen so often before in the long history of the empire – once the emperor had departed to attend to other problems (he would die in AD 211 in York, literally on the opposite end of the Roman world), the slow progression toward problems would commence again. The Roman position in the East would not remain indefinitely at peace, and a son of Septimius would soon be back to the scene of his father's magnificent achievements.

Chapter 7

Septimius Severus

The crisis of AD 193 was parallel in one aspect to that of 175: there was a would-be governor of the powerful province of Syria who hoped to attain the purple of imperial rule. That governor was Pescennius Niger, who evidently aspired to do better than his unlucky predecessor Avidius Cassius. The winner of the latest crisis in Roman imperial management would be Septimius Severus; he was extraordinary for his management (in person) of military operations that extended from Britain to Arabia. Septimius was among the most tireless emperors in Roman history. He fought enemies both foreign and domestic, and along the way found time for the duties of the administration of government and the maintenance of the empire he preserved and won by masterful application of the Roman sword. Like many other exceptionally talented emperors in Roman history, he was mostly unlucky in family matters. He would leave behind two sons, Geta and Caracalla, as his successors: the former would not long survive his father, and would die as a victim of fraternal enmity, while Caracalla would go on to be one of the worst of Roman emperors, a far drop in quality from the talents and spirit of his storied father.

Septimius Severus earned his purple by triumphing in the chaos that followed the assassination of Commodus. Rome entered a period of crisis that would be stabilized by Septimius' success and acumen. His reign until AD 211 would be violent in terms of the extent of military activity across diverse regions of the empire, but it would also be marked by tremendous victories and an expansionist imperial mindset that rivalled the days of Trajan. Still, in 193, Septimius was but one of five men who aspired to rule the bequest of Augustus' Rome.

The five emperors of AD 193 include Pertinax and Didius Julianus, as well as the rivals Septimius Severus, Pescennius Niger and Clodius Albinus. There is no evidence whatsoever that Arabia Petraea was sympathetic to Pescennius Niger. Indeed, Glen Bowersock (page 113) notes the inscriptional evidence attesting to the twin facts that the governor in Arabia in 193 during the reign of Pertinax – one Publius Aelius Severianus Maximus – was retained in office by Septimus Severus, and that the Legio III Cyrenaica received the special title *Severiana* – clear enough indications that Arabia had remained loyal to Septimius. A legionary title and the retention of a governor are impressive signs of favour and rewards for fidelity – but far more significant is the evidence that Septimius planned a reorganization of the Roman East that would in the end favour Arabia. The basic problem was simple and had long been discernible: Syria was too large and too powerful a province, and one too many governors there had grown eager to demonstrate that they could exercise power over the entire empire. Fergus Millar (page 122) notes that 'The reason for the division can be regarded as certain, namely to limit the forces available to any one *legatus* in the Near East to not more than two legions.' Herodian (2.7.4) writes that Syria was the largest province of its time, encompassing the entirety of Phoenicia and everything as far as the River Euphrates. Herodian, we might note, also criticizes the Syrians as being by nature given to reckless and erratic behaviour, fickle and of untrustworthy disposition (2.7.9). For Herodian, it was not surprising that the province would support Pescennius Niger against Severus – especially considering that Niger had a reputation for being a mild and generally easy-going governor.

We are not entirely sure of all the main players in the Roman East in the drama of AD 193. Publius Aelius Severianus Maximus was governor in Arabia, and his actions in the crisis occasioned by the death of Pertinax are not entirely clear. If he did support Niger, his favour was short-lived and of little significance. We also do well to remember that communications were often slow; it is uncertain when this or that governor/legionary commander became aware of news from the West. Syria, whatever the case, would pay a high price for the revolts of first Avidius Cassius and then Pescennius Niger.

Syria would be divided into two provinces, and the territory of Arabia would be enriched at the expense of Syrian land. Niger would survive into AD 194, before decapitation and the sending of his head marked the end of his efforts to be emperor. Syria was divided sometime the same year, or possibly very early in 195: the new territories were Syria Coele in the north and Syria Phoenice in the south, the latter of which was now the direct neighbour of the province of Arabia.

Pescennius Niger was Septimius' eastern rival; in the West he faced Clodius Albinus (Septimius is reported to have quipped that he was caught between the 'white' and the 'black'" with reference to the meanings of the Latin names *Albinus* and *Niger*. Clodius Albinus was finally defeated in battle in AD 197 at Lugdunum (modern Lyon) in southern Gaul. According to the author of the 'life' of Septimius in the *Augustan History*, the Arabian legion – the Legio III Cyrenaica – is said to have switched sides from Septimius to Albinus at some point before the climactic battle. Scholars have found the report to be highly suspicious, especially given that the very same legion had remained loyal during what might be thought to have been the far more tempting period of Niger's ascent. Bowersock (page 117) wonders if a report had been put out by Syrian supporters of Albinus that the legion had defected as part of a campaign of misinformation aimed at demoralization. Septimius was defeating Albinus in the West; word would have arrived that he had another problem on the opposite side of the Roman world. Bowersock at any rate considers the besmirching of the reputation of the Legio III Cyrenaica to be an entirely false tale.

Septimius certainly added territory from his newly constituted province of Syria Phoenice to Arabia. We have reason to believe that Septimius visited his Arabian province in person; he carried out significant fortification of the desert outpost. The mention of a visit of Severus to Arabia, however, leads to a confusing fact about some of our ancient sources. The Greek historian Herodian (who was born around AD 176/177) composed a history of the empire from the death of Marcus Aurelius to the accession of Gordian III in 238. At 3.9.3 of his history, Herodian asserts that Septimius visited Arabia Felix (i.e., south-western Arabia). We have no other record of such a visit, and the detail is indicative of a frequent ambiguous use of 'Arabia' in our sources (though here, 'Arabia Felix' is either a true, striking blunder on Herodian's part, or a testament to very extensive Severan travels indeed). Herodian places this visit to Arabia Felix as part of Septimius' great campaigns against Parthia after the defeat of Pescennius Niger. Herodian even explains the name 'Felix', connecting it to the aromatic spices and perfumes for which the region was famous. All that said, we do well to remember that there was indeed a functional land route in this period all the way to modern Yemen (i.e., Arabia Felix). It was immensely long and a no doubt quite difficult journey, but then again Septimius Severus was one of the most indefatigable imperial travellers in Roman history, and he lived to see many a remote corner of the empire. Without additional evidence we cannot be sure what exactly to make of Herodian's claim – but we might do well to note that it is very difficult to believe that Herodian did not know where Arabia Felix was located. Roman officials were stationed, as we have seen, as far south as the northern Hejaz of modern Saudi Arabia, and there is evidence that Arabs – both urban and desert dwellers – began to take their place in provincial government and local administration under the reign of the great African emperor. 'A few Arabs of uncertain provenance, emerging in the senate during the third century, may also have come from the more outlying parts of the Syrian and Arab territories,' writes Bowersock (page 118). Trajan had established the Arabian province, and Hadrian had visited it – only soon to be distracted by the serious crisis of the Jewish rebellion. But it would be Septimius Severus who would significantly reorganize the region, and who would fully integrate Arab families into the mechanisms of Roman provincial government. It may in some ways be considered the heyday of Roman Arabia. One imagines that Augustus would have been pleased with the developments in his romantic backwater of would-be imperial conquest and peace.

There were, of course, prices to be paid for the extensive military adventures of Septimius Severus. He was relatively rarely in Rome. Fergus Millar (page 121) notes that, 'When Severus celebrated the beginning of the tenth year of his reign in Rome in 202, he had spent at least half of it either in Syria or on campaigns across the Euphrates.' Septimius Severus is among the best examples of the slowly evolving reality in Roman imperial history that where the emperor was, there was the capital or seat of empire. Rome was not as significant as it had been in the days of Julius Caesar and Augustus; a global empire had other foci of power, and Syria was among the most prominent.

We may consider some additional sources on Roman involvement in Arabia in the Severan Age. Sextus Aurelius Victor, the fourth-century author of a collection of imperial biographies from Augustus to Constantius II (the *De Caesaribus*), speaks of how Septimius attacked the 'Arabs' and reduced them to a province: '*Neque minus Arabas, simul adortus ut est, in dicionem redegit provinciae modo*' (20.15). The reference is to the establishment of a Mesopotamian province, not to anything concerned with Roman Arabia proper (again, the vagueness of the appellation is striking). Eutropius (8.18.4) has the same confusion: '*Arabas eo usque superavit ut etiam provinciam ibi faceret*' ('He then conquered as far as the Arabs so that he could make a province even there'). Festus (21) too reports '*Arabas interiores obtinuit et Arabiam provinciam fecit.*' The author of the 'life' in the *Augustan History* reports that Septimius received the submission of the Arabs (18.1). In reality, there was no 'Arabian War' (at least strictly speaking), but the conflict Septimius waged against Parthia did offer a suitable occasion for the reconstitution of the borders of Rome's eastern provinces.

Septimius Severus is in many ways an enigma, though his treatment of Roman Arabia follows a logical and coherent path. Arabia was no longer a 'new' province, but the great Trajan had established it, and all subsequent emperors sought to emulate their renowned predecessor. Arabia had been peaceful, and had apparently conducted itself in a way that commended it to Septimius' favour during the potentially quite serious Niger revolt. Arabia was a wealthy region with attendant glory and romance. It was also relatively easy to maintain, at least based on the record of the past century: it had remained loyal under not one but two Syrian crises, and had helped to supply troops to suppress the Jewish emergency under Hadrian. Arabia was, in short, a province that more than paid for itself. In the cost-benefit analysis of Roman provincial administration, Arabia was in the black, a positive entry in the roster of imperial expenditures.

Further, we do well to remember that Septimus Severus was married to one of the most famous women in the later history of the empire, the remarkable Julia Domna. She was born at Emesa in Roman Syria (the modern-day Homs), to an Arab family. Septimius thus had significant family reasons for his interest in the whole region. Bowersock (page 114) notes the inscriptional evidence of a dedication set up by a soldier of the Legio III Cyrenaica in honour of the emperor's wife. Bowersock (page 118) sums up the new reality of late second/early third-century AD Rome: 'And thus, in an astonishingly short time, through the influence of the house of Septimius Severus, Arabs reached the pinnacle of Roman government.' It is no surprise, we might conclude, that Septimius enriched and enlarged the province at the expense of its more unmanageable, difficult northern neighbour.

Strict geography aside, Septimius did receive the title *Arabicus* in AD 195; to be precise, he was accorded the title *Parthicus Arabicus*, since the reference in the name was not to the Arabs of the Roman province of Arabia Petraea, but to subjects of Parthia to the east of the Euphrates who surrendered to Septimius. At the same time, the title *Adiabenicus* (again, technically *Parthicus Adiabenicus*) was bestowed on Septimius; the Adiabeni were an ancient Assyrian people. There were no fewer than three Septimian victories in battle in 195, for which he was thrice acclaimed *imperator*. Whatever the initial reaction of the Arabs and the Adiabeni, there was certainly fighting at some point for which Septimius merited his titles of military glory. The epitome of Dio says that Severus attacked the Adiabeni and the Arabians out of a desire for glory. An interesting detail about the emperor's mindset that is also preserved in Dio's epitome is that the Arabians at one point did not secure their reasonable offers because they sent envoys to Severus rather than visiting him in person. One develops the impression that Severus was a fundamentally reasonable man who quickly lost patience with those who gave offence or seemed to fail to realize and appreciate his generosity. In the final appraisal, he more than merits his reputation as one of the finest rulers of the empire.

For further material on Septimius Severus and his reorganization of the East, we may note the biography of Anthony R. Birley, *Septimius Severus: The African Emperor* (London–New York: Routledge, 1999, a paperback version of the 1988 Batsford revision of the 1971 Eyre & Spottiswoode original). Barbara Levick is the author of *Julia Domna: Syrian Empress* (London–New York: Routledge, 2007, part of the publisher's 'Women of the Ancient World' series). Pat Southern has a lucid history of the entire period that commences with *The Roman Empire from Severus to Constantine* (London–New York: Routledge, 2001). Highly to be recommended too is Nathaniel J. Andrade's *Syrian Identity in the Greco-Roman World* (Cambridge, 2013), with useful historical and ethnographic material. On all aspects of Septimius' involvement with Arabia, the masterful study of David F. Graf, *Rome and the Arabian Frontier: from the Nabataeans to the Saracens* (2018 Routledge reissue of the 1997 Ashgate original) has helpful material.

Among ancient sources, the history of Herodian is most conveniently accessible in a two-volume Loeb Classical Library edition by C.R. Whittaker (Volume I, 1969; Volume II, 1970), with extensive annotations and bibliographical references. In his volume on Septimius Severus (page 204), Birley memorably appraises Herodian: 'He has always had his fanciers, or defenders, but he was careless, ignorant, and deceitful, a self-concious stylist who wanted to write a "rattling good yarn" and happily adjusted the facts to achieve readability and excitement.'

We lament the loss of Septimius Severus' autobiography. Marius Maximus also composed an account of the emperors from Nerva to Elagabalus; he may have been contemporary with Septimius Severus, but his work is regrettably also lost.

Chapter 8

Caracalla

The emperor we know best today as 'Caracalla' is a good example of the confusing nature of Roman nomenclature. He was born Lucius Septimius Bassianus or Julius Bassianus, then as a child he was renamed Marcus Aurelius Antoninus as part of his father's dynastic plans. The name 'Caracalla' is derived from that of a Gallic hooded cloak that the young emperor popularized. We do not know for sure who his mother was: she was either the famous and celebrated Julia Domna or Septimius' first wife Paccia Marciana.

For all of Caracalla's life, and especially his military career, the Finnish historian Ilkka Syvänne has provided an extensively detailed, rich volume *Caracalla: A Military Biography* (Pen & Sword, 2017). This lavishly illustrated book provides an excellent resource on all details of the young emperor's life. Syvänne is open to the possibility that Caracalla was in fact the son of Septimius' first wife.

In terms of ancient sources, as for the father, so for the son we are indebted – more or less – to epitomes of Dio, to Herodian and to the 'life' in the *Augustan History*. The fourth-century Roman historians add some small details here and there to supplement the record.

Caracalla succeeded his father Septimius after the latter's death in York in February of AD 211. At the time of his accession he was joint emperor with his slightly younger brother Geta, with whom his relationship was quarrelsome at best (Syvänne argues that the sibling rivalry between the brothers is in part possibly explained by their having different mothers). Geta would in fact be murdered before the end of the year, and Caracalla would be in sole command of the empire. The surviving epitome of Book 78 of Dio commences with the note that Caracalla essentially commenced his reign in sole power; Geta was an irrelevant inconvenience. Caracalla's first major foreign policy decision was made almost immediately after the death of his father: he ended the war in Britain.

Such a pacific start to his reign was not to be repeated. Caracalla was destined to fight wars on both the northern and the eastern frontiers of the empire. It is his eastern wars that concern us as regards Roman Mesopotamia and Arabia, territories his father had left reorganized and largely tranquil in the wake of the great wars of the last years of the second century.

The spectre of Alexander the Great had haunted both Trajan and Septimius Severus, and it seems to have captivated Caracalla too. Unlike those previous emperors, Caracalla had the seeming advantage of being roughly the same age as Alexander. Born in Lugdunum in AD 188, Caracalla was only in his twenties when he assumed the purple. The dreams of Alexandrian conquest must have haunted him in those years, and perhaps he even had a Philip-like relationship with his father: the young Alexander was chomping at the bit, as it were, to outdo his aging sire.

Dio's account imprints a military character on Caracalla's rule from the start. He addressed the soldiers in language that assured them that he was one of them (and indeed, he had spent most of his life to that point in the camp and on the march with his father's military entourage). He offered them the customary donatives and presents to earn their favour and support. Septimius' revered memory certainly favoured his son; Julia Domna was also still a quite powerful presence in her own regard.

The appraisal of Caracalla's character that survives in Dio is an unremittingly negative one. For Dio, Caracalla possessed none of the virtues of his mixed races. He was bloodthirsty, ordering the deaths of many for trivial reasons, and given over to indulgence in the blood sports and beast hunts of the arena. He was in this sense a second Commodus, another inferior son to a great imperial father.

And throughout, there was the Alexander obsession. Dio's epitomizer notes that he created an actual phalanx of 16,000 Macedonians, which he referred to as 'Alexander's Phalanx'. He persecuted those philosophers who were devotees of Aristotle, on the grounds that Aristotle had been implicated by some in the poisoning of his one-time pupil. He was obsessed with using weapons and cups that were said to have belonged to his Macedonian mentor from beyond the grave; he was fond of elephants, in emulation of both Alexander and the great wine god Dionysus, who, like Alexander, had travelled to India. Macedonians were favoured above all others in the empire. Caracalla was determined, in brief, to replicate the spirit and deeds of the immortal fourth-century BC warlord.

Book 4 of Herodian's history does not do anything to improve the reputation of Caracalla. Here, he is a man of violent temper, one who preferred to rule by intimidation and threat rather than by persuasion and cajoling. He was obsessed with war and the world of arms.

It seems that Caracalla may have spent much of AD 212 – the first year of his reign – in his capital of Rome. There he established his power by both excessive flattery and presents to some, and the sword and ridicule to others. He left the city early in 213 at the latest, destined never to return. We cannot be sure of the exact whereabouts of the emperor for all of the busy months of 212 and early 213, but by the spring of 213, he was being hailed as *Germanicus Maximus*. (Syvänne thinks that Caracalla moved out of Rome much more quickly than our ancient sources would have us believe; he posits a departure for Gemania Superior early in 212).

Caracalla's first military exercises were conducted on Rome's northern frontier. He went to Gaul sometime early in AD 213; most of that year was spent in dealing with the threats on that long border. Military activity probably started even before the end of 212; certainly war preparations did, if not actual military engagements and victories. It seems that from the start, Caracalla simply intended to follow the Alexander model and launch a war against the East – if any emperor to date intended to destroy Parthia utterly, it was Caracalla. The Germanic campaigns of 213 were a prelude to this, which some scholars have speculated were actually designed to give the young emperor military credibility before he commenced a major war in the East.

There were also numerous very real problems. Rome at present faced – as Syvänne recites in grim catalogue (page 155) – 'the Franks, Alamanni, Chatti, the tribes of the River Elbe, the Marcomanni, Vandili (Vandals), Quadi, Goths, Dacians, Sciri, Bastarnae and Sarmatians'. From west to east it was a dizzying, near overwhelming roster of foes. The Rhine and Danube borders were almost constant sources of stress and strain for overtaxed Roman resources.

The German War was not only an opportunity for military glory and the pacification of Rome's northern borders. It was also a chance to recruit auxiliary forces (especially cavalry) for Caracalla's principal, eastern ambitions. Herodian (4.7.3) notes that Caracalla won the loyalty of the Germans and established not only military units but also a personal bodyguard recruited from their ranks; he also began to adopt northern styles of dress (cf. the infamous *caracallus* or hooded cloak whence his most popular appellation) and wore a wig of blond hair to emulate the

Germans – all of which won his popularity with the northerners. The soldiers of the Roman legions loved him too, mostly because he gave them generous pay, but also because he shared all duties with them and was moderate in his personal habits. He was ready to grab a shovel and join in the commonest of duties, shirking no work in the life of the army camp. He sometimes would even take up the legionary standards himself and carry them for long distances (no small task that). He preferred to be called their fellow soldier rather than their emperor.

In all of this, the lessons of Alexander had been absorbed. If there is a positive side to the depiction of Caracalla in our ancient sources, it is to be found in the conduct of his army life. Arguably (at least in Herodian's estimation) the best thing that had happened to Caracalla was his decision to depart from Rome; the army, it would seem, suited him well.

At some point in AD 213 or 214, Caracalla was back in Rome before his departure east. During this period, preparations were apparently in full operation for the planned campaigns.

Things soured a bit in his military reputation, we might think, once Caracalla actually proceeded toward the East. Herodian (4.7.8) says that as soon as Caracalla entered Thrace and Macedonia – the very soil of his revered hero – he began to act in a less than rational manner. The Alexander obsession took over completely, even to the setting up of ridiculous artworks where the head of an image would be biform, half Alexander and half Caracalla. Alexander now began to dress like a Macedonian of old, and he ordered his men to start to assume the names of Alexander's generals. Men were recruited from Sparta so that the new Alexander could have a Spartan cohort. Caracalla was planning to invade the East in exactly the same manner as his grand idol.

Needless to say, upon his arrival in Asia, Caracalla at once made for such sites as the tomb of Achilles – a visit that occasioned his wish to find some young man who could play the Homeric role of Patroclus to his Achilles. Herodian (4.8.4) records that a freedman of the emperor by the name of Festus died while they were at Troy. The story went about that he had actually been poisoned so that the new Achilles could have a Patroclus to mourn. Herodian adds that Caracalla greatly admired Sulla and Hannibal alongside Alexander – ominous infatuations indeed. Dio gives the detail that he sought out the tomb of Sulla and ordered it to be repaired.

Herodian's travel itinerary for Caracalla has him visiting Antioch, and then – of course – heading to Alexandria in Egypt, the city where he could gaze on the body of Alexander. The visit to Alexandria, we are told, had another, more savage purpose. The Alexandrians were reported to have been making fun of Caracalla – one imagines that they were amused at the associations the young Roman emperor was making between himself and their central tourist attraction figure. Caracalla, simply put, ordered a massacre. In typical rhetorical flourish, Herodian (4.9.8) says that the mouths of the Nile ran red from the great quantity of blood that poured forth from the mass slaughter. From Alexandria – his diverse purposes accomplished – the emperor returned to Antioch, ready to commence his great Parthian War.

For Herodian, this was yet again a case of an emperor seeking nothing save glory, an expedition that was designed to give an excuse for more honours and praise to be heaped upon the ambitious young man.

Dio's epitomizer (Book 78) gives a little more information about the early preparations for this campaign, especially the events that likely occurred in Rome in AD 213–214 (the interlude between Caracalla's German and Parthian engagements). Essentially, tensions developed between Rome and the client kings of Osroene and Armenia. Abgarus of Osroene is said to have behaved insolently toward his subjects, simply for the sake of his own power and dictatorship. His claims that he was merely seeking to have them adopt Roman customs fell on deaf ears (at least at home). Caracalla suggested a meeting, ostensibly on friendly terms; the king was instead arrested and imprisoned. Caracalla attempted the same trick against the Armenians, who responded more violently. The Armenian king in question is sometimes identified as Khosrov I, a Parthian royal. Khosrov is a somewhat mysterious figure. He was in power from 198–217, during the difficult years of Septimius Severus' war in the Near East. He was a neutral party in many regards between Rome and Parthia, it would appear – though he was ultimately a client king of Rome, placed under Rome's protection by Septimius. The reasons that provoked Caracalla's deposition of Khosrov are unknown. He was held in his Roman detention from 214–216. What is certain is that Caracalla's action provoked a significant uprising in Armenia, which may, after all, have been the emperor's intention.

Syvänne (pages 197–98) does an able job of trying to ferret out the truth concerning affairs in Armenia at this time from a study of both Dio's epitomes and Armenian and Georgian sources. He concludes that the king who was deposed by Caracalla was actually Tigranes/Tigran, a monarch who – if Syvänne's analysis is correct – enjoyed a long reign of some forty-two years before he was removed from office by Caracalla.

The epitome of Dio mentions that there was a 'Tiridates' who fled to the court of the Parthian king Vologaeses, thus instigating trouble with Caracalla – it is possible that this Tiridates is one and the same with Tigranes/Tigran, the Armenian king.

If it seems confusing, it is – but the chessboard of Parthian politics is reasonably clear. The Armenians were a wildcard in any internal struggles of the Parthian Empire. There were two rival claimants to the Parthian crown – Vologaeses and Artabanus. The Armenians were a potential source of support for one or the other. Like Osroene, Armenia (as another of the smaller players in the deadly game) needed to be eliminated first to simplify affairs. The ultimate plan was to absorb Armenia and Osroene, and then to appear to support Artabanus against Vologaeses. The fact that Armenia may have been inclined to support Vologaeses made the ruse all the more logical and effective in its execution. In the end, the goal was the complete conquest of Parthia. *Divida et impera* was thus practised on a grand scale by this son of Septimius, and it is possible that through the shadowy picture cast by our garbled and confused sources, a quite credible and bold plan was in the works.

For Caracalla was clearly practising deceit with Parthian monarchs. According to Herodian (4.10.1 ff.), in this busy period Caracalla also wrote to the Parthian king Artabanus IV or V, requesting a marriage of state with his daughter as a means of uniting the two great neighbouring empires by a nuptial union. Caracalla essentially proposed a grand alliance, one in which Romans and Parthians together would achieve global domination by invading all those powers not yet subjected to either of the two greatest empires.

At this juncture we should note that Herodian completely omits any reference to the serious internal divisions in the Parthian Empire that plagued the realm in this period. Artabanus was in serious rivalry with Vologaeses V or VI for control of the empire; Vologaeses was at Ctesiphon, and Artabanus in Media. According to Dio's epitomizer, Caracalla was delighted at this situation, in particular because he appreciated the notion of brother fighting brother – the image resonated with him not only because of his fatal quarrel with his own brother Geta, but because of the tradition of fratricide at the commencement of Roman history in the story of Romulus and Remus. Caracalla is even said to have told the Roman Senate that the dissension between the Parthian brothers would undermine and destabilize Parthia, as if this were a negative thing – in other words, Rome needed Caracalla to solve the crisis in the East. In attempting to solve that crisis,

Caracalla had taken clear sides in the internal Parthian dispute: he was favouring Artabanus over Vologaeses. According to what remains of Dio, one of the pretexts for war was that Vologaeses was harbouring enemies of Rome. The conflict between the brothers Artabanus and Vologaeses had clearly been a serious strain not only for Parthia, but also for such buffer states as Armenia and Osroene. Caracalla certainly took full advantage of the situation.

Artabanus was the younger of the Parthian princes, and thus in the inferior position of revolt against Vologaeses. The Parthians under Artabanus are said not to have welcomed the offer of a marriage alliance. The response was that Rome and Parthia did not share a common culture, a shared language or clothing (they evidently were not aware of Caracalla's penchant – in imitation of Alexander – of adopting local dress). The Parthians were not interested in mixing races; they wanted to preserve the purity, as it were, of Parthia and of Rome. The whole matter constituted an interesting reversal (at least in part) of the attitude displayed by the Persian king Darius toward the idea of a marriage alliance with Alexander.

Caracalla was not offended by the rebuff – he simply sent presents and pressed his case yet again. The Parthians this time agreed to the union, and an announcement was made that the two powers would soon be joined by a family tie.

Caracalla was thus able to cross the Tigris and the Euphrates 'in peace', as it were. We are not sure exactly where Artabanus was as Caracalla made his way to his prospective father-in-law – he was probably at Arbela, the modern Erbil in the Kurdistan region of modern Iraq, not far from where Alexander the Great had won his great victory over Darius in the Battle of Gaugamela. Celebrations were set in motion everywhere along the route for the grand wedding celebrations, and – just as in Alexandria – trickery and deceit were the order of the day. Artabanus would barely escape with his life, since Caracalla had apparently planned all along for a massacre of the Parthians. An attack commenced at once, and the surprise nature of the assault enabled Caracalla's men to wreak havoc against their enemy. The king survived, but his relatives and those of the Parthian nobility who supported him were cut down in a single action.

It is an incredible story, one that nearly defies belief. The epitome of Dio's Book 79 offers a different, more sober version of events. There it is recorded that Artabanus did not fall for Caracalla's tricks; he realized that the proposed marriage alliance was really nothing more than an excuse for the Roman emperor to seize the Parthian realm at a single stroke.

He thus refused the marriage plan, and in response Caracalla invaded Media and ravaged the countryside, capturing Arbela and desecrating the nearby royal tombs of the Parthians. The Parthians did not engage Caracalla, and the Romans were able to run amok unopposed.

It is very difficult to decide which version of events is the correct one. The dramatic story of the wedding ruse reported in Herodian may well have a basis in reality. It may be worth wondering just how Caracalla reconciled his apparent ready use of trickery in light of his Alexander fascination; one cannot imagine the Macedonian conqueror resorting to anything like what is reported in Herodian. Here we see a clear case of the problems inherent to source criticism, with the accounts in Herodian and Dio exceedingly difficult if not impossible to reconcile. The biography in the *Augustan History* provides only the scantiest of details with respect to Caracalla's wars, and offers no help with the Artabanus problem.

In Herodian's account, the aftermath of the Arbela massacre was unremitting plunder and looting that lasted literally until the Roman army was exhausted from slaughter and pillaging (4.11.8). The Senate was duly informed of the alleged great victories that the emperor had won over the Parthians. According to Herodian, the true story did not manage to escape the attention of the senators; the historian observes that everything done by an emperor is eventually discovered. All the same, the customary honours and triumphs were decreed for the would-be Alexander. Caracalla began to indulge in chariot racing and hunting pursuits, his great campaign at a pause if not a *de facto* conclusion. Surviving coins attest to the celebration and honour in commemoration of Caracalla's Parthian victory.

We have noted that according to Dio's epitomizer, the Parthians did not even challenge Caracalla over the conquest of Arbela. Indeed, Dio offers little in the way of information about the campaign, giving the excuse that the Parthian failure to engage Caracalla meant that relatively little happened worthy of note. There is a seemingly absurd story about two soldiers who came to Caracalla for his judgment in a dispute over a wine skin (Syvänne, page 251, draws attention to the interesting parallel of the story of Solomon from the Hebrew Scriptures, and wonders if there is evidence here that Caracalla was familiar with the Jewish lore).

In Syvänne's appraisal (page 252), the actions of Caracalla succeeded in keeping the Parthians divided – Vologaeses was given a new lease of life by the destruction of Artabanus' support – and the Parthian Empire was kept in a weakened, divided state. The Augustan 'life' does say that Caracalla advanced through the territory of the Cadusii and Babylonia,

a report that has occasioned ridicule from some scholars. Caracalla
allegedly engaged in guerilla warfare against scattered bands of Parthian
opposition, even employing wild animals against his enemies. We cannot
be sure, but there is no good reason to think that Caracalla did not indeed
wish to visit Babylon (again, the Alexander legend may be relevant) – and
Caracalla certainly faced a disorganized enemy that could provide little
in the way of effective resistance.

What survives of the epitomes of Dio notes that the Parthians and the
Medes did begin to assemble a large force to oppose Caracalla, and that
he was at once filled with terror in the face of actual risk. He began to
suffer the effects of the desert heat, being easily exhausted and unable
to endure much in the way of hardship. He continued to wear German
costumes and shoes in Syria and Mesopotamia, and ordered his men to
don the *caracallus* that he considered especially fashionable. The soldiers
under Caracalla were living increasingly dissolute lives, the Parthians
heard; the luxuries and ease of existence occasioned by plunder were
taking a toll on battle-hardiness and martial reliability.

It is a confused account, not made easier by the fact that there are
serious gaps or lacunae in the existing text of the epitomes. There are
strange tales, too: a lion is said to have run down from the mountains and
fought on Caracalla's own side in a sign of favour. Caracalla is said to have
fought in unusual and unprecedented ways, but other than the references
to wild animals employed in combat, there is regrettably no detail in
what survives of Dio's account.

Syvänne (page 255) offers a positive appraisal of Caracalla's military
operations in Mesopotamia: 'He achieved far greater success with far fewer
losses than Trajan and his father Septimius Severus ever did, and one
can only guess at what he would have achieved if he had been given a few
more years to live.' Syvänne argues that even the treachery of Caracalla
toward his would-be father-in-law Artabanus served a purpose, creating
such a resolve to fight that Artabanus did exactly what was in the Roman
interest – prepare for a pitched battle that would allow for a decisive
Roman victory.

This analysis is at odds with the account in Dio that Caracalla was
worried when he received news that the Parthians were massing – but our
ancient sources, as we have seen, simply cannot be reconciled. Both Dio and
Herodian move on quickly to the inevitable end of Caracalla, his assassination
in AD 217 and the accession of his prefect Macrinus. Perhaps appropriately
given the disaster that had been visited upon the Roman republican

general Crassus in the same region, the end would come near Carrhae in Mesopotamia, in the modern Harran in Turkey. According to Herodian (4.13.3), Caracalla wanted to visit a temple of the moon goddess Selene that was not far from the town, and decided to travel there with a few cavalry so as not to disorganize his entire armed force. The assassination came en route, when the emperor suffered from a stomach ache and needed to relieve himself by the side of the road. The assassin was a centurion named Martialis, who was angry because his brother had been executed a short time before, while he himself had been insulted by the emperor, taunted with being a coward and friend of Macrinus (whose relationship with Caracalla had taken on some of the fatal characteristics of that between Caligula and Cassius Chaerea in a previous age). Martialis would not survive the daring, fatal assault on the emperor; he was cut down by Caracalla's German cavalry bodyguards. Macrinus hurried to the site of the assassination and is said to have pretended to mourn the emperor whose death he was complicit in, while the army in general is said to have been in a state of extreme grief over the unexpected death of a man they had come to appreciate for all his bad qualities.

Word soon arrived that there were critical problems at hand: Artabanus had organized what we might call a revenge force that was bearing down on the Roman position. The Romans needed a commander if not an emperor; Macrinus was eventually selected as the man for the job. Artabanus arrived on the scene soon enough, ready to fight. His army, according to Herodian, consisted of a great cavalry force, many archers and armed riders who fought from camels with long spears to avoid the hazards of fighting at close quarters. Artabanus initiated hostilities in the ensuing great battle, attacking with a cavalry charge under the cover of archer fire. In terms of missile warfare, the Parthians were superior between the arrows and the camel-borne spears. But in melee combat, the Roman legionaries were supreme. It was, it would appear, a classic instance of the exercise of the best fighting qualities of each side – the Romans with their extremely formidable infantry, and the Parthians with their exemplary and fearsome cavalry.

The sheer size of Artabanus' force was at risk of overwhelming even the best of Roman foot soldiers, however, and soon Macrinus' men decided to steal a page from the book of classic Parthian tactics. They pretended to retreat, but the feint was only to allow the infantry to scatter caltrops and other fatal hazards to the Parthian force. The pursuing Parthian cavalrymen were severely discomfited by the trick; Herodian records that the camels in particular were much affected by this stratagem because of the soft pads of their feet. Herodian notes that the Parthians did well only so long as they were mounted; they surrendered or otherwise gave up very quickly once they were on foot. Even the folds of their loose clothing hampered their escape or manoeuvrability.

Herodian claims that the great battle near Carrhae lasted for two entire days from dawn to dusk. Both sides were still hopeful of victory. On the third day, the armies reassembled and the Parthians tried to encircle the Roman force. The Parthians certainly outnumbered the Romans, but Macrinus avoided the peril of encirclement by thinning out his ranks so that the Parthians were unable to envelop them. Absolute slaughter ensued in the forthcoming clash of arms, with the field littered with the dead – especially, Herodian notes, the dead dromedaries. The men were prevented from launching effective charges either on foot or on horse because of the clogged battlefield, choked as it was with the slaughter of animals and humans.

Once again the two armies retired to their camps. Macrinus is said to have realized that the only reason why Artabanus was putting up such a hard fight was because he was unaware that there was a new emperor: he thought he was fighting his treacherous foe Caracalla. Macrinus sent an emissary under a flag of truce with a message that explained the situation and announced the death of the man who had so fatally disrupted that marriage banquet at Arbela. Macrinus declared that he was not in support of what Caracalla had done, and that he was prepared to release all Parthian prisoners and make amends for plunder and rapine. Artabanus was in no mood to continue the fight in light of his heavy losses, and the fact that Caracalla was dead made him all the more convinced that he had sufficiently avenged his opponent. He agreed to make peace with Macrinus, and Rome's newest emperor hastily made his way to Antioch.

Thus far we have the account in Herodian of the events of what would appear to be the spring of AD 217, yet once again our sources are confused. The surviving epitomes of Dio offer more in the way of evidence about the events in Mesopotamia in the wake of Caracalla's death (79.26.2). In Dio, we are told that Macrinus was well aware of how angry Artabanus was in the aftermath of his mistreatment, and that he had massed a large army. Macrinus anticipated the trouble by sending prisoners and a note of friendship, announcing his desire for peace and the death of Caracalla – in other words, the exact opposite of what is reported in Herodian, where such initiatives come only after a hard-fought battle. Artabanus, not satisified by Macrinus' missive, demanded that all the demolished Parthian fortresses be rebuilt and that Mesopotamia be entirely evacuated by the Romans. The royal tombs that had been ransacked at Arbela would require restitution too.

According to Dio, Artabanus did not consider Macrinus to be worthy of much respect, and he was also trusting in the immense size of his own military force. Artabanus was not worried about anything: either Macrinus would agree to the terms, or he would be defeated in battle. Macrinus is said to have been on his way to Nisibis when he encountered Artabanus' army. The Romans suffered a defeat: the two sides were apparently encamped opposite each other, and a dispute arose over water supplies. Macrinus is said to have suffered the near destruction of his camp, which was saved only because of the quick action of his baggage handlers, who rushed out against the Parthians and so shocked the enemy by the unexpected assault that they drove them into flight.

There is nothing in what survives of Dio, then, that matches the dramatic description of the *triduum* of fighting in Herodian. There is also a question of date. What seems to have occurred in the spring of AD 217 in Herodian took place more toward the winter of 217/218 in Dio. Certainly the detail in Dio about the water dispute points to a more or less protracted period of peace negotiations, that broke down in a hair-trigger atmosphere and resulted in a full-scale battle. The Romans were effectively defeated in the ensuing engagement, but the quick action of the defence of the camp seems to have rendered the battle a technical draw. Artabanus withdrew, and so did Macrinus.

Macrinus would ultimately buy off Artabanus. Syvänne – who tries admirably and well to rehabilitate the near unremittingly negative picture of Caracalla we find in the ancient sources – argues that regarding Macrinus, 'Caracalla's judgment of the man was spot on' (page 278): he was a coward who was unable to defeat Artabanus. Syvänne speculates that Caracalla might well have been the Roman emperor who would finally defeat the Persians. He notes the rare positive appraisal of Caracalla from an ancient source – the *Liber de Caesaribus* of Sextus Aurelius Victor (24.8), where Caracalla is said to have represented the apogee of Roman greatness. Yes, Caracalla was a master deceiver – but deceit is a part of the art of war, and in that regard Caracalla was one of the most competent and impressive military masterminds in Roman history. Syvänne (page 278) argues that Caracalla belongs to the same class of Romans as Julius Caesar – i.e., men slain by those close to him – and blames his use of deceit against Parthia for the bad press he received from ancient sources. He goes on to note that if a quality of a good commander is to protect and preserve the lives of his men, then Caracalla deserves to be lauded for his tactics, given that by tricking the enemy he secured the safety of his armies. Syvänne is correct that by and large, Caracalla did enjoy the admiration and respect of his men. He was a popular emperor with many of the soldiers, to be sure.

It is not an argument that will win universal acceptance, perhaps, but it does deserve consideration on its merits. Certainly, Trajan and Septimius Severus had done much to lay the groundwork for Roman involvement in Mesopotamia. Caracalla capitalized on the work of his two great predecessors, and on the serious dissension in the Parthian Empire at the time of his accession. Even the hostile traditions in the epitomes of Dio, in Herodian and certainly in the Augustan 'life' point to the significant achievements that the emperor won during his desert treks – achievements that were, to be sure, won in large part because of mendacity and the force of feints. Alexander might not have been pleased with his would-be emulator, but the Romans were certainly in a powerful position in Mesopotamia on the day of Caracalla's fateful bathroom visit near Carrhae.

Caracalla is a difficult emperor to appraise in terms of his dealings with Mesopotamia and the Roman East. The Roman Empire after Septimius Severus was arguably more deeply invested than ever before in the vast expanses of Mesopotamia and Arabia. While Septimius had left behind a stable and remarkably well-ordered system, there were also the twin realities of expense and the weakening of the Parthian Empire that became all too apparent during the reign of Caracalla. The new impetus after AD 211 was clearly to eliminate Parthia entirely and to absorb its empire into Rome's dominions – it was a foolish idea, some might think, a plan worthy of a megalomaniac. But Alexander had of course envisaged similar scenarios for Macedonian expansion, and Caracalla was, after all, aspiring to follow in his footsteps.

We have observed that one of the early stages of Caracalla's involvement in the East was his deposition of King Abgar of Osroene. Osroene (with its capital at Edessa) was an interesting place, and may well merit its title of being the first Christian kingdom in the world. Osroene was absorbed into the Roman Empire as a province, approximately a century after it had become a dependency of Rome during the days of Trajan. There was certainly a significant Roman presence in the region now, shoring up the dual provincial structure of Osroene and Mesopotamia.

Caracalla was assassinated while officially still on campaign against the Parthians, thereby receiving the ignominious distinction of being the first Roman emperor to die under such circumstances. Even after Macrinus suffered his apparent losses to Artabanus, there was no question that Mesopotamia, at least, would remain a Roman province. The Parthian War of Caracalla was a case of a *status quo ante bellum* then, in the end – and that was a consequence solely, we might conclude, of the unexpected death of the emperor. The Battle of Nisibis in AD 217 had ended any dreams of finishing the war on terms completely favourable to Rome, and critics of Macrinus might well have argued that he paid indemnities more or less to see the map revert to its condition on the occasion of Septimius' death half a dozen years before. Macrinus himself would be dead in June of 218, murdered in Cappadocia as the latest short-lived emperor.

The man Caracalla had considered an effeminate coward – his doomed successor Macrinus – is said by Dio to have paid out something like the incredible sum of two hundred million sesterces to buy peace with Artabanus of Parthia. The Parthians were willing to settle accounts with the Romans because of their own discomfiture in terms of lack of supplies and the great distance of the battle front from their homes. Dio adds that Macrinus failed to send an account of what he had done to the Senate, such that at first he was awarded the title *Parthicus* and other honours, as if he had defeated the enemy – honours that he respectfully declined, one of the nobler actions of his life, we might think.

Armenian affairs were all settled in this period. Dio reports that 'Tiridates' received the crown from Macrinus – this would be the son of the king deposed by Caracalla. His mother was released from Roman custody – she would have been one of the hostages held in detention since the removal of the king from office. Armenia was once again a more or less stable client kingdom of Rome, another sign of the restoration of the *status quo*.

Book V of Herodian opens with the account that Macrinus allegedly sent to the Senate details of his actions in Parthia (we may compare Dio's report that there was no such information sent). Macrinus paints himself as successful in having ended a war on terms that were respectable with regard to Roman military might, and peaceful with respect to the relationship with Artabanus. Whittaker interprets the evidence of Herodian as indicating that the result of the campaign was more favourable to Rome than Dio would have one believe; Artabanus did not, in the end, receive so very much in the way of compensation. The Parthians were in a difficult situation at the time of Caracalla's death. Macrinus was arguably in a better position to supply his Roman forces than Artabanus was to provide for his Parthians. Syvänne (page 294) argues that Artabanus reasoned that the new emperor Macrinus would need to hurry back to Rome to defend his uncertain position, thus strengthening the hand of Parthia. Indeed, many a foreign power had realized that one effective strategy was always to wait until the Roman emperor and his large military forced had departed the scene. Biding one's time was a good idea in difficult circumstances.

There is an interesting additional note that should be added here to the story of Artabanus of Parthia. The king had had extensive dealings with both Caracalla and Macrinus, and had emerged on peaceful terms with Rome in the wake of the Battle of Nisibis – whatever the exact circumstances of that struggle. But what Artabanus could not have predicted was that Rome would soon be plunged into another crisis of empire, with the family of the Julias – Julia Domna and her children Julia Soaemias and Julia Mamaea, and the former's son Elagabalus – conspiring to regain the Roman crown for the Severan Dynasty.

The civil war that soon erupted would cost the life of not only Macrinus, but also his son Diadumenianus, his co-emperor for an exceedingly brief time. The son was sent to Artabanus for protection, but was killed en route, joining his father in death. The heads of both father and son would be sent to Elagabalus as trophies to commemorate the accession to power in AD 218 of the boy (he was barely 14 years of age) who would prove to be one of the most notoriously crazy of Roman emperors.

Dio's epitome is clear: the Roman soldiers who helped to overthrow Macrinus did more harm to Rome than the Parthians. The Parthians killed a few Roman soldiers, Dio notes, and overran Mesopotamia. But the killers of Macrinus and his son were responsible for the deaths of many Romans in a new civil war, and they were complicit in the reign of an emperor who did nothing that was not base and disreputable (for a case could easily be made that Elagabalus was the worst of Roman emperors, outdoing Caligula for insanity). In a ruse that was perhaps not surprising at all, the story was put out that Elagabalus was actually the illegitimate son of Caracalla, and thus that he had every right to succeed his assassinated father. Whatever negative appraisal of Caracalla one might hold, Elagabalus certainly made his 'father' seem all the better in comparison.

We may note here that an additional source of information we possess about this period is the 'life' of Macrinus in the *Augustan History*.

The 'life' is a poor source of information about Macrinus' brief Parthian War. It argues that Macrinus suffered from something of an inferiority complex because of his low birth and relatively poor social status; for him, a successful war against Parthia would give him the glory that birth and fortune had not. The 'life' laconically says that after one engagement with the Parthians he was killed in a revolt by the legions, with nothing in the way of detail about the progress of the campaign. The 'life' does go on to make clear that Macrinus been been defeated in the Parthian engagement, since Artabanus was interested in incurring revenge for all he had suffered under Caracalla. The Parthians are said to have been willing to agree to peace principally because that previous emperor was now dead. Macrinus is charged with having pursued a life of luxury in Antioch in the wake of the peace treaty, such that his own assassination was understandable in light of his poor conduct as emperor.

There is also a brief 'life' of Diadumenianus in the same imperial bio- graphy collection. Like that of Macrinus, the Diadumenianus 'life' does not offer much of interest for the study of Rome's relationship with Parthia in this period.

That said, there is one odd detail that must be mentioned in connection with the lives of the *Augustan History*. At *Macrinus* 12.6, there is the briefest citation of the emperor's wars against the Parthians and the Armenians (with no details appended), and of operations in Arabia Felix (in other words, modern Yemen). We have absolutely no information whatsoever about what was going on in southern Arabia in this period. Some might well argue that the anonymous biographer is in error here, and that there was no Roman war in that region – it was not, after all, even a part of Trajan's (or Septimius') province of Arabia Petraea. If it is not an error, then it is a precious detail about the extraordinary extent of fighting in this period in which the Roman military was engaged. Syvänne (page 295) argues, 'My own educated guess is that Macrinus also ended the Arabian war ... mentioned by the SHA [i.e., the *Scriptores Historiae Augustae*] ... at the same time as he ended the Persian and Armenian wars. It is unfortunate that we do not know the result of the war waged in Yemen and on what terms the war was ended.' It is, however, one of the scanty bits of surviving evidence that we possess for continuing Roman involvement in the remote territory that had been the object of the Aelius Gallus expedition so many decades before, and one of the only indications of any military actions in the Arabian theatre during the course of the Parthian War of Caracalla and his successor.

An indispensable guide to the complicated history of the period from AD 217 and the reign of Macrinus (and his ill-fated son) is the Society for Classical Studies/Oxford University Press publication of Andrew G. Scott's *Emperors and Usurpers* (2018). The volume offers historical commentary on the relevant books of Dio 79(78)–80(80), covering the history of Rome between 217 and 229 (i.e., into the reigns of Elagabalus and his cousin and successor Alexander Severus). On the difficult question of whether or not Herodian can be trusted for his unforgettable account of Caracalla's wedding massacre, Scott takes a sober, middle-ground approach.

In different ways, both Caracalla and his would-be successor Macrinus are enigmas. We have seen how by the time the literal dust had settled on affairs in Mesopotamia, things were more or less back to the way they had been upon the death of Septimius Severus. Caracalla had a vision, and a grandiose one, while Macrinus was a more practical man. Polar opposites, they both succeeded in doing something that would ultimately prove ruinous to Rome – they weakened the Parthian Empire. Artabanus and Vologaeses would come to represent the last fraternal struggle in the long and eventful history of the Parthian Empire. Artabanus was clearly the 'winner' in the struggle with his brother, though he never succeeded in destroying him. He would precede him in death, as Parthia – and Rome – faced a new challenge in the years to come. The Sassanian Dynasty of Persia had been born under Ardashir I (who more than earned his title of 'Ardashir the Unifier'), and the Persian revolt within the Parthian Empire would spell the end of the history of that great power.

Caracalla could not have known that within something like seven years of his own death, Parthia would cease to exist. What replaced it would pose an even greater threat to Rome than its predecessor. The responsibility for the rise of Persia must in part rest with Caracalla and Macrinus, the man of action and the man of diplomacy. Unwittingly and largely unknowingly, both men contributed to what would prove to be the ultimate destabilization of Roman Mesopotamia and the eventual weakening of Roman power in the Near East.

In order to appreciate the great significance of the coming of a resurgent Persia, one must recognize the tremendous historical ironies at play. Caracalla – like Trajan and Septimius Severus before him – had aspired to be a new Alexander. Alexander had come to power on a claim that he would avenge the Persian invasion of Greece – indeed, that vengeance would mean taking the war to Persia, and ultimately defeating the Persian Empire. This he did, and with enormous successes that should not be minimized even in light of the ultimate failure of his plans, cut short as they were by his premature death. The Persian Empire had menaced Greece in the classical age of the fifth century BC, the age of such memorable military events as Marathon and Thermopylae. Alexander had vanquished the might of Persia at the Granicus, Issus and Gaugamela. He had devastated the power and majesty of the Persian Empire like no Greek before him had ever really dreamed.

The decline of Persia had been profound, and the rise of the Parthian Empire was a direct consequence of Alexander's achievements and the historical realities that followed his death. Now, after centuries of intermittent conflict and long rivalry, Parthia was splitting apart. That division did not come solely at the hands of the Persians who revolted early in the third century AD, but they were certainly the winners of the chaotic struggle for control of Rome's eastern neighbour. The weakening of the Parthian Empire by almost too successful Roman emperors had engendered unforeseen consequences.

The Persians would prove to be interested in more than mere conquest of their Parthian overlords. They would aspire to nothing less than the restoration of the most glorious days of Persian imperial sway. They would seek to retake the lands that had long before been lost to Macedonian sarissas as well as Roman legionary short swords. Persia would be resurgent, and Rome would in some sense be the new Parthia – an empire in decline, riven by internal struggles as well as unrelenting external pressures (we do well to remember that we have focused in the present work exclusively on affairs in the East – yet the Rhine and Danube frontiers were as vulnerable as ever). But in the final analysis, that ludicrous episode of assassinating an emperor as he happened to be relieving himself by the roadside may well have proven to be the most shattering event in the long-term military history of the empire – the death of Caracalla may have guaranteed that Rome would miss its best opportunity to crush both Parthia and Persia.

Thus, whatever was happening between Rome and Parthia during the reigns of Caracalla and Macrinus must be read in light of the background story of Parthian history, much of which is a mystery. Ardashir was said to have been born in Istakhr, a little over 3 miles north of Persepolis in modern south-western Iran. He seems to have been born around AD 180; there are different accounts of his lineage and background. What is certain is that he would eventually face Artabanus in battle, somewhere in what is today southern Iran. That meeting would end in the death of Artabanus and the beginning of the great success of the Persian uprising that Ardashir led. The name 'Ardashir' means something like 'He who rules in honesty and justice'. It was certainly an appropriately noble sentiment for the first monarch of a new dynasty.

Chapter 9

Elagabalus, Alexander Severus and the Rise of Persia

In one sense it is astonishing in itself that a boy emperor of the nature of Elagabalus managed to reign from AD 218–222. Macrinus had settled the wars in the East, and the new emperor and his family and entourage were no doubt eager to travel to Rome, there to demonstrate in more than one way that the empire was now more than anything a Syrian one. Elagabalus and his family would see to the institution of the worship of the sun god Elagabal, whence the emperor would take his notorious posthumous name – while emperor he was known as Marcus Aurelius Antoninus Augustus.

Once again we are mostly in debt to that trinity of sources: what remains of Dio, the histories of Herodian and the 'life' in the *Augustan History*. The last of these sources is a notorious catalogue of the vices and unimaginably disreputable deeds of the youth, an account whose veracity has been questioned on any number of points – though even if only a small portion of the 'life' were true, it would be enough to condemn Elagabalus as one of the most disgraceful of emperors. If many of the so-called bad emperors of Rome – from Caligula to Nero, Domitian to Caracalla – have enjoyed attempted rehabilitation, the same cannot be said of Elagabalus, whose defenders have been few and far between.

Elagabalus would never return to the Roman Near East. The army was certainly not one of the main focal points of his reign, and military action was not the order of the day. Any observer of the period might have expected that the extreme neglect of military affairs during his reign was enough to create a plethora of problems. And in the Roman East, a new threat was indeed emerging – the nascent neo-Persian Empire.

The Persians under Ardashir defeated Artabanus in April of AD 224 in what is today southern Iran. It is thus clear enough that for the four years of Elagabalus' reign, the situation in the Near East was deteriorating quickly. The Parthians were still in a state of disarray and recovery in the

The Arabian desert into which Aelius Gallus led his forces on his fateful march. (© *Katelyn McGarr*)

Desert landscape, Northern Arabian peninsula. (© *Katelyn McGarr*)

Camels then and now are a ubiquitous feature of the Arabian desert vistas and transport. (© *Katelyn McGarr*)

The royal tombs at Petra in modern Jordan, capital of the ancient Nabataean kingdom. (*carlalexanderlukas via Wikipedia*)

Legionaries of Legio II Parthica c.230 AD. (© *Graham Sumner*)

The Battle of Nisibis by Igor Dzis. (© *Igor Dzis for Karwansaray Publishers, first published in Ancient Warfare III.5*)

Roman tribune, Dura Europos c.230 AD. (© *Graham Sumner*)

Ruins of old Marib, capital of the Sabaean Kingdom near modern Ma'rib, Yemen. (*Tapio at en.wikipedia*)

Remains of the Temple of Awwam, near ancient Marib. (*H. Grobe via Wikipedia*)

Above and below: The Persian Gulf. (© *Katelyn McGarr*)

wake of Caracalla's great expedition. The Persians were on the move, in full rebellion against their Parthian overlords. A transformation was coming over the region, and Rome was not involved during these years; it was more consumed with the sexual proclivities of Elagabalus and the religious tensions inherent in the reign of this devotee of an eastern god even above the cult of Roman Jupiter.

Elagabalus was eventually perceived to be a liability even by members of his own family. His grandmother Julia Maesa arranged that Elagabalus should share power with his cousin, Alexander Severus (the son of Julia Mamaea). Elagabalus was smart enough to realize that there were powerful forces at play (not least the Praetorian Guard) that preferred Alexander to him, and he sought to eliminate his cousin. These efforts failed miserably, and by March of AD 222 Elagabalus and his mother were assassinated by members of the Guard.

Alexander Severus was the new emperor at the age of only 15. He would retain power until his own death in 235 – long enough to preside over the coming of the Persian menace.

Dio was a contemporary of Elagabalus, as was Herodian. For once, both historians are in general agreement about the tenor of times and the challenges of the boy emperor's reign. Dio's history ends in Book 80, which like the other latter books survives only in epitome. Dio's account of Roman history ends on an ominous note, with the coming of Persia. Cassius Dio lived until about AD 235, when he died aged around 80. His history thus continued more or less until his death, and he lived to see through the reigns of Elagabalus and at least most of his cousin and successor Alexander Severus.

What survives of Dio records that Ardashir – in Greek, Artaxerxes – conquered the Parthians and Artabanus in a series of three campaigns. It appears that the final destruction of Artabanus came in the spring of AD 224. These victories were of course in one sense Parthian problems and not Roman ones – but soon enough the Persians were the new neighbours of the Roman East. Ardashir contrived to seize the great fortress of Hatra, according to Dio to employ it as a base against the Romans. He was able to breach the wall, but just like more than one Roman emperor before him, he ended up abandoning the quest of taking the fortress when he lost too many men through an ambuscade. He then swept into Media and Armenia, conquering and threatening his way across vast tracts of territory in conquest.

Admittedly, all did not go his way. He suffered setbacks in his mighty expedition, in part, Dio records, at the hands of the sons of Artabanus.

There was clearly significant resistance to his initiatives of conquest, and he eventually either fled or engaged in a strategic retreat to allow for the planning of a larger force. This very preparation, Dio notes, struck fear into Roman hearts – for Ardashir now had a powerful army poised against Mesopotamia and Syria, and he was given to boasting that he would retake all the old possessions of the Persians right through to Greece. In other words, he aspired to be the Lord of Asia, a more formidable neighbour of Rome than any of the Parthian monarchs before him. By AD 230, he would be at war with Roman military units.

Dio notes that part of the problem was the general lack of order and discipline among the Roman armies in the East, observing that some soldiers were actually inclined to join him and not to defend themselves against Persian attack. Dio records that the military commander Flavius Heracleo was actually murdered by his troops when he tried to enforce traditional army discipline, and that Dio himself was the object of complaints because he governed his own forces in Pannonia with a strong hand.

Once again, the rule of a fool had spelled trouble for Rome. Brewing problems on the eastern borders were ignored while Elagabalus was busy with other pursuits.

Alexander Severus was another boy emperor of Rome, and rather a more successful one than his predecessor – though the bar had admittedly been set rather low. It is a testament to the enduring quality of what had been established by previous imperial administrations that Rome survived the various crises of the third century – anyone studying the period today is left with a strong sense of how overwhelming the various foreign and domestic threats to Roman security were, and how extraordinary some of the emperors of this period were in meeting the challenges of the day. Indeed, Alexander Severus is one of the more fascinating figures to emerge from the shadows of Rome's century of conflict.

Cassius Dio probably lived to see the entirety of Alexander's reign, but what remains of Book 80 covers only until AD 229 – just about half of the emperor's reign. We are left once again for primary source material with Herodian and the lives of the *Augustan History*.

Book 6 of Herodian (6.2.1 ff.) announces the great international threat that would dominate much of Alexander's foreign policy. The governors of Syria and Mesopotamia wrote to Rome with news that Ardashir had struck against the Parthians, defeating and killing Artabanus and absorbing the eastern part of the Parthian Empire into a new Persian kingdom. Numismatic evidence confirms that the coinage that Vologaeses had been issuing at Seleucia comes to a sudden end in around AD 222/223, which points to his defeat too – the two Parthian brothers who were rival claimants to the empire were both defeated by the rising Sassanian Persian Empire. Herodian also refers to other conquests by Ardashir in his subjugation of different parts of the Parthian Empire; certain peoples are said to have been conquered in this period and reduced to paying tribute to the new Persia. The River Tigris was no border for Ardashir; he had crossed the river and invaded Roman Mesopotamia, and was clearly a threat to Roman Syria as well.

It was a set of letters that essentially announced that everything that Trajan, Septimius Severus and Caracalla had established and defended was in peril. The Roman provinces of Syria were directly in the line of attack from Persia; Mesopotamia was merely the first territory on the map to come under fire. The letters to Alexander reported the news that Ardashir was intending to conquer all of western Asia, all the territory of Cyrus and Darius and those other storied names from ancestral Persian history.

The boy emperor and his female family handlers had the first real crisis of the Roman Empire, the stability of which had been dented by the years of neglect of foreign affairs under Elagabalus.

Herodian reports that Alexander was deeply discomfited by the news from the East precisely because he had been reared in peace and the comforts of urban life. This is true enough: Alexander Severus, like his cousin before him, had no previous experience of overseas affairs. Herodian's account would have us believe that Alexander was rather inadequate to the task, and that his response was half-hearted at best. He is said to have discussed the crisis with his advisors, and to have undertaken diplomatic initiatives to try to address the Persian menace. He addressed a letter to Ardashir in which he advised him not to think that the Romans were foes like those he had already conquered. Everyone, Alexander argued, should remain within their own borders, maintaining the *status quo* and refraining from unnecessary military action. Alexander further reminded Ardashir of the victories of Augustus, Trajan, Lucius Verus and Septimius Severus in the region.

It is an interesting list of emperors. Trajan and Septimius Severus certainly deserve to be on any such catalogue of great Roman victors in Mesopotamia and the East, while Lucius Verus had presided over a Parthian War and also earned mention. Caracalla was entirely left off the roster of worthies – an interesting omission. Augustus was of course the 'founder' of the Roman Empire – but as for the East, other than the ill-fated Aelius Gallus expedition to Arabia, he was not known for much in the way of conquest in Mesopotamia or elsewhere in the vast regions under immediate concern.

Ardashir, unimpressed by Alexander's letter, continued his conquests, overrunning Roman Mesopotamia and seizing an enormous amount of plunder. Herodian notes that Ardashir quickly fell under the spell of his seemingly unconquerable martial spirit. The historian offers a *précis* of the history of the region: Darius of Persia had lost his empire to Alexander of Macedon, after whose death the region was the scene of many battles of the wars of succession between Alexander's former generals and commanders. The Parthian Arsaces – founder of the Arsacid dynasty – had been the first to stir his people to rebellion against Macedonian hegemony. The dynasty endured until the times of Artabanus, who had now been defeated by Ardashir. For the new Persian lord, Rome was the obvious next target of imperial conquest.

The bleak news from the East arrived in Rome as a *de facto* response to Alexander's letter to the Persian court. The governors of the eastern provinces were said, not surprisingly, to have demanded that the emperor arrive to address the crisis – by this point in Roman history, it was taken for granted that an emperor needed to lead armies in person against critical threats. Alexander is said to have proceeded to this war with regret and no sense of martial spirit or vigour; there was no interest for glory or conquest.

Preparations were afoot throughout Italy, notably the raising of troops for what was certain to be a tremendous enterprise. Alexander would personally lead an immense Roman force from Italy to the East – Herodian cannot help but say that the emperor looked back on the city with tears in his eyes as he made his departure. The whole scene is one very different from the surviving descriptions of men such as Septimius Severus and Caracalla.

Herodian is not much interested in the route Alexander took. He is said to have visited the Illyrian provinces, where he raised additional levies of men, and then to have proceeded to Antioch. It seems that the year of the departure was AD 231, probably in the spring; scholars estimate that the emperor was in Antioch by the summer.

Alexander once again sent a diplomatic mission to Ardashir, urging him to agree to terms of peace. Herodian records that in response, the Persian monarch sent back 400 of his tallest and most impressive Persians, all adorned in gold and with horses and archery equipment, in an attempt to cow the young emperor into submission. The Persian demands were simple: the Romans must abandon Syria and indeed all of Asia. The traditional borders of the Persian Empire must be restored, right up to Ionia, Caria and the waters of the Aegean Sea. Herodian says that the 400 Persians were seized and divested of their sumptuous accoutrements; they were sent to Phrygia, where they were allowed to live in villages and become farmers. If true, this was clearly intended to ensure that Ardashir would have 400 fewer quality soldiers – and to send a message to the king that his insolence would no longer be tolerated.

Herodian preserves a note about the humanity and dignity of the young emperor: he did not think it right to kill the Persians, since they were not, strictly speaking, combatants. They were merely messengers, and it was punishment enough that they would never be allowed to return home.

As we have noted, Herodian is not much of a fan of providing reliable, precise geographical details: Alexander is said to have prepared now to cross the rivers – that is, the Euphrates and the Tigris. In point of fact, we have no way of knowing if he ever did cross both rivers. He was ready to launch an invasion of Persian-held territory, but is said to have suffered a mutiny at the hands of soldiers who had been based in Egypt, joined by Syrian supporters who were interested in a change of emperors.

We are woefully unaware of the details of this rebellion. Dio, as we have noted, preserves the detail that there were Roman army units who were not interested in fighting against Ardashir and who rebelled against their commanders, even to the point of killing the officer Flavius Heracleo. There was apparently significant and widespread discontent in the military.

The reasons for these episodes of mutiny may lie in the years of relative quiet and tranquillity in the aftermath of the peace settlement of Macrinus with Artabanus. There had been no fighting in the Roman East for some time, and now there was suddenly the prospect of war against a new and fearsome foe. Alexander Severus was no Septimius Severus or Trajan – he was not even a Caracalla or a Macrinus, one might think. The release of the 400 Persians may have also occasioned discontent. His gentle demeanour and calm nature – the lachrymose departure from Rome and openly expressed regrets about proceeding to war – may have contributed to a general air of dissatisfaction with the imperial command. In time of crisis and impending war with an enemy as strong as Persia, Rome did not need a 'nice' emperor who was interested time and again in making peace from a clear position of weakness. The hour called for a dramatic response, a massive application of military force to destroy the Persian threat and restore Roman dominions. All told, in the current crisis it was perhaps not at all surprising that there should be an outbreak of mutiny and open rebellion.

Herodian does not provide much in the way of explanation for how Alexander quelled the uprising. Some men are said to have been punished – the sarcastic wag might ask if they too were pensioned off to be Phrygian farmers – and others were transferred to other military units, where they might be useful, Herodian notes, in responding to barbarian incursions. This is a tantalizingly brief reference to Alexander's evident concern for maintaining security on the other vast frontiers of the empire while he was preoccupied with his eastern campaign, and an ominous foreshadowing of the other serious crises that would face him before he would meet his end.

Alexander reorganized his force and completed what he thought were adequate preparations for the campaign. Whittaker thinks that the preparations to confront Persia occupied most of AD 231, with the actual war commencing in 232.

Herodian is our best source for what happened next – which may give rise to concern among those inclined to distrust a significant portion of what the historian records. Alexander is said to have divided his force into three sections, the first of which was assigned to march north through Armenia and occupy Media. The second Roman army was sent east, with orders to investigate the marshes at the confluence of the Tigris and Euphrates. The third detachment would be commanded personally by Alexander, and would proceed along a more central route. The men in this force were to be the best soldiers the emperor had, presumably because they were destined to face the strongest enemy opposition. In point of fact, we know very little indeed about what this unit did.

On paper at least, the tripartite division of the army was a sensible one, indeed perhaps the best arrangement that one could have conjured to deal with the massive threat. Alexander is said to have reckoned that just as the Romans were admittedly now divided, so also the Persians would have to split up to face three threats at once. Herodian digresses briefly at this point (6.5.2 ff.) to note that the Persians did not have a paid, 'regular' army like the Romans. They were, in short, bereft of a disciplined, trained professional fighting force. When the king had given the order, all men – and sometimes women too – responded to the call to arms as they were. They were experts with the bow because they spent so much time hunting and engaging in related pursuits from childhood. However, they lacked garrisons and permanent military outposts, with everyone returning home as soon as this or that campaign was finished.

Herodian reports that luck and fortune were the undoing of Alexander's well laid plans. The northern force did indeed proceed to Armenia, and succeeded in crossing intensely difficult mountain terrain. This army managed to break into Media and launch destructive waves of attack as planned. Ardashir learned of the incursion, and tried to respond with both infantry and cavalry – but the terrain impeded his horsemen from overwhelming the Romans. Then the Persian king learned that the eastern detachment of Alexander's force was in Parthian territory, wreaking havoc there – the second Roman army was appearing on schedule to hamper Ardashir's plans for conquest. Ardashir was worried that this force was destined to invade Persia, and so he is said to have left a small force in Media to deal with Alexander's northern army. He then proceeded to meet what he considered to be the greater threat from the eastern force, which in the meantime was growing rather lazy and careless because they had met with almost no enemy resistance.

The eastern army, Herodian notes, assumed that the third Roman force under Alexander had met with the main body of Ardashir's army. They believed that Ardashir and Alexander were facing off in the third, central sector of the battle front – leaving the eastern army an easy path to plunder and conquer. Herodian records that all the armies had been told to make a flanking movement into the territory, so that once they had conquered in their individual theatres, they could arrive at an unspecified rendezvous point.

Alexander, however, is said not to have invaded in his sector (6.5.8 ff.). Herodian speculates that he may simply have been afraid, fearful that he would lose his life in a direct engagement with the enemy. Julia Mamaea is said to have been possibly worried about the health of her son, and to have argued that he should not take any unnecessary risks. She maintained that he was an emperor, and that it was the job of others to risk life and limb for him.

The situation is thus reasonably clear, even if Herodian does not provide the details we should very much appreciate. The northern army was doing the best of all, not least because Ardashir had taken his main body away from that theatre in pursuit of what he perceived to be the greatest threat to Persian security. The eastern army was growing lazy because they had seen little of the enemy, and were expecting the support of Alexander's central force.

Alexander's central force, however – hampered by the apparent cowardice of the emperor, coupled with the likely baleful influence of his mother – was doing nothing in support of the campaign. The result is not surprising. The Persians were able to attack the eastern army with the main might of their army. The Romans, encircled by Ardashir's force, were unable to do much because of the overwhelming size of the Persian force. They were transformed from an army on the march into a camp under siege, hiding behind their shields and suffering under a constant volley of enemy fire. Herodian says that the entire army was wiped out, a disaster, he notes, that no one liked to recall. It was a devastating loss, and one which filled the Persians with encouragement that they could indeed break the back of the Roman Empire in the East.

Alexander is said to have received the news of this disaster while he was not in the best of conditions (6.6.1). Herodian reports that he was either suffering from depression or from the inhospitable climate. One wonders how word of the crisis even reached the emperor – evidently some had survived the massacre of the army. Alexander had already suffered from the threat of mutiny, and it is hardly surprising that Herodian says the central force under the emperor's command was incensed with their leader, arguing that he had betrayed the eastern force by not keeping to the plan of attack. If true, the criticism was more than amply justified in the circumstances.

Alexander was battling sickness, as were the troops he had raised in Illyria – the summer climate in Mesopotamia was not helping the dire situation. Alexander decided to return to Antioch in Syria, sending word to the northern army that they should march home too. They had no support now, and the last thing the young emperor and his mother could endure was the loss of another force.

The northern army had been lucky. But now, on the return journey, many of the Roman soldiers who had seen Armenia and Media were dying in the mountains, suffering frostbite as winter set in. Alexander lost a significant portion of his own force on the march back to Antioch, further lowering the morale of both soldiers and emperor.

By the later part of AD 232, then, Alexander Severus had lost the better part of his three armies. One was entirely gone in action against the Persians, while the other two were suffering from the harsh conditions of mountainous winters in Armenia and the deserts of Mesopotamia.

Life in Antioch was, not surprisingly, comparatively much easier. Herodian reports that the emperor's health recovered quickly once he was able to take food and water in abundance. He started to try to pacify his remaining soldiers by generous distributions of money, aware that his reputation with them was by now dreadful. He prepared to mobilize another army, realizing that the Persians had enjoyed a dramatic victory and could be expected to launch another attack at any time.

Herodian at this point offers an interesting detail about the condition of Ardashir's victorious force. Word is said to have reached Alexander that the king had actually disbanded his army, having suffered significant losses in Media, not to mention the high cost incurred in Parthia in the destruction of the eastern Roman force. Many Persian soldiers were dead and many more were wounded. It was not, Ardashir reasoned, the right time to risk even more losses by pursuing the Romans. Alexander had inflicted serious losses on the Persians, checking their progress against Roman Syria. While the Romans had not achieved a victory, Herodian states, at the very least they had scored a technical draw.

Herodian further observes that the number of dead on both sides was about equal; it appeared that the only reason why the Persians had done as well as they had was because they had more men to throw into the campaign. For some three or four years, in fact, the Persians would refrain from any large-scale military operations. The more Alexander heard about the aftermath of the war, the more he is said to have begun to relax and to enjoy life in Antioch. It was increasingly clear that the spring of AD 233 would not bring a renewal of open warfare with Persia.

The very nature of the Persian force made it difficult to muster quickly. Herodian notes that once the men were discharged and sent home, it was an exceedingly difficult process to reassemble them for combat. Therefore, once Ardashir had disbanded his army, one could assume a significant period of rest and recovery were at hand. Alexander and the Romans would have time to recover on the Persian front, which was doubly fortunate as word was now also arriving from the Rhine and the Danube that major problems were afoot from barbarian incursions. Alexander was being summoned to another major war, one in which he would eventually meet his end.

We may compare the account of the Augustan 'life' with what we find in Herodian. The 'life' is complimentary to Alexander. He is said to have proceeded to the eastern war with such discipline that one would have thought that senators and not soldiers were passing through (*Severus* 50.1 ff.). Alexander was beloved of the provincials, and by his men. He was openly interested in emulating his namesake Alexander the Great, indeed of surpassing him – noting to his men that a Roman should be greater than a Macedonian. He had men armed with silver shields and employed a phalanx in imitation of his military forebear. He is said to have won 'many victories' in Persia, as if he were indeed a neo-Alexander.

Like many of his predecessors, he shared in the life of the army camp. He would dine in an open tent, and ate the ordinary food of his common soldiers. At Antioch, he learned that some of his men were overindulging in the luxuries of the city, so he tried to restore discipline and order – in consequence of which he suffered a mutiny.

The differences with Herodian are striking. There is a much more positive appraisal of Alexander, though even in the 'life' the fact of mutinies against his army command cannot be concealed – only the reasons given for the rebellion are different. The 'life' does not in fact provide anything in the way of a serious account of the Persian War. The 'many victories' with which Alexander is credited are difficult to explicate. The 'life' says bluntly (55.1 ff.) that the emperor defeated Ardashir. The biographer reports that Alexander commanded his army in person, directing the action from the flanks and personally encouraging his men. He was constantly exposed to missile fire and to the hazards of combat, and praised and directed the work of individual soldiers while under heavy fire.

In this climactic battle, Ardashir is said to have fielded 700 war elephants, 1,800 scythe chariots and many thousands of horsemen. And yet Alexander routed this mighty Persian cavalry force, driving the king off into an ignominious retreat. At last, Alexander was able to return to Antioch, where he shared with his victorious men the tremendous plunder that had been secured in the campaign. For the first time ever, the biographer notes, Romans now had Persian slaves – for Alexander allowed his men to keep personally whatever had been captured in the war. Ransoms were soon offered by Ardashir for the slaves, since it is said that the Persians were especially hateful of servitude; Alexander accepted the money and paid some of it to those who thereby lost their slaves, with the rest going into the public treasury to help to pay for the tremendous expense of the campaign. Alexander is said to have returned to Rome in AD 233, there to celebrate a grand triumph.

What are we to make of these two strikingly different accounts of the war? Coinage does attest to victory celebrations in AD 233. Alexander is crowned and has the Tigris and the Euphrates at his feet. Imperial propaganda could interpret events in creative ways, after all.

The Augustan 'life' records a purported address of the emperor to the senators regarding the Persian war. Thirty of the 700 elephants of Ardashir are said to have been captured, with 200 killed. Eighteen were led in triumph. Besides the alleged pachyderm victory, Alexander alludes to how 200 Persian scythe chariots could have been displayed in the triumph, but since they were easily faked, the emperor had refrained from including them. One hundred and twenty thousand cavalry are said to have been routed, with 10,000 horsemen killed in battle. Romans were now wearing Persian armour as the spoils of war. The lands between the two rivers – Mesopotamia – had been reconquered. Ardashir fled from the scene of battle and left behind his own standards in his hasty departure. *Parthicus* and *Persicus* were easy titles to award to an emperor who had done so much.

The biographer attests that all of what he reported about the Persian war had been found in annals and histories of the emperor's reign. Some authorities, he admits, asserted that the Persian king was not defeated, and that it was Alexander and not Ardashir who actually fled. There is a reference to a possible betrayal of the emperor by a slave. The 'life' even cites Herodian for the detail that much of the Roman army suffered losses from hunger, cold and disease – but the majority, we are assured, do not agree with this version.

The seemingly wildly disparate accounts, in other words, were already current in antiquity, and the biographer of the Augustan 'life' was certainly aware of the conflicting reports. It may well be that Herodian is largely correct: the Persians were more or less victorious, but it was a classic Pyrrhic victory. Like the Parthians of another age, there were other preoccupations for their king than the Romans, and the losses incurred in the engagements with Alexander's armies had taken a heavy toll. To launch a full-scale assault on Roman Syria would require significant additional preparations, and the bloodletting was sure to be even more intense – too sanguinary a price to pay, we might think, for a Persian king who had also already lost significant resources in defeating his Parthian foes.

If fortune and luck had failed Alexander Severus in some regards, they had also blessed him. The Romans now had other problems to confront on the Rhine and the Danube, and Ardashir was hardly bored as he continued to firm up his rule over a newborn Persian kingdom. By AD 233, it is quite possible that both sides needed a good long rest from Mesopotamian warfare. If Alexander had managed to halt what had seemed at one point to be an unstoppable Persian advance to the Aegean, then it would be easy to commemorate his victories and achievements with coins and triumphs. Augustus had, after all, received the same sort of praise and credit in a prior age for the recovery of the standards of Crassus from Parthia, and even Alexander had done more in the region than Augustus before him.

John S. McHugh has authored a comprehensive Pen & Sword study of every aspect of the reign of Alexander Severus, 2017's *Emperor Alexander Severus: Rome's Age of Insurrection, AD 222–235*. McHugh offers a detailed appraisal of the disparate source material available from 'both sides', as it were. He fixes certain dates that can be considered reasonably reliable chronological markers of events. Ardashir conquered Artabanus in AD 224. For the next three years, he was preoccupied with mopping up the remaining support of the Arsacid dynasty – again, we do well to remember that by the time Alexander and his mother Julia showed up in the East, Ardashir had been fighting nearly nonstop for some years. There is some evidence that Ardashir even carried out military operations in such distant realms as modern Azerbaijan. After this period in the north, the Persians seem to have turned their attention to the conquest of Roman Mesopotamia and more southerly regions. By 232, Alexander Severus was finally on the scene in Antioch with a massive Roman force.

There is a fascinating detail in the *Epitome de Caesaribus* of Pseudo-Aurelius Victor (157) that Taurinus was a rival emperor to Alexander, and that out of fear he cast himself into the Euphrates. McHugh wonders if this otherwise unattested Taurinus was a usurper who died while trying to flee to Persian territory upon news of the arrival of Alexander. What is certain is that there is ample evidence of serious resistance to Alexander's rule; while the young emperor and his mother were not nearly as offensive in their conduct as had been Elagabalus and his mother, there was almost certainly a lack of appreciation for some aspects of the rule of this Syrian overlord and his overbearing mother. With huge armies drafted for the massive campaign, there would have been ample opportunity for unrest and dissension in the army – disagreement of the sort that would have taxed the ability of even the most competent and seasoned of military commanders.

Eutropius (8.23) simply paints the deeds of Alexander as being those of an overwhelming conqueror of the Persians. There are no details beyond the simple report that the emperor engaged in a war against the Persian king ('Xerxes', i.e., Ardashir) and won a mighty victory.

The truth, as often, likely lies somewhere between the opposite poles of interpretation. For a young emperor under the domineering control of his mother, and who lacked any military experience, what was achieved in Mesopotamia was impressive. That said, the army was not impressed with the emperor, and justifiably so, we might think – whatever had been achieved against Persia had been won by their blood and sweat, not by any tactical or strategic brilliance of their emperor. Alexander was seen as having betrayed his own armies, and not without reason. He and his mother would survive the eastern wars to see conflict on another front – but the emperor's reputation by AD 233 was in tatters.

Alexander and his entourage needed to hasten to the northern threat. They did bring with them, Herodian records, help from the results of the eastern campaign (6.7.8): a huge contingent of eastern archers is said to have accompanied the emperor to his western war, mostly from Osroene, with some Parthian deserters and mercenaries who were apparently more eager to sign on with Alexander's Romans than to come to terms with Ardashir's Persians. The bare heads and large bodies of the German foe were said to have been ideal for the training of such an eastern missile force to combat a new threat.

The basic problem that Alexander faced in confronting the German peril was that he had lost so many men in Persia. His mother seems to have suggested the plan that money ought to be spent in an attempt to buy off the enemy, rather than risk any major engagement that would cost even more in men and scarce resources. This was of course exactly the sort of behaviour that displayed stunningly bad optics to an army that already apparently more than distrusted the competence of their commander and his mother. To buy off the enemy was against every tenet of Roman doctrine and tradition; it was an embarrassing gesture that was unbecoming of the armies of the great empire that had just faced such a massive threat in Persia. Coming as it did from an emperor who was already thought to have essentially betrayed his fighting men in the deserts of Mesopotamia, it was all a bit too much to handle.

Alexander was losing control of his army, and whatever tendencies he may well have had to be gentle, less than autocratic rule did not help. Was he indeed tutored in Christianity in Antioch by such a theological luminary as Origen? Was he indeed given by disposition and inclination to dislike the clash of arms? Whatever the rationale behind his actions – and simple cravenness and servitude to his mother no doubt played major roles in the whole matter – Alexander was doomed probably before he even arrived in Germany. He would be assassinated – together with his mother – at a meeting with his generals on 19 or 22 March AD 235 in Moguntiacum (the modern Mainz). It was a military coup, plain and simple – and it was a military coup that was long in the making, one might think. The man who would replace him as emperor – Maximinus Thrax – represented a dramatic swing of the pendulum from the world of the Syrian emperors. One could not, in fact, imagine a greater contrast between emperors.

Maximinus Thrax was, as his name indicates, a Thracian. He was of low birth, a man who in the eyes of the senatorial aristocracy would have been considered a barbarian and little more. He had risen through the ranks of the Roman army, and thus enjoyed the battlefront credibility that came from a lifetime's service in the army. According to the Augustan 'life', he was a shepherd and a bandit leader before he joined the military.

Nevertheless, the opening of Book 7 of Herodian records that Maximinus attempted an almost overnight transformation of the Roman Empire, one that would now be marked by his bloodthirsty character and naturally savage disposition. He is said to have suffered something of an inferiority complex, all too conscious that he was considered by many to be beneath the glorious heights of Roman supreme power. Our sources agree that he was physically an extremely imposing, tall and powerful man. He was given over to the exercise of discipline and harsh military judgments. He was already in his 60s when he took power, and he would reign for something like three years until his downfall in AD 238.

Those were years during which the new emperor was compelled to address the German crisis that had been unfolding in the last phase of Alexander's rule. In a fascinating detail, however, that has emerged from the pages of archaeology, scholars working in the Golan Heights region of occupied Syria in the spring of 2019 announced the discovery of a Roman milestone that bears the name of Maximinus. In a garden in Moshav Ramot, the name of the emperor was found on a cylindrical mile marker. Gregor Staab of Cologne used paper rubbings to decipher the monument and uncover the name of the first emperor of what is sometimes called the 'Crisis of the Third Century' (some would say the crisis started earlier than Maximinus, for example with Elagabalus).

The mile marker evidence is an extraordinary indication of the efficiency and cohesion of the empire even in a time of crisis. Maximinus never launched any campaigns in the East, and he was more than busy with affairs in Germany and threats to his own regime – the very threats that would end in his destruction. Roads were clearly being repaired and renovated during these years, however, and the emperor's name was duly recorded on the refurbished or new mile marker in what is today occupied Syria.

McHugh (page 243) asks the key pertinent question about the events of AD 235: how did Alexander Severus manage to hold on to power for as long as he did? Admittedly, there was no serious disturbance that he was aware of until probably around 228, but in all he managed to hold on to power for over a dozen years, with half of his reign spent in comparatively serious turmoil, with crises on both perennially troublesome Roman fronts. There are parallels between the downfall of Alexander and that of Macrinus. In both cases, the army clearly yearned for a serious commander who was bold and brilliant, someone who would lead them to glorious victories in the East and the North. In some sense, Maximinus would fulfill some of that wish, and his conquests in Germany are impressive to study.

We may now proceed to consider the situation in Roman Mesopotamia in the years after the assassination of Alexander. Maximinus may have been honoured on a mile marker, but he never dealt with any eastern crisis. The situation in the East, however, was in some sense deteriorating with every passing year.

Chapter 10

Persia and the Crisis of the Third Century from Maximinus Thrax to Philip the Arab

The year AD 238 spelled the end for Maximinus Thrax. His appreciable victories in Germany and at least temporary resolution of the problems Rome faced on its northern borders were greeted with the news that there was open rebellion to his rule in the wealthy and comparatively stable province of Africa Proconsularis.

The aged governor of that province would be the emperor known to history as Gordian I, and his son would be Gordian II. The story is in some sense one of the usual tales of provincial corruption and greed. There was discontent over the extortions being practiced by a lower official in the province, and before long he was murdered and Gordian was proclaimed the new emperor. There is obviously a story behind the revolt, and the seeds of the rebellion no doubt lie in the unpopularity of Maximinus with the nobility throughout the empire. The Senate never appreciated him, indeed never had any real respect for this barbarian monarch – and the aristocracy in Africa was likely equally unimpressed with a man they clearly considered to be a Thracian thug.

In order to have been even considered, let alone chosen to be a new emperor, Gordian must have been seen as part of the opposition to Maximinus. Clearly, the procurator who was assassinated because of alleged extortion was on the 'wrong side' of the growing divide between emperor and nobles. The problem was complicated, however, by the fact that dissension in the empire was significant. The governor of Numidia, for example, hated Gordian and his family, and was more than willing to use his single legion to march on Africa and deal with the rebellion. Gordian II was destined to die in battle, and Gordian I would commit suicide when he learned of his son's death and the fighting between the legion from Numidia and the militias that were defending the African capital of Carthage.

As soon as news of the African problem reached Maximinus, he was on his way to Rome – where the Senate, which had sided with the Gordians, could expect no mercy from their battle-hardened enemy. The Senate decided to nominate two of their number as co-emperors – we might think of the classic republican arrangement of the joint consuls – but Pupienus and Balbinus were destined to be short-lived emperors indeed. Some, however, in Rome preferred the grandson of the Gordians – that is, the future Gordian III – and there was soon fighting in the streets over the question of who should be supported as emperor in lieu of Maximinus. Pupienus and Balbinus decided to compromise with the Gordian faction by declaring Gordian III to be Caesar to their Augustuses – but meanwhile, Maximinus was still on his way to Rome.

Maximinus was murdered in May AD 238 by soldiers of the Legio II Parthica. The city of Aquileia in the extreme north-east of Italy had refused to open its gates to Maximinus in his march toward Rome, and during the ensuing siege of the city there was discontent among the army. Maximinus' son Maximus was also killed. The year 238 was thus one of six emperors – Maximinus, Gordian I, Gordian II, Pupienus, Balbinus and Gordian III – and the old one-time shepherd and bandit leader now joined the first two Gordians in death. Half of the emperors of the latest 'long year' of multiple emperors were thus dead before the year was even half over.

We may mention one interesting episode in the history of this period – the case of the military units which had been brought back from Osroene for use in the German campaigns. We have relatively little information about apparent trouble, indeed rebellion among these archer forces. Herodian (7.1.9 ff.) is our main source, although some relatively meagre information can also be collected from the *Augustan History*. It would appear that the contingents from Osroene were less than happy about the death of Alexander Severus, and when they found a suitable candidate in a friend of Alexander's who was of consular rank – one Quartinus – they resolved to support him in a bid for the purple. We do not know exactly when this episode took place; it may have been a revolt of at least half a year or so, perhaps if not likely in AD 236. Quartinus was murdered in his sleep one night by a certain Macedo, a supposed friend of Quartinus who had been a former commander of the Osroene contingent. According to Herodian – who is indeed our only source of knowledge about this assassin – Macedo had absolutely no reason for his evident hatred of Quartinus. He assumed that Maximinus would be greatly pleased by the killing, and so he decapitated Quartinus' body and took the head to the new emperor. Maximinus was indeed happy about the murder, but he still ordered the execution of Macedo – after all, he had been one of the ringleaders and orchestrators of the Osroene plot. Maximinus was also displeased that a friend would backstab a friend in such a way. (We might think of the reaction of King David to the news that someone had agreed with Saul's wish to kill him – David could not countenance that anyone would dare to raise their hand against the anointed of God, and Maximinus could not tolerate a false friend.)

Osroene had thus figured in some small way in the history of the brief reign of the man who never launched an eastern campaign of his own. There is some evidence to corroborate the scant literary record, with indication that the Osroene unit was indeed disgraced. Herodian reports that the episode left Maximinus even more embittered and hateful than he was already naturally disposed to be; the would-be revolt of the archers only hardened his resolve to inflict severe military discipline on his forces.

After the death of half of the emperors of the 'Year of the Six', Pupienus and Balbinus were literally left to squabble between themselves. Pupienus had assumed control of the campaign that was planned against Maximinus, while Balbinus remained in Rome to maintain order. After the Aquileia siege and the death of the Thracian emperor, the two senators quickly came to argue about their power. There were joint suspicions and recriminations – and the Praetorian Guard finally put an end to the division. They were both killed in the summer of AD 238, on 29 July, with Gordian III thereby the winner of the lottery of half a dozen imperial candidates. Having been born in 225, he was at the time of his accession the youngest sole Roman emperor in the history of the empire: just 13 years of age, younger even than the notorious Elagabalus.

In one sense, despite the Praetorian Guard assassination of the two quarrelling senators, Rome was more in 'republican' hands than it had been for some time. Maximinus Thrax clearly represented the voice of the army, indeed of the common soldier – a fickle audience that had proven more than ready to turn on the emperor from its own ranks. Gordian III was in no condition to rule the empire, but the powerful aristocratic families of the Roman nobility were. Gordian III was a constitutional monarch of sorts, a figurehead for some, a boy who was no doubt thought to be easily manipulated.

Gordian would reign for six years – not a bad record in the dark period of the crisis of empire. But the problems in the East that had haunted his young predecessor Alexander Severus had not been resolved. Rome's attention had been diverted by the great internal imperial crisis of AD 238, and of course Maximinus had prosecuted major wars in Germany. In the meantime, the Persians were regrouping, rearming and preparing for the next stage of the execution of the dream of Ardashir – the conquest of all the lands that had traditionally been held by the Persians of antiquity.

Herodian's history of Rome closes in its eighth book with the coming of Gordian III. The very last sentence of the work announces the salutation of the boy as custodian of the empire. Herodian would be one of the few sources to speak well of the otherwise seemingly unremarkable Pupienus and Balbinus, noting that they had deserved their power and brief reign. The *Augustan History* is a source for the emperor's life – indeed, there is one surviving biography of the 'Three Gordians' – and it announces simply that war erupted with the Persians, probably around AD 241. Gordian – still a teenager – married before he departed to conduct the Persian War in person. His wife was the daughter of Timistheus, the praetorian prefect, and the biographer notes that the emperor now had the wise counsel of his father-in-law.

The *Augustan History* is hardly a reliable source for the progress of wars and military affairs. Even where it does try to describe them, it rarely provides much in the way of detail. Gordian is said to have opened the gates of the Temple of Janus to mark the commencement of a great war – he could not have known that it would be the last time in the history of the empire that this would be done. The army with which he proceeded to Persia was so large that it is said that victory could have been achieved either with the regular force or with the auxiliaries. An enormous amount of gold was also brought for the campaign.

Gordian is said first to have marched into Moesia, a region of the Balkans south of the Danube that includes large portions of the former Yugoslavia. He is credited with having vanquished enemies in this region before proceeding to Antioch, which by then had fallen to the Persians. It is claimed that he fought and won repeated battles, before finally driving out the Persians under their new king, Sapor. Antioch, Carrhae and Nisibis were all retaken. Sapor is said to have been in complete fear of the new king, such that he evacuated cities and restored them to their inhabitants without harm or pillaging.

Timistheus is said to have been the real man of the hour, the figure responsible for the conduct and progress of this incredibly successful military campaign. The Persians had run amok to such an extent that there was fear that they might even cross into Europe and threaten Italy, yet thanks to Gordian's father-in-law Timistheus, they are said to have been forced to evacuate all the Roman territories in the East that they had seized.

The Augustan biography purports to record the praise that Gordian showered on his prefect in dispatches to the Senate about the war. Antioch and Carrhae, he announced, had been retaken. Nisibis had been reached, and the young emperor expected that soon the Romans would be in Ctseiphon. The Senate decreed that chariots drawn by four elephants should be provided for Gordian, so that he might conduct a Persian triumph; a six-horse chariot was to be provided for Timistheus.

At this juncture, the 'life' annotates, Timistheus died – either from disease or by the plotting of his successor as prefect, the man known to history as the future Roman emperor, Philip the Arab. It was now AD 243, and the lowborn Philip is said to have begun to plot even against the emperor – if he had succeeded in removing the prefect, he might well wonder why the boy emperor should be a problem.

The succeeding story of the 'life' is almost as difficult to believe as what preceded it. Philip began to manoeuvre to discredit Gordian and win the support of the army. Gordian was forced into the pathetic position of asking for this or that subordinate role under Philip, indeed even to begging for his very life. Philip is said to have been prepared to grant that request, though consideration of how popular Gordian was with the people began to weigh on his mind. Gordian was ultimately taken away and murdered, and Philip the Arab assumed the purple. Philip wrote to the Senate that Gordian had died of disease; officials in Rome were, at least for the moment, ignorant of the true state of affairs in the East.

Thus far we have considered primarily the evidence of the *Augustan History* concerning the dramatic events of the reign of the boy emperor and his expedition to Persia. The basic narrative is frustratingly vague and difficult to absorb. Allegedly, the Persians had been resurgent to such an extent that they managed to overrun almost the entirety of the Roman Near East. Gordian is said to have arrived on the scene with his praetorian prefect, and in a relatively brief time to have utterly restored the situation, with recovery of all that the Romans had lost. Soon thereafter, an ambitious Arab by the name of Philip is said to have successfully orchestrated the elimination of the emperor, such that by February AD 244 he was in sole command of the empire.

The man known to history as Philip the Arab was certainly the first Roman emperor to originate from the province of Arabia Petraea. The province had come into its own, one might say, with the accession to power of its first native son. Philip was born in what is today Shahba, Syria, a city some 54 miles to the south of Damascus. We cannot be certain that

Philip was of Arab origin, although Glen Bowersock argues that he was indeed the first Arab emperor of Rome (the Byzantine historian Zosimus concurs; cf. *Historia Nova* 1.18). The Augustan 'life' and other ancient sources attest to his being of low birth, but this need not have been at all true. Certainly, Philip came to power under a cloud of suspicion, at least if our relatively meagre ancient sources can be trusted. Bowersock argues (page 123) that we need not believe the claim that Timistheus was killed by the connivance of Philip, while the report from Pseudo-Aurelius Victor's *Epitome de Caesaribus* (28.4) that Philip was exceedingly humble in birth, his father a leader of a band of brigands, is also dismissed as an example of Roman prejudice against the Arabs (the whole account has something of the flavour of the stories about the origins of Maximinus Thrax, who was also said to have originated from bandit stock). Eutropius (9.2.3) joins in the allegations that Philip was somehow involved in the death of Gordian III. The *Breviarium* (true to its nature) does not offer anything in the way of details, but simply notes the victories of Gordian over the Persians, and then the killing that resulted in the accession of Philip. Zosimus (1.18) notes that the Arabs were held in ill repute, and argues that Philip certainly had attained power by no noble ends.

What is certain is that Philip was the man who ended the war with the Persians. Fittingly enough, the eastern war was concluded by a man of eastern origin. Philip would return to Rome and serve as emperor for some five years, during a period that was marked by the millennium of Rome's founding: from 753 BC to AD 247. As Bowersock does well to sum up (page 125), 'An Arab negotiating a Roman peace with the Persians was notable, and an Arab presiding over the millennial celebrations of the foundation of Rome was even more notable.' Further, there is some evidence that Philip is to be numbered among the Christian emperors of Rome – a tradition that is known to Eusebius (AD 260/265–339/340), the author of a celebrated ecclesiastical history.

We are left to ferret out the truth – however impossible a task that may be – about two major problems. First, what happened during the great Persian War in which Gordian III took part; and second, how did Philip the Arab come to power? In some sense, these two episodes represent the fusion of the worlds of Roman Mesopotamia and Roman Arabia by the coincidence of Philip's origins.

Ardashir had died – it would have been in either AD 241 or 242, as best as we can determine – and he was replaced by Sapor/Shapur, who was by all accounts a more militaristic and determined monarch than even his ambitious predecessor. There is inscriptional evidence that attests to Gordian III leaving from Misenum on an easterm expedition in 242. It is reasonably clear that he travelled through the Balkans toward the usual eastern imperial destination of Antioch. There is a passing reference in the great fourth-century historian Ammianus Marcellinus (23.5.17) to a victory won by Gordian III over Sapor at Reshaina. In other words, there is good reason to believe that Gordian III – or Timistheus, we might argue – achieved a significant victory over Sapor sometime in 243. What is less certain is what exactly the Persians were doing in the last years of the reign of Ardashir and the early days of Sapor's tenure. There is reason to believe that there may have been Persian incursions into Roman territory even as early as the reign of Maximinus Thrax. Thus, 243 was a busy year for the Romans in the Near East: Gordian launched his apparently successful enough campaign against Sapor, and his trusty prefect died. He was certainly replaced by Philip, but the early career of the future emperor is mysterious indeed. The Roman campaign against Sapor did not end with the Battle of Reshaina, but continued into 244. The Battle of Misiche was a terrible loss for the Romans, probably fought not far from the modern Fallujah in Iraq. A great surviving inscription of Sapor attests to the victory, and mentions that Gordian III was killed in battle. The Romans with Gordian were destroyed, we are told in the Persian inscription, and Philip was made emperor. He then came with money to pay for the safe exit of the Romans.

No surviving Roman source admits to any such defeat in the deserts of what is today central Iraq. The Roman sources instead report the murder plot that Philip orchestrated to remove Gordian; the story of a battlefield death is not mentioned. Peace was certainly struck between Rome and Persia under Philip, and the peace was secure enough that Philip was ready to leave for Rome and stay away from the scene of his Persian adventures and early life in Arabia. The peace that had been arranged with Sapor would last for years.

We cannot, in the end, be certain about the true course of events. It is entirely plausible that Timistheus was indeed the mastermind behind early Roman achievements in Persia, and that after his death Gordian was at something of a loss as to what to do. By then the Romans were deep into Persian-held territory in Mesopotamia, in another veritable graveyard of empires. Philip may have decided that he wanted to be more than praetorian prefect; he may have thought the time was right to eliminate Rome's latest teenage emperor. If there had been a defeat at Misiche, the army may have been ready to go along with the convenient removal of Gordian – and of course everyone was far enough away from Rome that the truth could easily be manipulated. Bowersock (page 124) acknowledges that a military coup is certainly within the realm of possibility in light of the inability of Gordian to handle complicated affairs in Persia. Bowersock argues that the war had been 'wasteful and debilitating', and that however humbling the terms were on which the Romans left for home, the decision to get out was in the end for the best: 'The five years of Philip's reign were a time of uncommon stability and repose in a century that was notorious for turbulence.' The war in the desert had no doubt once again taken a huge toll on the resources of both the Romans and Persians, and neither side was probably much interested in a bloody fight to another stalemate. History was indeed repeating itself in the sands of the Near East, and this time it would be a native, Arab emperor who would decide that it was time to step back.

AD 244 was thus in some sense another year of a re-established *status quo ante bellum*. There was certainly no interest on Philip's part in being a new Alexander, with dreams like those of Caracalla to destroy the Parthians and the Persians. There was a weariness, to be sure, after the destructive realities of the 'Year of the Six Emperors' and the turmoil on the northern borders of 238 and after. There were the heavy losses in the East – even a rebellion in Africa that also confronted Gordian during his youthful reign. Rome was the prey of chaos, and once again we do well to step back and marvel that there was not only restoration and survival, but success and recovery. There would be more wars in Persia, indeed against Sapor – but for the moment, there was a surreal atmosphere, no doubt, as Rome prepared to celebrate its 1,000th birthday. The empire's borders were largely intact, and the games and fanfare in the city were likely unprecedented.

If there were storm clouds yet again gathering, there was at least a joyful respite to enjoy a festive atmosphere. Philip would soon enough fall prey to yet another internal insurrection, like so many other would-be saviours of Rome during this long and difficult century.

For those interested in the fascinating life and reign of Maximinus Thrax – an emperor whose story does not much concern us with our look at Roman Mesopotamia and Arabia – one may recommend Paul N. Pearson's monograph *Maximinus Thrax: From Common Soldier to Emperor of Rome* (Pen & Sword, 2016). Pearson provides a convenient appraisal of the state of the empire in AD 235 and a careful look at every aspect of Maximinus' tenure.

Zosimus is not accessible in the Loeb Classical Library. The best modern edition is the muli-volume Budé edition of the Greek text, with French translation and commentary. There is a very good 1982 English translation with notes by Ronald T. Ridley, *Zosimus: New History (Byzantina Australiensia 2)*. For much of the chaotic history of the later Roman Empire, we are very much dependent on Zosimus as one of our only extant pagan sources. The first book of his history is devoted to the history of Rome from Augustus to Diocletian. By the close of the sixth and final book, we are in the year AD 410. Certainly Zosimus offers an invaluable account of the decline of Rome, a source easy to deride but without which we would be much the poorer in our knowledge of relatively inadequately documented events.

Chapter 11

From Philip the Arab to
Renewed War with Sapor

I t is not the purview of the present volume to consider the complicated
question of the place of Christianity in the third-century crisis of the
Roman Empire. Religious considerations certainly were a significant
part of the imperial problems of the reign of Elagabalus, whose insistence
on the fanatical worship of the Syrian sun god was a major element of
the growing irritation with and eventual rebellion to his rule. There is
some evidence, as we have seen, that Rome's first Arab emperor was
also a Christian – at the very least, there is good reason to believe that
whatever Philip's own religious views, he was certainly more tolerant of
Christianity than many of his predecessors.

Some scholars have disputed the extent of imperial persecutions of
Christians and the attendant number of martyrs to the Christian faith from
Rome's crisis years of the third and early fourth centuries AD. History and
tradition alike agree that Philip's imperial successor Decius was one of the
more notorious persecutors of Christians in Roman history. He did not
reach the levels of savagery that were seen during the 'Great Persecution'
of Diocletian some decades later, but it is to the reign of Decius that the
martyrdoms of some of Christianity's most famous saints belong. Saint
Agatha, the Sicilian patroness of Catania (invoked against the eruptions of
Mount Etna), was one of the casualties of his reign.

Decius' coming to power was the climax of the process of unravelling
of both domestic and foreign affairs for the empire in AD 248 and 249.
Almost as if the celebrations of Rome's 1,000th birthday were a brief
respite before the resumption of chaos, troubles began to emerge for Philip
in Rome's 1,001st year. Certainly, the situation on the northern frontiers
was soon critical. The Quadi were on the move again; so also the Goths.
Pannonia would be invaded and the barbarians would once again be
across the Danube frontier.

There is also good evidence that there was an uprising against Philip in the East – once again, in fact, in Syria. Marcus Jotapianus – Jotapian – was a rival claimant to empire. Aurelius Victor mentions this episode (*Liber de Caesaribus* 29.2) alongside other snippets of extant sources. Philip had appointed his brother Gaius Julius Priscus to be *Rector Orientis*, or 'Ruler of the East', during his absence in Rome. Priscus apparently angered Jotapian and others over matters of taxation and financial indemnities. History does not record the ultimate fate of Priscus; he may have been killed in the ensuing uprising in Syria. There is reason to believe that Philip and his brother may have shown special favour to Arabia Petraea at the expense of other eastern provinces. Whatever the case, alongside the northern crisis it was an internal problem that was likely beyond the ability of Priscus to resolve, though we cannot be sure – some would say that there is reason to believe that Priscus did quell the revolt.

Jotapian was one of several usurpers attested during the reign of Philip. The world of numismatics is the source for much of what little we know about these shadowy figures of Philip's reign. Indeed, some scholars even question how much weight should be put on the evidence of (in some cases at least) a single coin. Jotapian at least has both numismatic and literary evidence to secure the historical fact of his usurpation – the record does not allow, however, much in the way of certain information about what happened and how it was ended. According to Aurelius Victor, Jotapian claimed that he was descended from Alexander – perhaps a reference to Alexander Severus. Antioch was his briefly held capital, and he probably did survive into the reign of Decius, the ultimate winner of the gambits to replace Philip.

Gaius Messius Quintus Decius was one of the men entrusted by Philip to deal with upstarts. The beginning of Philip's end came when he entrusted Decius to deal with the revolt of Tiberius Claudius Marinus Pacatianus on the Danube. Although Decius was sent to tackle the crisis, Pacatianus was killed first by his own men, and Decius' troops proclaimed him emperor – a gesture that he accepted. One irony of the whole situation was that there is evidence that Philip actually proposed his resignation to the Senate as report after report arrived of uprisings. No doubt the twin problems of domestic turmoil and foreign crisis offered ample reasons for abdication. Decius is said to have been among Philip's most ardent supporters (which is why he was sent to deal with Pacatianus in the first place). Philip would ultimately be killed in the Battle of Verona in September AD 249, after the breakdown of any hope of reconciliation between Decius and his former emperor.

The cause of death is unknown; he was either killed in the engagement or murdered by his own soldiers.

It was a stunning reversal for the man who had presided over Rome's millennium some two years earlier, and the commencement of yet another period of uncertainty for the empire. By January AD 250, Decius would be issuing edicts of persecution against Christians. There was an outbreak of plague that served only to increase the general sense that the Roman world was unstable and indeed on the verge of collapse – the millennium was, after all, not only a source of celebration, but also of ominous worry that Rome had been destined to last but a thousand years. Christian eschatology may have been a significant factor in Decius' decision to persecute them: the Christians were convinced that the plague and the general breakdown of order in the empire was a clear indication of the coming return of Christ and the final judgment of the world.

Meanwhile, the Goths were overrunning the Balkans. Decius would in fact be killed in combat against them, a casualty of the Battle of Abritus in what is today north-eastern Bulgaria. The Gothic king Kniva had won an enormous victory, and Decius' body was never found. His son Herennius Etruscus died in the same battle, a conflict that ranks among the worst disasters in Roman military history. Decius had been able to field three legions; it was uncertain what the exact casualty toll was, but the losses were no doubt extremely heavy.

Decius was succeeded by the former governor of Moesia Superior, the short-lived emperor Trebonianus Gallus. We need not be much concerned in our story with the reports that Gallus was somehow complicit in his predecessor's death, working in connivance with the Goths to secure his own power. Gallus initially accepted the co-rule of Decius' surviving son Hostilian, who would reign with him for a few months until either the plague or the conspiracies of Gallus eliminated yet another would-be emperor before the end of the eventful year of AD 251.

Gallus made peace with the Goths, evidence enough for some that he had been working with them all along in some sort of dishonourable collaboration in his own best interest. Gallus – like Decius before him – was certainly preoccupied with the northern crises, not to mention the challenges of securing power in the face of a host of candidates in the army and government ready to take on the purple.

While we cannot be certain if Trebonianus Gallus was indeed responsible in some way for the deaths of Decius and his sons, we can be sure that his reign was one of absolute disarray. Barely two years into his rule, Rome would once again experience a year of multiple emperors. For the purposes of our focus on Roman Mesopotamia and Arabia, we need not be overly concerned with the renewed fighting against the Goths that soon broke out – save to say that the man of the hour was the governor of Moesia Superior, one Aemilian, who would enter the pages of history because he won great victories over Rome's enemies and was more than willing to accept the acclamation of his imperial dignity by his men. Students of the later history of the Roman Empire are often amazed that so many men seemed willing to risk their lives in the exceedingly perilous gamble of trying to secure the job of Roman emperor. The emperor in this period had to deal with enormous internal chaos and threats, not to mention an unimaginably vast and restive northern border – and this is not to account for the presence of Sapor's Persia in the East. And yet there was always another governor or general who was ready to try to do what so many before him had failed to accomplish.

Regrettably, given the paltry state of our sources, the *Augustan History* lives of Philip the Arab, Decius and Trebonianus Gallus do not survive. Neither does that of Aemilian. Aemilian defeated Gallus in a battle in southern Umbria in central Italy in August AD 253. Aemilian himself would be killed by his own troops in Umbria the following month; by October, Rome's new emperor was Valerian, the Roman governor on the Rhine who had been summoned by Gallus to aid him against Aemilian's usurpation of power. It was thus a year that saw at least three emperors: Gallus, Aemilian and Valerian. Publius Licinius Valerianus – the greater part of whose 'life' in the *Augustan History* is also missing – was the 'winner' of the civil wars of 253. His victory would be short-lived, however, given that the Roman East would once again demand the personal attention and military acumen of an emperor.

For during the Roman civil wars that accompanied the Gothic crisis, King Sapor in Persia was also busy. The new foe he would face in Rome was from a noble senatorial family and had a distinguished lineage – no doubt a significant factor in the willingness of Senate and army alike to rally behind him (not to mention the fact that there was probably another period of exhaustion in the wake of so much internal dissension, coupled with the terrible losses incurred in the Gothic War). Valerian also had a son, Gallienus, and he was quick to appoint him to the role of 'Caesar' to his Augustus. A new dynastic arrangement needed to be established quickly, after all, so as to secure the family's hold on power.

The chronology of what happened in the Near East in this period is difficult to determine with exactitude, but Sapor was clearly sometime on the march. There is every reason to believe that Sapor's Persians took advantage of the internal mess in Rome to launch a more or less massive invasion of their favourite target, Roman Syria. After all, the avowed intent of the Sassanid Persian Empire was to reclaim all the ancestral lands of Persia; they intended for Persian sovereignty to extend to the waters of the Aegean Sea, if not beyond. We need have no doubt that Sapor was an expansionist monarch, and the time was right to take advantage of Rome's civil wars. If Decius had been too busy in his short reign to honour the full terms of whatever Philip the Arab had signed with Sapor, there was even more provocation – but the Persians needed very little instigation in the current hour of crisis.

Inscriptional evidence helps to fill in the dearth of anything approaching extensive, coherent literary accounts. Sapor's invasion was overwhelming, and before long the Persians had seized the great Syrian city of Antioch. The Romans were in disarray throughout the region.

In the collection of lives from the *Augustan History* known as the 'Thirty Pretenders', brief notice is given to one of the most mysterious and fascinating men from this period of transition and chaos. Antioch was apparently betrayed to Sapor by a disgruntled adventurer named Mariades, who was distinguished early in life mostly for his excesses and love of luxury. He defected to the Persian side and is said to have urged Sapor to make war on the Romans (we might well think that Sapor needed no encouragement). The Augustan 'life' claims that he was eventually proclaimed emperor – yet another usurper, in other words, from the East – but there is no good reason to believe this. He is said to have been put to death by his own followers, though not before he added parricide to his ledger of crimes.

What seems clear is that Sapor launched a significant operation against Roman Syria and that there were certainly people on the Roman side willing to cast their lot in with the Persians. There is also evidence that Sapor suffered a setback at Emesa, where his attempt to take the city was hampered by an Arab priest of Aphrodite, Sampsigeramus (see here Bowersock, page 127). Everything, in other words, did not go according to Sapor's wishes, but he had succeeded in once again altering the balance of power in the East.

In a world that laboured under the reality that communications – while remarkably efficient by ancient standards – were less than rapid, it is perhaps not surprising that coins attest to a Roman imperial usurper in Emesa, one Lucius Julius Aurelius Sulpicius Uranius Antoninus (the possessor of what Bowersock justly calls a 'magnificent name' – page 128). Bowersock argues that 'Uranius' is the Hellenized version of the name Sampsigeramus, and that the priestly Arab saviour in Emesa was also the would-be emperor. Our knowledge of the setbacks suffered by Sapor in this age relies on such sources as the sixth-century Byzantine chronicler John of Malalas and the *Thirteenth Sibylline Oracle* – not the easiest sources to evaluate.

In other words, the history of Arab versus Persian conflict that has dominated so much of the history of the Middle East was alive and well in the time of chaos and disorder after the death of Philip. There were no doubt Arabs who deeply resented the loss of their native emperor and were eager to take charge against the Persian threat that, after all, imperilled them more than anyone. The understandable-enough distractions of the Roman emperors subsequent to Philip with affairs both internal and Gothic only increased the size of the eastern vacuum that Sapor was eager to fill at Roman (and Arab) expense. The famous ancient numismatist and historian Michael Grant opens his 1999 Routledge study, *The Collapse and Recovery of the Roman Empire*, by stating, 'One of the main problems with the Roman empire was its incessant changes of emperor.' Sapor would no doubt have agreed with the observation.

Eutropius sums up what happened to Valerian with his characteristic brevity (9.7): *Valerianus in Mesopotamia bellum gerens a Sapore, Persarum rege, superatus est, mox etiam captus apud Parthos ignobili servitute consenuit*; 'Valerian waged war with Sapor, the king of Persians, in Mesopotamia. He was conquered and soon captured, and grew old in an ignoble servitude among the Parthians.'

There had been emperors who died in battle against foes both foreign and domestic, but there had never been a Roman emperor who was captured by the enemy and held in captivity. The *Breviarium* of Eutropius records the bare facts without embellishment: Valerian was not only a failure in his war against Sapor, but he lost something more precious, some might argue, than his very life.

What happened to bring Rome to such a dire state of affairs in AD 260? The fourth-century historian Festus, in his own abridgment of Roman history, says that Valerian was *infaustus* – unlucky and ill-starred. He observes that it is wearisome even to relate the disasters that were experienced in Valerian's Persian campaign. Since we know that Valerian was another indefatigable persecutor of Christians, one imagines that the

Christians of the era were convinced that Valerian's losses in the East were the verdict of God. To Valerian we can ascribe the dramatic story of Saint Lawrence on his gridiron, and of the martyrdom of Pope Saint Sixtus II and his companions. It was a fresh time of anti-Christian persecution in the empire, and it came before the apparent defeat of the imperial enemy of Christians – like Decius before him, Valerian went to what some no doubt considered his just reward. Festus offers no more detail than Eutropius as to how Valerian's defeat and capture came about. Eutropius says that the captured emperor's servitude was *ignobilis*; Festus labels it *indecorus* – 'unbecoming', to say the least.

What survives of the Augustan 'life' of Valerian is actually the very close of the joint 'life' of the 'Two Valerians', that is, of the famous father and his far less famous, equally unlucky son Valerian (often referred to as Valerian the Younger), Gallienus' half-brother. The 'life' commences in the midst of a purported missive sent by the emperor's son to Sapor. Valerian the Younger notes that the Gauls once sacked the city of Rome, and yet now they served the Romans, while Mithridates of Pontus was once lord of Asia, but he too was defeated and his lands taken over by Rome. The son is arguing on behalf of his father that if Sapor is wise, he would release the emperor to the Romans. Velenus, the king of the Cadusii in Media, is also recorded to have written to Sapor, urging him to release Valerian. Velenus notes that the Romans are never more dangerous than when they have been defeated; to hold Valerian in custody would mean constant peril for the Persians. King Artavasdes of Armenia is also said to have written to Sapor, noting that the Persians had succeeded in capturing one old man and thereby turned the entire world into their foe. The Bactrians, the Hiberians, the Albanians and the Tauroscythians are all said to have snubbed Sapor in the wake of his actions against Valerian, and to have written to Roman commanders promising that they would do all they could to secure Valerian's release.

Valerian would die, in point of fact, in Persian captivity. There would be no rescue, no grand army of revenge from Rome. The 'life' briefly announces what would indeed happen: it would be from the Kingdom of Palmyra, that desert realm of Syria, that salvation – after a fashion – would come for the Roman East. The story of Palmyra would now represent a dramatic new page in the history of Rome's involvement in Mesopotamia and Arabia, and offer a true episode of real recovery in the otherwise seemingly unremittingly bleak history of the third-century AD.

We may also consider briefly the evidence of the Byzantine historian Zosimus for Valerian's reign and downfall. With respect to Persia, he notes first that Valerian entrusted the West to Gallienus so that he could take the field against Persia (1.30). While the Scythians were busy overrunning Bithynia – reports of which reached Valerian – he was preparing to deal with Sapor (1.36). He is said to have gone in person from Antioch into Cappadocia, only to suffer a plague that destroyed much of his army, thus giving Sapor a perfect chance to attack. Zosimus condemns Valerian for being lazy and effeminate, and records an effort to try to buy off Sapor – but the Roman ambassadors were rebuffed. Sapor is said to have duplicitously suggested to the emissaries that Valerian should come in person, thus giving him the chance to kidnap his enemy. The Byzantine historian concludes his brief account of the whole matter by noting that the disgrace of the Romans was enduring – and that disgrace was largely the fault, in his appraisal, of Valerian.

Chapter 12

Palmyra and Roman Resurgence in the East

almyra is a celebrated ancient realm of Syria that was tragically in the news during the rise and spread of the Islamic State of Iraq and the Levant, which destroyed much of the archaeological remains of the old city in the early twenty-first century.

It was one of the wealthiest of the desert cities of the Roman East. Its power was unquestionably centred on its mercantile economy. The residents of Palmyra were men of practical mind, focused on the tremendous financial success of their economic endeavours.

Palmyra was a client state of Rome, a valuable ally in the defence of the vast deserts of modern Syria. When the Augustan 'life' of the 'two Valerians' says that Odenaethus of Palmyra gathered a large force and restored Roman power to its previous condition, one sees, perhaps, more than a glimpse of a weary client state of Rome that was tired of Persian encroachment and the threats to economic stability occasioned by renewed warfare in the East. If the Romans were not going to solve the Persian problem for them, the denizens of Palmyra would mind their own house and backyard, as it were.

Palmyra had been part of the Roman system of provincial and client-state government since the early days of the empire under Tiberius. The Palmyrenes had endured clashes with Rome before – including conflict with none other than Mark Antony in 41 BC – but once the region came under the government of the Roman province of Syria, it entered a period of real prosperity and economic growth. Trade and commerce were more valuable enterprises for the residents of Palmyra than rebellion and war against Rome. While a part of the provincial structure of Syria, it appears that some measure of independence was still respected. The region was clearly defined, and may have operated in a way not entirely dissimilar to contemporary autonomous and semi-autonomous regions of larger powers. Palmyra was, in several aspects of its governmental and management structure, something of a hybrid between provincial and client kingdom.

What had been a minor stopping point on desert trails grew into a major city during the first century AD. In some ways that century was a heyday of Palmyra, the time in which Roman rule was certainly seen by most of the region's inhabitants as tremendously beneficial. When Hadrian visited Palmyra in AD 129, he declared it 'free' and celebrated its accomplishments and loyalty to Rome. When Septimius Severus divided the province of Syria into two, Palmyra was assigned to the new province of Syria Phoenice.

Alexander Severus visited Palmyra in AD 229 – a century after Hadrian's stopover. During the Severan Age, Palmyra certainly experienced a transformation of sorts. There was an increased concern about military development and the defence of the trade routes that ensured the livelihood and success of the city. There was a greater emphasis on adopting Roman customs of law and government. In short, Palmyra became a more integrated part of the governmental and military apparatus of the Roman East. It was independent, and yet not independent.

And one thing is certain: the rise of Sassanian Persia was a source of major and immediate stress for Palmyra. The coming of the Persians and the resultant wars with first Parthia and then Rome were all bad for business. The Palmyrans were increasingly left to their own devices in terms of fending off Persian threats – they were, after all, in the very hinterland of the Roman Empire, and more or less expected to do much to secure their own defence and safety.

Odenaethus of Palmyra is one of the 'Thirty Pretenders' of the *Augustan History*, an interesting analysis of a man of action at a critical point in Roman history. Odenaethus is credited by his anonymous biographer with nothing less than being the man most responsible for the rescue of Roman affairs in the Near East. He declared himself a king, and proceeded forth with his wife, the celebrated Zenobia. He had an elder son, Herodes/Herodianus, and younger ones named Herennianus and Timolaus (the later pair sons by Zenobia). He captured Nisibis and the entirety of Mesopotamia from Persian domination. He drove Sapor and his sons into flight, chasing them as far as the legendary city of Ctesiphon – the very site of so many previous clashes between Rome and the East. He captured Sapor's concubines and tremendous plunder from Persia's king, only to be slain around AD 266 or 267 by his cousin Maeonius, who also killed the king's son Herodes. Maeonius seized the Palmyran kingdom – an action that Odenaethus' biographer ascribes to the wrath of some god or other who was so angry with Rome that he was unwilling to safeguard Odenaethus after the death of Valerian in captivity.

For his gushing biographer, Odenaethus and Zenobia would have been able to restore not only the East, but the entire world – so competent and devoted to excellence and hardship were the powerful husband and wife pair. Maeonius earned a disreputable place of his own among the 'Thirty Pretenders', as his own soldiers would eventually kill him. Sources are so confused for this period and these individuals that we should not be surprised to read that Maeonius may have acted in concert with Zenobia in the death of her husband; she was apparently angry that Herodes should be favoured over her own two sons. Herodes too is one of the Thirty; his exceedingly brief biographical note states that Zenobia treated him like a classic Roman stepmother of yore – in other words, as a bitterly wicked woman bent on his destruction.

We do not know for sure when the Emperor Valerian died in captivity. It was certainly before the end of AD 264. His reign was thus shy of seven years in all before his capture by Sapor in 260. The great inscription of Sapor at Naqsh-e Rostam in what is today Fars Province, Iran, depicts the submission of Valerian to Sapor. The inscription was trilingual: Greek, Middle Persian and Parthian. It is thanks to this inscription that we know, for example, that the Romans suffered a major defeat at Barbalissos in Syria (not far from Aleppo). This battle in 253 seems to have resulted in the ruin of a Roman force of some 60,000, and was directly consequential to the fall of Antioch and Dura-Europos some years later.

We may take stock of what can be reconstructed from our scanty evidence of what were appreciably confused events. David Potter, in his mammoth study *The Roman Empire at Bay, AD 180–395* (London–New York: Routledge, 2004; second edition, 2014) observes (page 242) that 'The political situation that followed upon Decius' demise was deeply confused.' Troubles in Persia may have never truly ended after the settlement of Philip the Arab, and certainly the actions of such upstarts as Jotapian and Mariades in Syria did not help. Sapor's inscription – perhaps not surprisingly – says that the Romans lied with respect to Armenia. The Barbalissos engagement cost 60,000 Roman lives in a single battle, and led to the overrunning of Syria. The list of towns and cities invaded by Sapor is impressive – thirty-seven in all, according to the Persian side of the tale.

Potter argues (page 244) rightly that if there had been 60,000 Romans concentrated in one place, there must have been a plan for direct engagement with Persia in the wake of the growing troubles in the East. The subsequent aforementioned victory of Uranius/Sampsigeramus over Sapor is mysterious. But the rise of men like Uranius, and the outfitting

of the Palmyran 'kingdom' with its own armed force, is a testament to
the reality that the Roman legions were in no position to be of much help
against Persia – not least in the face of alleged losses like 60,000 in one clash.

We know from inscriptions that Valerian was in Antioch by AD 255,
ready to be yet another emperor on the scene to try to deal with the latest
crisis of empire. He was there again in 258. Sapor probably launched
renewed attacks on Roman Mesopotamia and its environs in the spring of
260. The so-called Battle of Edessa involved Valerian's personal command
of an army of some 70,000 Romans; the defeat of this force – even apart
from the resultant capture of Valerian by Sapor – would have been a
devastating blow to Rome's position in the East. Lurid stories would come
to be told of how the aged emperor would be used as a stepping block
for Sapor as he mounted his horse, and how after the death of the emperor
his flesh was flayed and hung in a temple as a grisly monument to the
Persian defeat of the Romans.

Valerian had thus failed miserably in his attempts to deal with Persia.
In past engagements with the Romans, we have seen how at a moment
of seeming total victory, the Persians either withdrew or began to suffer
setbacks. No doubt in this crisis, too, there was serious loss and impairment
on the Persian side that made the eventual Roman recovery possible.
The revival that came was not the result of any massive imperial response,
but rather due to the impressive work of men like Odenaethus and other
ad hoc commanders of the ongoing struggle against Sapor.

Those extraordinary men included yet another pair of the 'Thirty
Pretenders' of the Augustan lives, the treasury official Macrianus and the
praefect Callistus/Ballista. They are said to have been contemptuous of
Valerian's son Gallienus (who was, in any case, far off in the West at the
time of his father's capture). Macrianus was in possession of significant
financial resources because of his fiscal responsibilities, and Callistus
brought with him significant military respect. The fact that Macrianus
had two sons – Macrianus the Younger and Quietus – made the plan
for imperial takeover all the more possible. Macrianus was said to have
been deformed in one of his legs and thus unable to take power himself;
the plan was for his two sons to assume joint power with the support of
their father and Callistus.

Quietus and Callistus would remain in the East, while Macrianus and
his son proceeded to Europe. Father and son would be doomed to meet
another usurper (not to say pretender), the Roman military commander
Aureolus. Aureolus would defeat Macrianus Maior and Minor in the

central Balkans in AD 261 – whatever 'reign' they enjoyed was short-lived indeed. Odenaethus of Palmyra is said to have seen to the death of Quietus, also in 261. Callistus was another victim of Odenaethus, also probably meeting his death in 261; there is a possibility that their own men killed both would-be emperors. Aureolus (at the behest of Gallienus) also found time in this intensely confusing period to defeat two other upstart governors in the Balkans, Ingenuus and Regalianus. By the end of the summer of that fateful year of 260, Gallienus also faced the aftermath of a major internal rebellion in the West, with Postumus – governor of Lower Germany – in full-scale revolt. Postumus seized control of much of Gaul, the Germanies and Britain.

If the events of these years from AD 253–260 are difficult to follow, we may rest assured that they were equally difficult for the leading men of the age to navigate. The Persian side of the story is perhaps the easiest part of the drama to encapsulate: Sapor attacked Mesopotamia at some point after the death of Philip the Arab; he won impressive victories at least twice against major Roman armies; and by 260, he had definitively defeated and captured Valerian, only to suffer serious setbacks and reversals at the hands of comparatively minor Roman officials and a resurgent Palmyra. Odenaethus' exact job description in the aftermath of Valerian's capture is difficult to explicate. Was he indeed a more or less freelance Palmyran who had come to throw in his lot with Rome rather than Persia, or was he a Roman governor with official control over Roman forces in his domain? These are questions that are difficult if not impossible to answer in light of the surviving evidence. Fergus Milalr (page 169) notes that there is inscriptional evidence than even in the seemingly quite troubled years of 262–264, there were public works/fortification projects underway in Roman Arabia, at Adraa in modern south-western Syria, projects that were dedicated to the health and security of the emperor Gallienus.

And yet while technically Gallienus was emperor of Rome from AD 253–268 – an impressive fifteen years in a century where a year could seem like a lifetime – Valerian's son was unable to prevent the breakup of the Roman Empire. Numerous revolts had occurred, not least of which was the Postumus uprising that resulted in the so-called Gallic Empire that would endure until 274 – years after the death of Gallienus.

Odenaethus is a key and enigmatic figure in all of this. There is some reason to believe that as he gazed on the collapse of the old order in the East, he was willing to make common cause with Sapor in the best interests of Palmyra – but Sapor was not interested in making deals.

Odenaethus would certainly turn to favouring Rome, though always, we might think, with a first concern toward Palmyra. Bowersock notes (page 130) that the Palmyrenes were far better trained and acclimatized than the Romans at desert warfare; they were certainly capable of giving Sapor's Persians a good fight. Bowersock analyzes the significant problem not only of the Roman and Palmyran response to the Persian threat, but also the attitude of other towns in Arabia Petraea and its environs to the nascent growing might of Palmyra. It was an era of tremendous instability, one in which rival powers were jockeying for any opportunity to rise above the pack in the restoration of a single, dominant authority in vast and critically strategic regions. And throughout, one marvels that Rome survived at all.

Our sources do not permit us to be certain as to when Palmyra became a dominant player on the confused chessboard of the Near East. Fergus Millar (page 167) makes the good observation that for the entirety of the dozen years from AD 260 (i.e., after the capture of Valerian) until 272, 'no recognised emperor' came to the East.

A dramatic event in AD 267 was the aforementioned murder of Odenaethus of Palmyra. Odenaethus was killed at either Heraclea Pontica in Bithynia or at Emesa in Syria. At the time of his death he was engaged in two campaigns, technically – one against Sapor's Persia and another against Germanic invaders of Bithynia. We see in these reports evidence of the reality that in terms of effective Roman control of the eastern provinces, Palmyra was indispensable in the years of crisis. The death of Odenaethus paved the way for his widow Zenobia and her son Vaballathus to succeed to power. Vaballathus was at this point perhaps barely 8 years old, thus leaving his mother in a position of particular authority – the seeds had been sown, one might say, for the rise of a new Cleopatra in the Roman East.

Chapter 13

Zenobia and Aurelian

Whatever the exact status of Odenaethus, until the day of his assassination (which he shared with his son Herodes/Herodianus) he was – at least 'on paper' – loyal to Valerian's son Gallienus. One wonders if in the story of his death there is some real plan to assert Palmyran independence at the expense of Rome – after all, Postumus' breakaway empire in the West had shown that the empire was more than capable of successfully fragmenting.

The years from AD 267–269 were frightful ones for the Roman Empire in terms of Gothic invasions. The Heruli – an eastern Germanic tribe – even ravaged as far as Athens and Sparta in Greece after launching a naval attack on the eastern empire. Gallienus was reasonably successful in responding to the many crises that confronted him, though in 268 he would be murdered during the siege of Mediolanum (modern Milan) in the complicated sequence of events surrounding the usurpations of Postumus and Aureolus. Gallienus would be replaced by Claudius II, better known to history as Claudius Gothicus – like Maximinus Thrax before him, another emperor of barbarian lineage. The idea that he was a bastard son of Gordian II was believed by some; it rests on a citation in the fourth-century Pseudo-Aurelian *Epitome de Caesaribus*.

Claudius was a military tribune, the first of the so-called Soldier or Barracks Emperors. Not surprisingly, there were accusations that he was complicit in the death of his predecessor. The Roman Empire of Gallienus in AD 268 had essentially broken into three pieces: the Gallic Empire of Postumus in the West, the rising kingdom of Palmyra in the East and all that was left in the middle as it were.

Claudius' very appellation *Gothicus* points to what he would be most famous for – the defence of the empire against serious Gothic incursions. He also faced the need to settle the breakaway empire in the West, and would live to see appreciable accomplishments in this regard too. His death in AD 270 from plague cut short another fascinating imperial life and the reign of another emperor who might well have lived to achieve much more had he enjoyed several more years in power. His dream was to reunite the empire – and it was a vision that would be accomplished by his successor in no small part because of the foundation that was set by this latest 'barbarian' ruler of Rome.

There is great uncertainty as to the breakdown of Rome's relationship with Palmyra in this period. Perhaps analysis of the situation shows the simple truth that the Palmyrans under Zenobia were interested in independence, in exercising their own foreign policy toward Persia and in being able to fashion their own destiny. We do well to remember Millar's aforementioned point that there had not been a Roman emperor 'on the ground' in the East since Valerian's humiliating defeat and capture in AD 260. The Palmyrans – whether in league with Gallienus' Rome or not – had done the lion's share of the work in 'fixing' the problems occasioned by Sapor's devastating invasions.

Claudius was reputed to be an ancestor of Constantius Chlorus, and thus a great luminary of his age if only because of the noble imperial progeny destined to emerge from his line. The *Augustan History* is highly commendatory in its reports on both Claudius and his successor Aurelian, and conversely harsh against Gallienus. Gallienus is said to have rejoiced when his father Valerian was captured – his defeat had, after all, secured sole power for his son – and to have largely ignored the growing power of Palmyra under Odenaethus and his ambitious wife. The Augustan biography openly argues that Odenaethus of Palmyra achieved his immense power largely because he was actually a competent man of action, in contrast to the lazy and dissolute nature of Gallienus' rule. The war waged by Odenaethus against Persia is explicitly cast in this tradition as being an exercise of the vengeance for Valerian that his son was unwilling to practise. In Roman tradition, one of the most important of concepts and values is *pietas* – a word that is impossible to translate accurately into English (the English noun 'piety' does not give the full sense). Basically put, *pietas* speaks of the relationship between men and gods, or between men of different hierarchical positions – for example, a father and son. Gallienus should have rescued his father Valerian on the grounds of mere *pietas*, military and strategic considerations aside. The Trojan hero Aeneas was the master *exemplum* of *pietas* in his rescue of his father Anchises from the ruins of Troy. Gallienus, however, had failed to seek to help his father in his own hour of supreme crisis.

We may well question the Augustan tradition that Odenaethus was endeavouring to set Valerian free by his war against Sapor. Equally suspect is the record that Gallienus was willing to declare Odenaethus an 'Augustus' and to share power with him. The Scythian invasion of Bithynia that is reported in this same period, in any case, added additional complications to both Palmyran and Roman initiatives in this intensely troubled age.

Odenaethus' wife Zenobia is said to have outdone Gallienus in cleverness and competence, though the Augustan biographer notes that 'any girl' (*quaeque virgo*) could have done better than the incompetent emperor. Gallienus is said to have reacted to the news of Odenaethus' death by making plans for his own war against Persia to rescue his father. He is reported to have marshalled a force that set out on this grand expedition, only to suffer a defeat at the hands of Zenobia's Palmyrenes.

This is a mysterious detail, one that is difficult to reconcile with other surviving evidence and the general course of relations. The general cited in the Augustan 'life' as suffering a defeat the hands of Zenobia is one Heraclianus, and he was certainly with Gallienus at Milan in AD 268. The report from the Augustan 'life' points to the future reality: Rome would face a breakaway Palmyra in the East, under the dominion of Odenaethus' widow Zenobia.

The Augustan 'life' of Claudius provides some information for what Zenobia's Palmyrenes proceeded to do, alongside the fifth/sixth-century historian Zosimus. Claudius' reign was certainly marked by a Palmyrene attack on Egypt. Claudius' biographer says that the Palmyrene generals Saba and Timagenes launched an invasion that was repelled, though the Egyptian commander Probatus was killed by a trick of Timagenes. Egypt, however, is said to have declared its loyalty to Claudius. Zosimus (1.44) reports that Zenobia's Palmyrene force numbered some 70,000 men, who faced 50,000 Romans and allies in Egypt. The Palmyrenes are said to have been victorious, and to have left behind a garrison of 5,000 men to defend Egypt. Claudius' admiral Probus (i.e., Probatus) had been assigned to anti-piracy efforts in the eastern Mediterranean; when he learned of the Palmyrene assault on Egypt, he drove on to recover the province, which prompted the Palmyrenes to muster fresh forces. Probus secured a second victory over Zenobia's forces, and drove the enemy out of Egypt and even on to Babylon. Timagenes – who knew the country far better than Probus – launched a surprise attack on Probus' mountain camp with some 2,000 men, and won a victory that cost Probus his life. Egypt soon fell entirely to Palmyra in AD 269.

For Zosimus (1.39), Zenobia's conduct of the expansion of Palmyra was in every way equal to the work of her storied husband. One could do an interesting study of the appraisals of Cleopatra of Egypt and Zenobia of Palmyra in our extant sources – Zenobia would come off the better in several regards. Claudius, as we have seen, also comes off well in the sources – and whatever the later Constantinian tradition that may have improved his reputation, there is every reason to believe that he was indeed a competent commander and efficient military strategist.

But he was to be far overshadowed by his successor Aurelian, the man who was destined to do what may well have seemed impossible – the reunification of the Roman Empire. Aurelian would be one of the rare luminaries of the dark age of the third century, a soldier emperor who was both competent and blessed with sufficient time to achieve impressive goals in responding to the diverse problems of the empire.

Aurelian was another man of comparatively humble birth who would work his way through the ranks of the Roman Army to emerge as emperor. He would succeed in many regards where others of similar aspiration and background had failed. He would end up receiving the extraordinary title *Restitutor Orbis*, or 'Restorer of the World', and there would be few who would try to question his worthiness for such a grand appellation.

By the time of Claudius' death, Aurelian was already in his fifties – he was born in either AD 214 or 215. Much of his life was thus lived in the years of intense crisis that followed on the decline and fall of the Severan Age and its aftermath. Before his own end, he would have five years to rule Rome – and those five years would be well spent indeed.

Alaric Watson's *Aurelian and the Third Century* (London–New York: Routledge, 2004) may be considered a standard scholarly biography of this great emperor, while John F. White is the author of the Pen & Sword volume *The Roman Emperor Aurelian: Restorer of the World* (2015). We also possess a lengthy 'life' of Aurelian in the *Augustan History*, as well as some material in Zosimus.

What did Aurelian face in Palmyra at the height of its power? Cleopatra might well have been impressed with Zenobia's holdings at the zenith of empire: she controlled Egypt, Asia Minor and Syria. It was a vast area to reconquer, and the operations would require much investment in both men and materials.

King Sapor of Persia had been defeated by the Palmyrenes, and he seems to have closed out his reign in relative quiet after a long career of military action. He would die in May AD 270, months before the death of Claudius Gothicus and the accession of Aurelian in September of that year. In the ebb and flow of military affairs in recent decades in the Near East, Persia was in a period of relative inactivity.

It remains uncertain what exactly were the intentions of Zenobia with respect to Rome. We have noted the likelihood that Palmyra had decided on a course of *de facto* if not *de iure* independence, with the view that the Palmyrenes were better equipped than their western neighbours to handle the problems of territories that bordered on Persia. Victories over Sapor and a general period of Persian inactivity in the military arena might well have contributed to a growing sense of resolution that Palmyra should be independent. Aurelian came to power in the autumn of AD 270, and he seems almost at once to have divided his forces in two to deal with the eastern crisis. He conveyed one army into Bithynia, while his military colleague Probus – not to be confused with the Claudian admiral who had lost his life fighting the Palmyrenes over the conquest of Egypt – would seek to avenge his namesake's loss by taking naval units south to recover the ancient land of the pharaohs.

Our sources point to a relatively easy retaking of Asia Minor. The ability of Aurelian to succeed at essentially no cost in his march through the region may well be attributed to the unclear relationship between Rome and Palmyra. The odds are good that most of the inhabitants of the region – accustomed as they were to Roman rule – had no interest in fighting and dying for Zenobia in what they would consider little more than a needless civil war. The Augustan 'life' records the legend that the city of Tyana in modern-day south central Turkey was (alongside Byzantium, the modern Constantinople/Istanbul) one of the few places that resisted Aurelian. Tyana is memorable for the legend preserved in the Augustan history that during its siege, Aurelian had a mystical vision of the first-century sage Apollonius of Tyana, who begged the emperor to show mercy to his city. Aurelian was apparently a great fan of Apollonius, and was more than willing to heed the plea of the dream apparition. The whole story is reminiscent of Alexander the Great's willingness to spare the house of the celebrated lyric poet Pindar in the destruction of Thebes.

Zosimus (1.50–56) narrates the course of the Palmyrene War. He says that all the cities between Tyana and Antioch surrendered to Aurelian. Antioch was the real prize in the region, and Zenobia's army was nearby (the Augustan 'life' says that the decisive engagement came near Emesa, though the interlude at Antioch, including the battle near there, is not mentioned). Zosimus for one is willing to provide military details about the battle. As the Palmyrenes were especially strong in cavalry, Aurelian ordered his own cavalry not to engage immediately with the vigorous, skilled horsemen of Zenobia. Instead, they were to wait for the Palmyrenes to attack, and then – borrowing a Parthian tactic – pretend to flee, only for the purpose of wearing down the enemy horse. Since the Palmyrene cavalry were heavily armoured, the combination of heat and armour would weary and weigh down the enemy.

The ruse worked, such that Aurelian's cavalry were able to secure a great victory over Zenobia's forces. The queen's army fled to Antioch, where her general Zabdas is said to have tried to borrow a tactic from Sapor. Worried about the possibility of a mutiny in the city against the queen's rule, he chose a man who resembled Aurelian and dressed him in garb resembling the emperor – all for the purpose of claiming that the Palmyrenes had kidnapped Aurelian. Zabsdas, Zenobia and their forces were thus able to buy some time before they stole away to Emesa. Antioch was thereafter retaken by Aurelian without a fight.

The Palmyrenes had occupied a steep position near the city, hoping thereby to hamper and block the progress of Aurelian's forces. But the emperor ordered his men to march in close formation to help mitigate the threat from missile weapons and the Romans thus succeeded in taking the hill position, winning another victory. The Palmyrenes still had the main body of their army – Zosimus numbers it at 70,000 – encamped near Emesa. Aurelian is said to have faced this enemy with Dalmatian cavalry and a polyglot force of auxiliaries and legionary recruits.

At first the Palmyrenes seemed to be doing very well in the ensuing Battle of Emesa. The Roman cavalry deliberately sought to retire at the beginning of the engagement, so as to avoid being encircled by Zenobia's expert horsemen. The Palmyrenes pursued them with unexpected ferocity, however, and the Roman infantry was forced to try to carry the day. The Palmyrenes had broken ranks in their overly enthusiastic pursuit of the Roman cavalry, so the Romans and their allies were able to secure a great victory, driving Zenobia's forces off in flight – many of which sought refuge in Emesa.

Zosimus records that at this juncture in the war, Zenobia was beginning to lose heart. Indeed, her counsellors advised her to abandon Emesa (not least because the inhabitants of the locale were said to be unfavourably disposed to her), and to retreat to Palmyra and regroup.

The Augustan 'life' – perhaps not surprisingly – credits literal divine intervention for helping to secure Aurelian's victory at Emesa. Aurelian's cavalry were said to have been on the point of absolute exhaustion and flight when a supernatural being inspired the Romans with new hope for victory. The end came quickly thanks to the aid of the god – and once Aurelian entered Emesa, it is said that he enjoyed a divine apparition of the same deity, such that the emperor was careful to remember to fulfill all the rites and demands of religious worship in the wake of his victory.

Any army that has fought in Syria might appreciate the detail in the 'life' that Aurelian's march to Palmyra was hampered by brigands and local marauders. Palmyra would be the scene of a major siege to settle the course of the war; according to the 'life', Aurelian would even receive an arrow wound during the engagement. Zosimus tells a more colourful story: the Palmyrenes were in the habit of mocking the Romans from the safety of their walls, and on one occasion a Palmyrene was particularly offensive in his taunts against Aurelian himself. At this, a Persian who was standing near the emperor offered to kill the man with a missile weapon – and upon receiving the emperor's consent, this is exactly what the Persian did.

If anything, the episode is an interesting detail about the 'Persian' element in the current war. And it is prelude to another 'Persian' detail in Zosimus' account of the war.

The Palmyrenes shared the hope of all besieged parties: perhaps the Romans would give up because of lack of provisions. A council of deliberation, however, decided on another course of action – the Palmyrenes would attempt to flee the city, cross the Euphrates and appeal for help from the Persians against Aurelian.

Zenobia is said to have fled the city on an especially swift mount – a female camel. Aurelian, enraged when he learned that the queen had escaped, immediately sent men on horseback in pursuit of her. She was captured as she was in the process of crossing the Euphrates in a boat, and brought to Aurelian.

The Augustan 'life' adds some details to the dramatic story. A letter purportedly sent from emperor to queen is cited, in which Aurelian promised to spare the queen's life and respect the rights of Palmyra – on condition that Zenobia agree to live wherever the emperor and Senate should decree.

Zenobia's alleged response invoked Cleopatra, noting that she preferred death to dishonour. The queen further threatened that Persia would join with Palmyra – and even observed that the guerrilla marauders of the Syrian desert had taken a toll on Aurelian's army. We are told that Aurelian's letter to the queen was in Greek, and that her reply was dictated in Syrian to a scribe who translated into Greek – an interesting detail about language proficiency.

The 'life' reports that the Persians did, in the end, send reinforcements to Palmyra, but Aurelian cut these off and prevented the relief of the city. Squadrons of Saracens and Armenians were taken either by force of arms or by cunning. At this point, Zenobia proceeded to flee from the city on that infamous camel. She was captured by Aurelian's cavalry while attempting to make her way to Persian territory.

There are interesting elements here with respect to the Persian relationship with both Palmyra and Rome. Evidently, Zenobia had decided that peace with Persia was a key desideratum of her rule, and that Persian support against Aurelian was of paramount importance. It is uncertain what she intended to do in terms of the ultimate disposition of Palmyrene affairs with both neighbouring empires.

Zosimus says that Zenobia and her followers were brought to trial, and that the queen argued that she had been taken advantage of by her counsellors – quite a contrast from the haughty tone of the alleged letter in the Augustan 'life'. One of the most prominent of her counsellors was Cassius Longinus, a Greek philosopher and rhetorician. Aurelian evidently accepted the queen's version of events, and Longinus lost his life.

In Zosimus' account (1.59), Zenobia and her son (together with some surviving members of her court) were to be taken to Europe by Aurelian, but the queen died either of disease or hunger on the journey and the rest of her entourage were drowned in the strait between Chalcedon and Byzantium.

The Augustan 'life' relates that Aurelian's soldiers were demanding the punishment of the queen, but that Aurelian concluded that it was inappropriate to order the death of a woman. The deaths of her counsellors are mentioned in this source too, with criticism of the execution of Longinus (the 'life' says that Aurelian was told that the arrogant letter from Zenobia had been the idea of the philosopher – even though, the biographer reminds his readers, it had been composed in Syrian).

The Byzantine chronicler Malalas says that Aurelian had Zenobia paraded around on a female camel in mockery of how she had attempted to escape him. She was displayed in his eventual triumph and then decapitated. The famous story that she was spared and actually given a villa in Tibur, where she lived with her children, is found in the Augustan 'life'; some would claim she ended up marrying a Roman senator, and the house in which she had lived became a tourist attraction. Speculation is fruitless given the conflicting evidence – but it is certainly likely that she was paraded in Aurelian's triumphal procession.

There is also a vague mention in the 'life' that Aurelian dealt with the Persians, Armenians and Saracens in the immediate aftermath of his Palmyrene campaign. It would seem that the emperor was interested in demonstrating to Persia that he was well aware that they had sided with Zenobia, and he did not want to appear to lose face. He was also obviously not interested in any major engagement against Sassanid Persia – he still had the Gallic breakaway empire to contend with, alongside other problems in the West.

Whatever her ultimate fate, Zenobia had in many regards represented in her queenly rule the rise and fall of the Palmyrene Empire – though the final word had not yet been written on her kingdom. It is clear that Palmyra had been one of those powers that arose in the classic circumstances of a vacuum occasioned by the 'break' in tensions between Persia and Rome once Valerian was captured and Gallienus was preoccupied with a long roster of other concerns. Palmyra was more than useful to Rome for a while, though of course the growing power of that realm was soon enough the source of yet another serious threat to Roman domination in the East.

Roman Arabia had emerged largely unscathed from the struggles between Rome and Persia – it was not the battleground that Roman Mesopotamia and Roman Syria would become. Palmyra would ultimately use Arabia as a virtual launching point for its conquest of Egypt. The Palmyrenes were more than willing to sweep into Arabia and conquer Rome's distant desert province. Bowersock (pages 130–37) surveys surviving Arab and other sources to consider the tense relationship between Zenobia and the Arab populations to the south and west of Palmyra. In Bowersock's estimation, it was a combined Roman–Arab force that took on Zenobia once Aurelian had arrived on the scene, and not without the support of those in Palmyra who were less than pleased with the ambitious neo-Cleopatra.

Scholars have also drawn attention to the relationship between Zenobia and her circle of literary mentors and colleagues. There is good evidence to think that Zenobia really did consider herself to be as much an intellectual as a military strategist and desert ruler. She was clearly seeking to follow in the steps of Ptolemaic Cleopatra, and thought that she might achieve a different fate than her doomed predecessor – in point of fact, no matter the version of her end, she did indeed achieve that dubious goal.

Our sources agree that Zenobia's removal was soon followed by another roll of the Palmyrene dice. Zosimus states (1.60) that the Palmyrenes began trying to convince the new Roman official in Mesopotamia – Marcellinus – to support their plan to engender a new revolt against Aurelian. Marcellinus was quite loyal to his emperor, and on the pretext of saying that he needed more time to think about the complex proposals, he took the chance of informing Aurelian of what the Palmyrenes were plotting. The Augustan 'life' says that the Palmyrenes went so far as to kill one Sandario, whom Aurelian had entrusted with the command of a military garrison, and alongside the commander some 600 archers. The result of the treachery and rebellion was that a kinsman of Zenobia named Achilleus was said to have been declared ruler (although Zosimus identifies Antiochus as the new would-be king).

We cannot be absolutely sure, but this second Palmyrene revolt probably occurred in the early summer of AD 272. It was a perfect example of the sort of problem that so often confronted a Roman emperor, especially in an age where the personal presence of the emperor was deemed essential for dealing with all manner of crises. When Aurelian departed for the West, trouble resumed almost at once. Aurelian was probably back in Palmyra in the spring of 273 – again, the exact chronology is difficult if not impossible to reckon.

The Augustan 'life' would have us believe that Aurelian quickly taught the Palmyrenes a lesson they would not soon forget. He returned at once, ready to vent his wrath against those who would not keep faith with Rome. A letter purporting to be from Aurelian to an otherwise unknown Cornelius Bassus is preserved in the biography, in which the emperor finally calls for a halt to the slaughter, noting that soon there would be nobody left in Palmyra if the anger of Rome was allowed to continue unabated. The temple to the sun god Bel at Palmyra was ordered to be restored – long considered one of the best preserved ruins from Palmyra, it was destroyed by ISIL terrorists in August 2015.

Zosimus (1.61) offers more information about the failure of the renewed Palymrene uprising. He says Aurelian hastened back to Antioch, where he surprised a crowd that was attending a horse race. He then went to Palmyra, which he captured and sacked without a fight. Antiochus was dismissed from office (not executed, we might note – the historian states that Aurelian did not think this nobody worthy of being punished).

There are significant mysteries attendant on the mission of Aurelian to the Roman Near East, riddles that defy solution in the absence of better evidence. When Aurelian took power in the wake of the untimely death of Claudius Gothicus, the main problem in the East was the violent expansion of the Palmyran Empire of Zenobia. Persia had been relatively quiet – we were, after all, in the last days of Sapor, and the Persians had to contend with a new monarchical transition. Yet Persia was also more than willing to support Zenobia, and Aurelian would have recognized all too readily that Persia remained a formidable threat to Roman security in the East. We lack information about one of the most important aspects of Aurelian's work in Mesopotamia and Syria – his punitive expeditions against Persia in the wake of the defeat of Zenobia.

John White (page 106) argues that Aurelian more than demonstrated his ability to respond with alacrity to every manner of crisis in the speed with which he returned to Palmyra to deal with the rebellion of Antiochus. Palmyra would not rise again as a threat to Rome; Aurelian had destroyed that city's hope to be a major power broker in the Roman East. We shall mention Palmyra again when we study the work of Diocletian, but for all intent and purpose, the city no longer entered the pages of the story of Rome's involvement in the region. Palmyra would, however, be front-page news for its tragic history under ISIL in the mid-2010s – a sad new chapter in the long life of the desert city.

Survivors of the fall of Palmyra would be present at Aurelian's triumph, the Augustan 'life' says – even Arabs from Arabia Felix. Aurelian did much in AD 273 and 274 alongside the reduction of Palmyra. There was the need to recover Egypt, as well as the reunification of the so-called Gallic Empire in the West with Rome. There could have been precious little time for the new emperor to enjoy any rest, but by the end of 274 he could at least rest assured that he had successfully put back together the pieces of the Roman Empire. Some would argue that Aurelian is largely responsible for the fact that Rome would endure more or less intact for another two centuries.

In Persia, Sapor was succeeded by his son Hormizd I. He would have assumed power in May AD 270, but all too little is known of his reign. He would rule, as it turned out, for only about a year, succeeded in June 271 by his older brother Bahram I. Bahram's reign would last until September 274, when he was succeeded by his son Bahram II.

For the purposes of our story, the main thrust of Persian history in this period was one of relative weakness in the aftermath of the great reign of Sapor. His sons Hormizd I and Bahram I were not destined to leave marks comparable to their father in terms of westward expansion and recovery of old Persian domains. Whatever support the Persians gave to Zenobia and her Palmyrenes, it was probably on a small scale and certainly easily checked by Aurelian.

Aurelian had left the East to deal with the many other pressing problems of empire. But he had every intention of returning in the autumn of AD 275, when he joined that long catalogue of other assassinated emperors. In some sense, the death of Aurelian offers an unworthy and ignominious footnote to a glorious and successful career. He was said to have been unduly strict in handing out punishments, and a minor official was worried that a lie he had told would result in serious consequences. The official forged a document that was essentially a 'death list' of men the emperor was allegedly planning to kill. It was more than enough to engender a conspiracy, such that the Praetorian Guard was willing to murder Aurelian to save their own lives.

Aurelian's death had one consequence that the emperor could not have foreseen: the brief *de facto* restoration of the Roman Republic. The army apparently experienced significant remorse in the wake of Aurelian's killing. He had, after all, been one of the most successful and accomplished emperors in memory. On the eve of his death, he was planning to return to the Roman East to deal with Persia once and for all.

The army thus entrusted the Senate with the power to choose the next emperor. Ironically, they chose an aged senator named Tacitus, who claimed descent from the line of the famous historian of imperial Rome. While the emperor's boasts of Tacitean lineage may well be a total fabrication, what is much more likely is that we owe a debt of gratitude to the emperor Tacitus for the preservation of the historical writings of his namesake. Tacitus is one of those authors who barely survived late antiquity and the Middle Ages, and the short reign of the emperor Tacitus (he would be dead in June AD 276, after less than a year in office) may be best remembered for the preservation of those invaluable historical works. The Senate would never again select an emperor.

The Augustan 'life' of Aurelian reports that the emperor had declared war on Persia before his assassination, and he was slain in Caenophrurium in Thrace – modern north-western, European Turkey. The events that precipitated that war are not well documented, and the Tacitean aftermath to the unexpected assassination of Aurelian is also the source of confusion in our sources. It appears in general outline that Tacitus was forced to deal first with eastern problems, only then to be summoned to address renewed western crises – the see-saw pattern of imperial management that had become all too common. Tacitus died at Tyana in Cappacodia of a fever – at least according to the Augustan history and the fourth-century historians Eutropius and Aurelius Victor. In Zosimus (1.63), he is said to have been murdered. He had appointed his cousin Maximinus to Syria, and his relative had angered the Syrians to such an extent that in collaboration with the killers of Aurelian, they conspired to murder Maximinus, and soon thereafter Tacitus also.

The accounts are irreconcilable, not least because there is good reason to believe that Tacitus had done away with the murderers of Aurelian as part of the usual imperial/monarchical practice of making sure that regicides never survived to provide an example to other would-be rebels. Of greater interest to our story is exactly what was going on in the Roman East in the last days of Aurelian and during the brief rule of Tacitus.

Why would Aurelian plan to attack Persia? Some scholars have wondered if part of the issue was a desire once and for all to avenge Valerian's humiliating defeat and capture in AD 260 – an event that some, at least, would still remember all too ruefully. It is conceivable that there was a resurgence under Persia that followed the usual pattern of pendulum swings; the Roman emperor had been busy in the West, and Persia was able to regroup and step into the relative vacuum of power in the East once again. It may simply be that Aurelian considered business to be unfinished in the East, but that the restoration of the Gallic Empire and other western problems had demanded critical attention.

Did Aurelian intend utterly to subjugate the Persian Empire? We can only speculate. Certainly there is reason to believe that he intended a significant expedition at the time of his death. Tacitus would be preoccupied with crises in Asia Minor, allegedly because barbarians who claimed that they had been recruited by Aurelian for service in his Persian campaign were discomfited by the emperor's death and their suddenly being without a job. Bereft of pay from Aurelian's coffers, they decided to take their own money by pillaging Asia Minor. Tacitus would thus have been busy dealing with that crisis when he met either fever or assassination in the summer of AD 276 in Cappadocia.

If it is true that the crisis in Asia Minor was occasioned by discontent among foreign auxiliaries and mercenaries who had been recruited for what would have been a massive anti-Persian campaign, then the assassination of Aurelian had far-reaching consequences indeed. Tacitus would be replaced by his praetorian prefect Florian, who may have been the brother or half-brother of the aged emperor.

Florian is certainly one of the least memorable men who could claim that they had died an emperor. He had more or less declared himself emperor in the wake of Tacitus' death, and while he was recognized quickly and widely, a veteran army commander of Aurelian's and Tacitus' – Probus – would challenge the prefect's claim to the purple. This was the Probus who had been entrusted by Aurelian with the recovery of Egypt from Zenobia's Palmyra.

Florian probably should have analyzed the situation a little better, and recognized the precarious situation in which he found himself. Probus had an impressive record as a military commander, and extensive army support. By September of AD 276, Florian would be killed either by his own troops or after having been captured by Probus' forces. Florian would never leave what is today Turkey for the extent of his three-month imperial tenure.

In the dangerous game of third-century imperial politics, Probus would be one of the more successful players. He would have a longer time in office, in fact, than his former employer Aurelian. He would distinguish himself as a commander of great aptitude, with a strong sense of respect for the Senate and the republican traditions of Rome. He would, in short, be one of the better emperors in a mediocre age.

Probus had extensive experience in the East, and yet after his settling of the succession question and the death of Florian, he did not proceed to any grand commencement of Aurelian's Persian plans. He moved west, ready to deal with the myriad problems in other theatres of the far-flung Roman world involving the Alamanni, the Franks, the Burgundians, the Longiones and the Goths. Probus would enjoy the titles *Gothicus Maximus* and *Germanicus Maximus* before the end of those campaigns. Zosimus (1.65) tells the lurid story that Probus did see to the deaths of the killers of both Aurelian and Tacitus, inviting them to a banquet where he ordered their deaths – with the sole survivor of the dinner massacre then having been captured and burned alive.

Probus was a busy ruler during his reign from AD 276–282. And before he would meet the doom of so many emperors before and after him, Probus would also face the prospect of renewed war in the East.

Chapter 14

From Probus to Diocletian

'The decade after the death of Aurelian is one of the most obscure in the annals of the Roman Empire.' Such is the verdict of David Potter in his great history of Rome from AD 180–395 (page 271). The ultimate bringer of stability would be Diocletian, who would assume power in 284. The period from 275 to the coming of Diocletian was one of internal crisis and continuing foreign threats to the stability of an incredibly fragile empire.

Zosimus (1.66) tells of two uprisings against Probus, on opposite sides of the Roman world. Saturninus in Syria rose up against his emperor and former benefactor, but is said to have been put down by his own men. There is also evidence of troubles in Roman Britain. We have little information on the Saturninus uprising of AD 280, and even less on the British crisis of the same general period. Names like Proculus and Bonosus add to the catalogue of 'pretenders' who allegedly aspired to imperial power in a confused and confusing age. What is certain is that whatever plans there were for dealing with Persia – in other words, the dream of Aurelian that had been cut short by his death – Probus was more than preoccupied with other problems by the time he celebrated a triumph in the winter of 281. By then, Probus had achieved appreciable victories against both foreign and domestic foes, and in an eerie replay of history, was ready to do exactly what Aurelian had done in the same situation – prepare for a campaign against Persia.

While on the march in Illyricum toward this eastern expedition, the Augustan 'life' says that Probus was treacherously murdered, perhaps by his own men. It would have been the autumn of AD 282.

The actual story of the death of Probus is fraught with conflicting and disputed accounts. The Augustan 'life' says that Probus' problem was that he never allowed his soldiers to be idle. When not fighting, soldiers were to be assigned to all manner of labour and hard work. Further, Probus allegedly made comments about how in the future there would be no need for a standing army in Rome. In other words, once all of Rome's enemies were vanquished, the huge expense of maintaining such a massive Roman military could be foregone.

If such remarks were made, they were clearly meant either in jest or as some rueful comment on the incredible demands of fostering and preserving the unwieldy, cumbersome Roman military apparatus. Alternatively, they could simply be a legitimate lament about how Rome's emperors of late seemed to proceed from one crisis to another with little chance for repose. At Sirmium – the emperor's birthplace – he is said to have invested many thousands of his men with the laborious and unpleasant task of draining a marsh. The men rebelled and killed their taskmaster of an emperor, though the Augustan 'life' reports that he was buried by his very killers with honour and respect. With this account of the emperor's death, we may compare the account in Eutropius (9.17), which offers little detail.

Zosimus' account of the end of Probus is lost, but there is evidence of another version of the emperor's demise. The praetorians are said to have acclaimed their commander Marcus Aurelius Carus as emperor. In this version, Probus' men rebelled against him and sided with Carus. It is of course possible to reconcile these versions – Probus may have irritated too many of his men with an insistence on military discipline and a strong work ethic. What is certain and most relevant for our story is that it would be Carus and not Probus who would inherit the huge problem of facing Persia in war.

Carus was another of those emperors who came to power with the added strength of having sons ready to aid him and, potentially, to succeed him in the purple. Carus' sons Carinus and Numerian offered a new miniature dynasty of the sort that Rome had seen so often before. Whether or not Carus was complicit in the end of Probus, he found himself in the autumn of AD 282 with his chance to demonstrate that he could be a new Aurelian, a new emperor who would earn a place among the finer rulers of an empire in undeniable crisis.

The author of the Augustan 'life' of Carus and his sons opens his account of the aftermath of Probus' death with a powerful essay on fate and Roman history. The troubles of the empire had been largely solved by Aurelian, and Probus had lived up to his name – the Latin adjective means 'upright' – and now his maddened soldiers had slain him. One might have expected a tyrant now like Domitian (whose brother Titus before him had been one of Rome's better emperors), Vitellius or Nero. Rome was still suffering the aftermath of the disgrace of Valerian's capture and the dissolute rule of his son Gallienus.

The biographer proceeds to give a long account of all the blessings of fortune that had been visited upon Rome, even in times of crisis. Carus would not be a tyrannical figure – he would be mediocre, to be sure, but in the estimation of his biographer he was destined to be numbered among the better emperors, cursed only in his son Carinus (another commonplace of Roman historiography – the emperor who is undone by a markedly inferior son).

In point of fact, Carus would be emperor for less than one year. The Augustan 'life' says that he launched an invasion of the East and recaptured Mesopotamia, even joining the ranks of those Roman emperors who managed to reach Ctesiphon. The Persians are said to have been troubled by internal strife that hampered their resistance to Carus' armies; he was soon able to be acclaimed as conqureror of Persia. There seemed to be no reason why he should not continue his eastward advance, capturing more and more before him in a vigorous assault such as had not been seen in the East for some time.

And then, at the height of his power and glory, he died – either of disease or by a stroke of lightning – sometime in the summer of AD 283, somewhere beyond the River Tigris. At the age of 61, he had done more against Persia than even Aurelian before him.

Bahram II had proven to be no Sapor, not even perhaps a Hormizd or a Bahram I, having failed to secure his empire against Carus' ferocious assault. Carus had been hailed as *Persicus Maximus* before his death, and not without cause. There is no confused tradition here that Carus may have suffered this or that defeat before more or less restoring the *status quo*. Before Carus had entered the Near East, the Persians largely held sway across what had once been Roman Mesopotamia. After Carus, they had once again lost Ctesiphon, it seems, and were in danger of suffering a massive invasion of territories no Roman before Carus had realistically been able to contemplate seizing.

Despite Carus being emperor for less than a year, in that time he managed to a very high degree to restore Roman prestige in the East. The disgrace of the defeat and kidnapping of Valerian had largely been erased, with Roman authority restored in areas that had become Persian playthings. We would give much to know exactly how the obscure emperor had managed to do what so many before him had failed to achieve.

It seems that the internal divisions in Persia must account for some of the problem. Bahram is said to have been preoccupied with rebellions in what is today Afghanistan. Persia, like Rome, was a vast empire that had many conflicting crises at any given time. It is easy in studying the history of Roman Mesopotamia and Arabia to forget that Persia had more problems than simply whatever Roman army or garrison was stationed in modern Syria or Iraq.

The story of the lightning strike that killed Carus is the sort of tale that occasions suspicion from modern historians. Certainly it could have been true, and if it was, there should be no surprise that the death was seen as the judgment of the gods on an emperor who had perhaps advanced too far, too fast. Carus would be destined to suffer something of the fate of Trajan – almost as soon as he was succeeded, the Romans relinquished much of what they had captured. The River Tigris was seen by some as a divinely set barrier and boundary between the two great empires. Festus states it simply (24.2): the victory of Carus was seen as excessively powerful in the eyes of heaven: '*Cari imperatoris victoria de Persis nimium potens superno numini visa est.*'

The Augustan 'life' gives a lurid, allegedly eyewitness account of the tempest and storm that accompanied Carus' death. Ctesiphon was seen as a limit of conquest. There were tales of a violent peal of thunder, and then shouts from his entourage that the emperor was dead. Whatever really happened – and we do well to remember that he may have died simply of disease – the event was dramatic, and it spelled the end (at least for the moment) of the great Persian War.

Carus' son Carinus had been entrusted with maintenance of western problems while his father was preoccupied in Persia. His other son Numerian was with him, and was compelled now – whether ready or not – to take on the burdens of empire.

The most powerful men in the Roman Near East on the day of Carus' death were his son and successor, and the praetorian prefect Arrius Aper. The Augustan 'life' of father and sons does not have much to say about Numerian's conduct of the war in Persia, noting first that he began to suffer an ailment of the eyes occasioned by too little sleep (certainly the breathtaking speed of the campaign must have been exhausting), and then that he was killed by the connivance of Aper.

The 'life' omits the fact that Numerian apparently organized a retreat westward from Persia and that his death came in the second half of AD 284, about a year after he had assumed power. According to the twelfth-century Byzantine chronicler Zonaras, Numerian suffered a defeat (*Epitome Historiarum* 12.30). There is evidence that he was alive and at Emesa in March of 284, with his withdrawal from Persia already well underway. At some point in either Bithynia or Thrace, Aper and his officers began to report that the emperor needed to be carried in a covered litter because of his eye problems. One day, the stench from the litter proved impossible to conceal any longer. The curtains were opened and the decaying body of the young emperor was discovered.

If the triumph of his father Carus is a story that we wish we knew far more about, the downfall of Numerian is even more mysterious. Like Hadrian and Trajan, he seemed eager to be done with the Persian War, and indeed he may have suffered a setback that did not cement his security with the army. Their confidence in him may well have been undermined by a powerful prefect like Aper, who likely wished the imperial chessboard to be simplified once again. Numerian may well have been given more to the bookish pursuits that are reported in the Augustan 'life' – certainly campaigns against Bahram II were not much on his mind.

The verdict of heaven had been pronounced upon the overly successful Carus, and the Augustan 'life' asserts that heaven also avenged the death of Numerian. In the wake of his demise, the army in council met to decide who should replace him and the choice fell on Diocletian, the commander of the cavalry wing of the imperial bodyguard. One of Diocletian's first actions as would-be new emperor was to eliminate Aper; if the prefect had indeed orchestrated the death of Numerian, he offered yet more proof that regicide was an exceedingly hazardous enterprise.

Diocletian is said to have quoted Virgil in his personal slaying of Aper, a fact that the Augustan biographer notes as surprising to some because of a soldier emperor's evident literary knowledge. Of course there is the inevitable story that an omen had been given to Diocletian that he would attain great power after slaying a wild boar – the meaning of *aper* in Latin.

Concealed in the brief and obscure account of Numerian's short hold on power is the reality that Rome decided to abandon its Persian expedition yet again. History was repeating itself in more than one way. The relative brevity of Carus' rule points not so much to a grand imperial strategy at work as to the vicissitudes of the changing wearers of the purple. Bahram II was busy with the consolidation of his own power, which he would achieve soon enough – he would hold the coveted title of *shahanshah* of the Persian Empire until AD 293. Whether Numerian himself had ended the Roman campaign or his soldiers had demanded the cessation of hostilities, the end result was the same: Rome was once again in retreat from the East.

Numerian's brother Carinus was not destined to be a rival of Diocletian's for very long. He would be defeated in July AD 285 at the Battle of the Margus River in Moesia (present-day Serbia). Carinus certainly has a reputation in the surviving sources for having been one of the worst of emperors, a man whose support in the Senate was much affected by his penchant for adulterous affairs with senatorial and military wives. Indeed, in one version of events Carinus was actually slain by a military tribune whose wife had been one of the emperor's innumerable affairs. Carinus' short tenure and history's verdict of a disreputable life – whether justly deserved or the result of Diocletian's quite effective propaganda in the wake of his assumption of sole power – has little relevance, in any case, to the story of the Roman East.

Diocletian is famous as one of the most successful of Roman emperors. He is renowned for his establishment of the so-called tetrarchy, or rule of four men – the two Augustuses and the two Caesars – who would share power in a complex arrangement of joint responsibilities and a mechanism for succession. He is also, however, infamous for his great persecutions of Christians.

Diocletian is generally considered to be the next restorer or saviour of Rome after the reign of Aurelian. Certainly Rome achieved new-found stability under his rule; he would remain in power until the spring of AD 305 as the senior Augustus in the tetrarchy, with special responsibility for the Roman East. He shared his power with Maximian as the western Augustus, with Constantius Chlorus and Galerius as the junior partner Caesars.

He was another Balkan emperor, having been born within the borders of modern Croatia. It is remarkable that we know so very little about the first forty-odd years of the life of the man who would do so much to transform the empire. In point of fact, we really have no certain evidence of his career or whereabouts until an appointment by Carus in AD 282. His name was Diocles until he changed it to Diocletianus (whence the English 'Diocletian'), a more Latin-sounding version of his Greek birth name.

Diocletian was exceedingly busy in the early months of his reign, and not least because of the conflict with Carinus. He would be fighting the Sarmatians in the Balkans in AD 285. By the winter of 285 into 286, he was back in the East, however, ready to make his mark on that vast and troubled region of Roman conquest. His visit to the East did not take on the characteristics of an invasion or renewed war with Persia. On the contrary, it seems to have been a journey of consolidation, reorganization and diplomatic manoeuvring.

Diocletian seems to have enjoyed particular success in his eastern adventures in AD 287. King Bahram II was not interested in a war with Rome, and Diocletian had no ambitions to be a new Alexander the Great. Diplomacy was the word of the hour, and soon enough the two great empires were officially at peace.

Of course in some sense there were significant parallels between Diocletian's experience and that of Bahram. Both men knew all took well the problems of internal threats to one's rule. They understood that Rome and Persia had expended enormous resources in ongoing wars that had done little to change the map of the Near East. It is quite possible that both men were in complete agreement on the need to make an official peace between the neighbouring superpowers.

Diocletian admittedly came to the borders of Persia (in name if not in person) in a position of relative strength. The memory of Carus' victories would have been fresh, while Bahram was still recovering from his serious internal crises. Diocletian had a respectable reputation and a long history of military experience, and there was thus a credible threat of renewed war.

Persia definitely ceded Mesopotamia to Rome as a consequence of the Diocletianic treaty of AD 287. There was also possibly a surrender of any claim to authority in at least part of Armenia, that troublesome buffer state that had so often been the locus for serious hostilities.

Sources for the reign of Diocletian are plentiful enough, but problematic. The *Augustan History* gives out after the deaths of Carus and his sons, while gaps in Zosimus' history prevent a detailed account of Diocletian's reign from that source. Sextus Aurelius Victor and Eutropius continue to provide the same abbreviated account of imperial affairs. There are various Christian sources (coloured of course by the interest of those writers in Diocletian's religious policies and edicts – not without reason are the pages of the liturgical *Martyrologium Romanum* peppered with references to the Christian victims of this era). The Latin panegyric tradition provides additional help in explicating this complicated period in imperial renewal and reorganization.

Diocletian managed to solve the Persian question relatively painlessly and easily. The River Euphrates was now a fixed border, and the throne of

Armenia was in the hands of Tiridates III – a Roman supporter and nominee (this is the Tiridates who would traditionally be hailed as the bringer of Christianity to Armenia in AD 301). The establishment of a peace treaty guaranteed that there would be no need for a massive investment in men and materials to launch a major eastern campaign at a time when the Roman Empire had a plethora of other problems to address. Rome had recognized Persia as a peer empire; there was to be no plan to try to conquer that vast realm in the spirit of fourth-century BC Macedonian imperialism. Gifts were sent to Rome on behalf of Bahram II – it was all the sort of thing that would play well in panegyric composition and Roman imperial propaganda. Given the reality of Carus' impressive conquests, it certainly could be presented as a legitimate act of submission on the part of Persia to its mighty western neighbour.

Indeed, the panegyrics speak of some sort of victory over the *Saraceni*, or Saracens, from this period – certainly to Diocletian's successful settlement of the borders of Roman Syria. The peace that Diocletian secured with Persia would endure for several years without any interruption worth noting (at least according to our extant sources). Carus had launched a major war, and Diocletian had ended it on terms quite favourable to Rome.

Bahram II would remain on the throne of Persia until AD 293, when his death spelled the beginning of a period of relative unrest in that empire. He was succeeded by his son Bahram III, but the young emperor enjoyed nothing like the confidence that seems to have been placed in his father. The legendary Sapor I had one surviving son – Narseh – and he soon assumed power, apparently with the agreement that Bahram III – who did not seek to contest the change of power – would be spared. At some level, it seems clear that Narseh was interested in restoring something of the prestige that Persia had known under his father after years of relative imperial decline.

Sometime in AD 295 or 296, relations between Rome and Persia definitively soured yet again. We cannot be sure of the exact sequence of events, or of the reason for the breakdown of relations. The death of Bahram II and the rise of a son of Sapor might have been cause enough for the resumption of hostilities.

Narseh seems to have struck hard against Tiridates' Armenia, with resultant success for Persian arms. Osroene was next, and soon Roman Syria was under direct threat. Diocletian responded to the threat, with his Caesar Galerius able to support him in force. They split their forces, with

Diocletian seeking to secure Syria and Galerius responsible for proceeding towards Osroene.

Officially, Rome and Persia had been at peace, and at first there must have been a question as to the relative severity of the incursions. But Tiridates' Armenians (the remnants of whom soon met with Galerius' force) were able to tell the tale of just how catastrophic the Persian advance had been. Rome was once again suddenly embroiled in a major war in the East, some eight or nine years after peace had been struck with Bahram.

We have relatively little information on what happened to Galerius' campaign; Eutropius and Festus, as we have seen, are not given to much in the way of detail. Suffice to say Galerius was soundly defeated. The battle was fought – ominously enough – somewhere south of Carrhae, where Crassus had suffered his legendary defeat. The Persians employed *clibanarii* – heavily armoured cavalry. Tiridates survived – just barely – and Galerius was able to secure a successful retreat under the ignominy of defeat. We cannot be sure why he lost – he may simply have been overwhelmed with impossible numerical odds. Galerius had failed miserably in his first chance to prove his mettle as a Roman conqueror and military officer. There are traditions that Diocletian was so incensed with his junior partner's performance that he subjected him to public humiliation. But likely enough he realized that anyone – himself included – might have suffered a setback in similar circumstances.

There was no question of total retreat or settlement: Diocletian realized victory needed to be won. To add to the chaotic eastern scene, there was soon news of a major revolt in Egypt that likely resulted in massacres of Roman officials in Alexandria. Fortunately, yet again history repeated itself in that the Persians did not press their victory against Galerius – it is possible that they, too, had suffered considerable losses. Antioch, for example, remained safely in Roman hands in this crisis. AD 297 was a critical year, and the Romans needed fresh armies in the East to deal both with Persia and the civil unrest in Egypt.

Progress and proper preparation were necessarily slow. Galerius would be able to take the field against Persia in AD 298, this time with a reinforced army that included Goth mercenaries. It may come as a wearying bit of news to report that once again, Roman armies would reach Ctesiphon. Galerius' campaigns in 298 certainly redeemed his reputation, but as with Carus' impressive work years before, we could wish for more in the way of surviving detail about the progress of his advance. Nisibis was recovered in this campaign – we have no certain sense of when it had been lost.

One particularly impressive victory of the war was Galerius' defeat of Narseh at the Battle of Satala in Armenia, in which Narseh himself was wounded and his wife captured. She would spend her captivity in Daphne, a suburb of Antioch – it was not quite the same as having captured a Persian king in evocation of Valerian's disgrace, but it was close.

By the end of AD 298 or early 299, it seems the Romans were in a position to dictate new terms to Narseh – a new treaty between the two empires was to be struck. The Tigris would now be the border between Rome and Persia, and Nisibis was established as the place for economic intercourse between Rome and Persia.

It was certainly another favourable settlement from the Roman perspective, and one that had been bought by the blood spilled in Galerius' campaigns. The so-called Treaty of Nisibis would last far longer than the settlement of AD 287, enduring for some forty years.

Diocletian was no fool, and he evidently knew his eastern Roman history well. He followed up on the treaty with an elaborate amount of work on the fortification of the Roman East, including the defence of the *limes Arabicus* with a heavily defended road, the *strata Diocletiana*. Forts were erected from the southern bank of the River Euphrates down into north-eastern Arabia. This provided employment for workers and soldiers, but most all of it defended Roman commerce and political interests. If anything, Diocletian had shown the perfect balance between conqueror and settler: he had proven that military might could be displayed in conflict against Persia, and had also shown that he was extremely interested in the consolidation and development/defence of the holdings he had won by force of arms.

What Diocletian did in the Roman East with the help of Galerius was long-lasting and secure, allowing for a relative period of peace to ensue on Rome's long border with Persia. Diocletian's reign inaugurated a real period of prosperity and peace in Roman Syria and Mesopotamia, one that would last long after his death and the breakdown of the tetrarchy system. Diocletian would launch his great persecution of Christians from Nicomedia in February AD 303; by 305, he was ready to abdicate (his colleague Maximian joined him in this act, though apparently rather less willingly). Galerius became the Augustus responsible for the maintenance of the eastern provinces, while his nephew Maximinus Daia became his Caesar. Galerius would live until the spring of 311, dying at last of some bowel or gastric complaint that may have been cancer.

The Diocletianic – and, to be fair, Galerian – settlement with Persia would work for some time. But cracks were soon to emerge, even as the tetrarchy system itself showed real signs of strain. Diocletian died in December AD 311, having never agreed to yield in his resolve not to take up power again. There is some evidence that there was a campaign against Persia in this period (perhaps in 310), but in truth the military history of the Roman Near East in this period is largely an obscure mystery. Whatever happened against Persia at this time could not have been on a grand scale. Rome, in any case, was soon enough preoccupied with the internal problems of the strained tetrarchic arrangement. Alongside the frayed and soon-to-be-unravelling nature of internal affairs in the empire, renewed troubles in the Roman East would return.

For further research on Diocletian's remarkable achievements, Stephen Williams' *Diocletian and the Roman Recovery* is a good start (first published by Methuen and Batsford, 1985; Routledge edition, 1997).

Chapter 15

Roman Mesopotamia and Arabia in the Fourth Century

I ngilene, Sophanene, Arzanene, Cordoene and Zabdicene are said to be five territories that the Persians ceded to Rome as a result of the Nisibis treaty of AD 299. The new century would commence with a new reality in the Near East, one in which Rome had more than amply demonstrated the upper hand in the actions of the eastern partners in the tetrarchy. Armenia becoming Christian in 301 under Tiridates was a direct consequence, we might think, of this settlement. The culture of Syrian Christianity that spread rapidly through the region was the result of the Romanization of the Near East (or re-Romanization, in some areas) after the treaty with Narseh.

It is not the purview of this volume to consider the entire history of the empire, and books have justly been written about the circumstances under which the tetrarchy broke down. The death of Galerius came soon after he published an edict in toleration of Christianity; the religious freedom accorded to Christians was a positive note on which to end a reign that would also bring with it a serious blow to whatever stability the tetrarchy enjoyed in AD 310.

Soon in the West, the ultimate winner of Rome's new romance with civil wars – the immortal Constantine the Great – would be fighting Maxentius. In the East, Galerius' nephew and Caesar Maximinus Daia would be upset that his uncle chose for Licinius to be promoted to Augustus after him. Why we hear that Maximinus was busy campaigning in Armenia in AD 312 is as mysterious as whatever engagements with the Persians took place in 310. There were clearly rumblings of trouble in the Near East a little over a decade since the Peace of Nisibis, yet the origins for the problems are lost to history. Certainly they represent yet another unfolding of well-established patterns in Rome's relationship with its eastern neighbours. Maximinus Daia and Licinius would soon come to blows, and the former would be dead in August 313 – perhaps, as some modern researchers have argued, of Graves' Disease (which causes an overactive thyroid).

Licinius and Constantine would make their peace that same year, a year that was also famous for the Edict of Milan that granted toleration to Christianity throughout the empire. One wonders what Diocletian would have thought of the empire that he had sought to recover not so very long before. The relationship between Licinius and Constantine would prove to be a see-saw of peace and war, indeed of an enmity that would last more or less until Licinius' final defeat in AD 324 and his ignominious hanging in 325.

Licinius seems to have engaged in some fighting against Persia around AD 313–314, though as Fergus Millar notes (page 207), 'a ... strictly military history of the period cannot be written'. We are left with tantalizing titbits of information about the breakdown of relations between Rome and Persia, but we cannot be certain if the clashes represent something serious or simply a comparatively unimportant set of developments. Narseh of Persia died in 303, and was succeeded by Hormizd II, his son; his comparatively short reign was marked largely by internal divisions in Persia that mirrored the problems of Rome – he was murdered in 309, to be succeeded by a son who was also murdered after a few months in power (if indeed he even reigned at all – our evidence is inconclusive).

What followed in AD 309, however, is among the legends of Persian/ Iranian history, and may account for the troubles that begin to be dated not long after. Hormizd's wife was pregnant when her husband was murdered, and that unborn child would become Sapor II, a king certainly worthy of that revered name. The exact events of his accession are unknown – scholars have noted that the gender of Hormizd's unborn child would not have been known in advance – but Sapor would emerge as king and rule until his death in 379, thereby ensuring that he would dominate the fourth century and be emperor for longer than any Persian monarch in history.

Whatever military actions took place between Rome and Persia in AD 310 and 313–314 – and however serious – they may well reflect the chaotic situation of transition in the Persian Empire. Sapor II would be a neo-Alexander in some ways, dominating the scene in Persia from as young as the age of 16 with deeds of military valour. Once again, though, it seems that an uncertain era of transition had ushered in a period of strain between Persia and its western neighbours.

Matters were further complicated by the fact that Hormizd had another son – of the same name – who at some point in this succession drama fled for his life to the Roman side of the border. This Hormizd would have a fascinating career, eventually being welcomed and received with honour by Constantine. He would be given a palace on the shores of the Sea of Marmara, and would serve in the Roman Army.

In one sense we ought not to be surprised by the general sequence of events in the Roman Near East in this age. The Treaty of Nisibis was a humiliating one for Persia, even if it secured the peace and avoided large-scale destruction and hardship. It is no surprise that Sapor II would grow up eager to repudiate the treaty, and the escape of Hormizd to Rome would add a personal note to the whole matter. Much of the history of Rome's relationship with Persia in the fourth century would be the result of the efforts of Sapor to rewrite the treaty of AD 299.

Constantine the Great amply earned his honorific appellation. A man of striking personal and political contrasts, he was if nothing else an indefatigable and inveterate survivor. His death in late May AD 337 marked the end of one of the longest tenures in Roman imperial history, and came at a time of remarkable stability for an empire that had been riven not so very long before by such internal and external crises. He had transformed Rome, not least in the matter of religious adherence and toleration. His veneration as a saint by some Christians to this day is a striking contrast with the Antichrist-like role of Diocletian in the history of the same faith.

Constantine died, however, aware that there were troubles afoot with Sapor's Persia. The degree to which Constantine himself was responsible for those tensions is impossible to assess with anything approaching complete certainty. What is clear enough is that the clash Constantine envisaged between Rome and Persia was cast in religious terms. Valerian, for example, had been a notorious persecutor of Christians. Any defeat he suffered – and in the annals of imperial history, few defeats could be compared to his disgrace – was seen as surely the result of the judgment of the Christian god. It was a verdict that had apparently not been pronounced on Diocletian, who had been responsible for far worse persecutions of Christians than anything Valerian had managed to accomplish, but it was still easy-enough propaganda to declare about the plaything of Sapor I's mockery of Rome.

Christianity was certainly spreading on the borders of Persia, and Constantine would be but the first civil ruler in history who saw it as a key element of his job description to be responsible for the protection of Christians. Any future war with Persia would now be a religious one in ways that had not been true in the days of pagan Rome.

The ecclesiastical historian Eusebius is our source for the letter that Constantine is said to have written to Sapor II in which he proclaimed that he was the protector of Christians living even outside the borders of the Roman Empire. It was a striking assertion of power that is not altogether out of character for the man we know from our sources. It would also have been taken as an immense provocation, one that was perhaps quite deliberate. Eusebius' 'life' of Constantine (4.8–13) offers a record of the dramatic declaration. The date of the letter is uncertain, but if we can believe Eusebius, before Constantine died he learned from emissaries of Sapor that the Roman emperor's wishes were to be respected – there would be peace between Rome and Persia yet again, this time on the substance of imperial demands and thinly veiled threats.

Constantine was certainly aging, and he could have harboured no serious plans about launching a major war in the East in that fateful spring of AD 337 when he finally received baptism and was cleansed of his many sins in the purifying waters of the Christian sacrament of regeneration. We know that in the years shortly before his death – 335 or 336 – his son Constantius was assigned to be responsible in particular for the defence of the Roman East. But none of these snippets of information tell us about the grand plans of the emperor, if indeed any had been definitively formulated. Rome upon the death of Constantine was in a tense situation with Sapor's Persia: the king was by now in his twenties and eager, we might think, to prove a point against Rome, but things had been far more tense before, and with little appreciable consequence.

There are numerous books and articles on Constantine. Highly to be recommended is David Potter's 2013 Oxford monograph, *Constantine the Emperor*, with reliable coverage of every aspect of the reign.

Roman history would enter a dramatic new phase in the aftermath of Constantine's death. Some years before he died – probably around AD 330 – somewhere in the Roman East (possibly Syria), the man who has been called the last of the classical historians was born. Ammianus Marcellinus would live until the last decade of the century whose history is known largely because of his efforts. He was a soldier and military man, as well as a writer of no small merit. His *Res Gestae* was a massive Roman history that commenced with the death of Nerva in 96 and proceeded to his own day. Regrettably, only the sections that cover the years 353–378 survive – a period in which Ammianus was an eyewitness to much of what he reported.

Ammianus had experience in the wars with Persia that would erupt under Sapor II. What he accomplished in both public and private life is astonishing, not least given the extreme difficulties of his age. The fact that Books 18–31 of his history survive at all is miraculous. To be fair, his extant work has not survived all too well – the manuscript tradition and the ravages of time have not been kind to this would-be successor of Tacitus. Yet the Austrian historian Ernst Stein did not hesitate to call Ammianus the greatest genius of letters to emerge between Tacitus and Dante.

Ammianus is conveniently available in a three-volume Loeb Classical Library edition. To read through the surviving history is an exercise in growing admiration for the towering rhetorical achievement of the man, and a harrowing journey through some of Rome's most difficult hours. After a gap in available sources for the military history of the empire, it is especially delightful to work through Ammianus (whatever his faults – and they have often been overemphasized).

Constantine's death was followed by the ill-fated joint rule of his three sons, Constantine II, Constans and Constantius II. The last of these brothers had been assigned, as we have seen, to command in the East, and he would inherit that region of Rome as his initial domain. Destined to die of natural causes in AD 361, he would actually enjoy an appreciably long period in power – though not a tenure that was bereft of serious challenges, both foreign and domestic.

Constantius II had the usual serious succession concerns to busy him in the spring of AD 337 and beyond. He would travel to Sirmium in Pannonia to meet with his brothers and discuss the partition of the empire. Sapor II – not at all surprisingly – is said to have launched an attack on the Roman East almost as soon as the new co-emperor had departed from Asia. It was a pattern we have seen time and again. This was certainly the great chance for Sapor, the king might well have thought, so he launched his gamble. Before long, Persian armies were besieging Nisibis, the city of Diocletian's now-forgotten peace.

Peter Crawford has authored an immensely detailed life of Constantius II for Pen & Sword, with the provocative title *Constantius II: Usurpers, Eunuchs and the Antichrist* (2016). This volume studies every aspect of his reign, not least the significant religious turmoil of the age occasioned by the theological views of a notorious Christian priest from Alexandria, Arius. Crawford provides a very helpful summary (pages 41 ff.) of the history of Roman–Persian relations before Constantius' war with Sapor II. He also provides an introduction to the religious issues of Zoroastrianism and Christianity that are relevant to appreciating better the problems confronted by Persia in the early to mid-fourth century. Ilkka Syvänne's

Military History of Late Rome, 284–361 (Pen & Sword, 2013) is another book that provides equally comprehensive coverage of the period; a 2018 companion volume continues the story from AD 361–395.

The early days of Sapor II's active majority were apparently spent fighting against various Arab tribes. The mutual disdain of Arabs and Persians was alive and well on the fringes of Sapor's empire. The death of Tiridates III of Armenia in AD 330 – allegedly poisoned by a conspiracy of his own nobles – added to the instability in the region. Festus (27) gives a summary of the many military actions against the Persians with which Constantius is credited. In addition to minor border skirmishes, he is said to have engaged with Sapor's armies nine times in all, seven times through his subordinate commanders and twice in person. He was wounded once in combat. Nisibis is said to have been besieged three times by the Persians, with heavy losses to Sapor's forces. At the Battle of Narsara, Sapor's general Narseh was among the dead. Constantius was present at a night battle at Eleia near Singara, where the emperor saved the occasion by calling back his overly enthusiastic men from an ill-timed assault.

Our sources do not provide a definitive account of the early stages of Sapor's westward incursions. We have observed that after the death of Constantine, Persia seems to have taken the opportunity to strike against Rome. Indeed, Sapor seems to have targeted Armenia even before the great Roman emperor was dead, sending his general Narseh to invade in AD 336. Amida, in what is today south-eastern Turkey, was captured. Constantius' victory at Narasara and Narseh's death belong to this period, in which the young Caesar was earning his military reputation the hard way against Persia.

By the time Constantius was back on the scene in the East after settling his succession, Sapor had already done significant damage in a subsequent series of attacks, this time on a larger scale – and now Nisibis was under heavy siege. The city was able to resist valiantly – there is some evidence that the Romans may even have employed a primitive form of biological warfare against the Persian invaders, as there are reports that swarms of insects attacked Persian pachyderms and men alike (there may have been a plague). By AD 338, Constantius was fully invested in the war against Sapor and ready to take the initiative, at least in some fashion. His brother Constantine II would soon fall in conflict against Constans (in 340).

The years surrounding the death of Constantine, then, can be identified as a time of Persian resurgence, but with Constantius' response more than checking Sapor's ambitions. What happened after AD 338 is extremely poorly documented. There were certainly military engagements, but it seems that mutual cavalry raiding was the order of the day for both sides. There was a decisive Battle of Singara between Constantius and Sapor, but our evidence is so poor that we cannot even be certain when this crucial engagement occurred – it was perhaps in 343 or 344, or even as late as 348. This was certainly the occasion on which the nocturnal attack described briefly by Festus took place, which was fought to what appears to have been a highly costly draw.

Singara seems to have convinced Constantius that he needed to wear down Sapor by a defensive strategy, seeking to compel the Persians to throw their resources against heavily fortified towns and military bases. After all, as Crawford notes (page 56), 'From 337 to 353, Constantius had to face down the most bellicose and skilled of Persian kings with what amounted to a third of [the] Empire's resources and little help from his brothers.' Indeed, sibling rivalry in this period may well have meant that Constantine II and Constans were hopeful (until their respective deaths) that Constantius would fail in his eastern campaigns.

Sapor seems to have launched yet another strike against Nisibis, perhaps in AD 346. The first siege had lasted for something like two months; this one apparently endured for seventy-eight days and thus clearly cost Sapor dearly in men and materials. A third great siege of the city would come in 350, the same year that the usurper Magnentius made his bid for power in the West. Magnentius' forces would be responsible for the death of Constantius' brother Constans near what is today Perpignan in southern France.

One of our sources for the dramatic events of Sapor's third attempt to take Nisibis is the lengthy panegyric authored by Constantius' successor Julian in praise of his predecessor. Needless to say, whatever the truth of the herculean wonders reported by Julian and other sources, Nisibis survived a third time against Persia. Constantius would be distracted with Magnentius' quest for power, but Sapor had incurred frightful losses in his campaign. Sapor, just like Constantius, had problems elsewhere in his own vast empire to contend with in this period – neither ruler had any time to pause. Magnentius would not finally be overcome until AD 353, when his suicide after defeat in battle finished his page in imperial history. The decade from 350–359 was thus an interwar period for Rome and Persia, a time when both Constantius and Sapor turned aside to deal with internal threats to their rule.

It appears that there were negotiations between Rome and Persia in this period, culminating around AD 356 in the commencement of a serious attempt to negotiate a renewed peace. Sapor was militaristic and no doubt felt that he could argue from a position of some strength. He wanted Rome to evacuate Mesopotamia and to relinquish once and for all any authority over affairs in Armenia. However, Constantius was not interested in considering the conditions of what would have been a humiliating peace for Rome: the treaty of 356 would have been just as bad for Rome as that of 299 had been for Persia.

It is in this interwar period that the surviving portions of the histories of Ammianus Marcellinus begin to offer a better, more reliable picture of events. Book 14 covers the years AD 353 and 354. We learn (14.3) that the Persians had been warring with wild border tribes and were preparing another attack on Mesopotamia, in advance of which they were sending out reconnaissance parties. Roman Mesopotamia was guarded by numerous outposts because of the frequency of Persian raids. Sapor's subordinate Nohodares attempted to attack Osroene, but he was betrayed by his own men who deserted to a Roman garrison (at this juncture in his narrative, Ammianus provides a brief, valuable digression on the Saracens – in the Roman estimation, the historian notes, they were a people desirable neither as friends nor as enemies).

The Persians are said in this period to have persisted more in raids and desultory engagements than in any attempt at major military operations (16.9). Ammianus preserves what purports to be the negotiations between Persia and Rome that continued into AD 357/358, including an arrogantly worded letter of Sapor to Constantius. We can only speculate on whether the Persians seriously thought that Rome would give up Mesopotamia and Armenia. It may well have been a deliberate provocation to push the issue of war. Certainly in principle, the demand was impossible for any Roman emperor to countenance, whatever the other pressing concerns of empire (and the pages of Ammianus are replete with descriptions of those myriad problems). The devastation of Nicomedia in this period by an earthquake (17.7) only added to the burdens of the surviving son of Constantine's long and troubled reign.

Book 17 closes out the description of the events of AD 358 by noting that the negotiations between Rome and Persia were at a total standstill. The Romans were proposing that there should at least be a treaty of friendship on the basis of not disturbing the current state of affairs in

Armenia and Mesopotamia. Sapor, for his part, was insistent that the territories must be definitively relinquished to his control. If Persia had once dreamed of recovering all the land once ruled by Darius, no doubt Armenia and Mesopotamia seemed to be a concession. But it was not a demand that Constantius would ever be willing to grant.

AD 359 would thus be the year of renewed full-scale conflict. Ammianus describes Sapor's preparations (18.4). The very border tribes he had subdued during the period of relative peace with Rome now supplied conscript auxiliaries for his ever-growing military force. Ammianus is our only surviving source for one of the more disreputable figures to emerge from our story: the Roman traitor Antoninus (18.5). He had been a merchant, eventually joining the imperial government as a relatively low-level official. Embittered by corruption and personal affronts, he grew tired, to put it simply, of his lot in life and decided to cast in his lot with Sapor's Persia. He crossed the River Tigris and offered himself as a counsellor and advisor to Sapor. We are told that he eventually came to adopt the customs of the Persians, essentially joining the ranks of those figures in history who shockingly defect to the enemy and more or less fully embrace the customs of their new home.

Antoninus is said to have urged Sapor repeatedly to trust in fortune and to take the field against the Romans (18.5). The king, we might well imagine, needed little encouragement.

Ammianus was in Nisibis in AD 359, when the city was preparing for the hazard of a feared fourth siege. He eerily records how he and his fellows saw the fires in the distance from large-scale Persian plundering as Sapor mobilized and moved his forces. A dramatic story unfolds in vivid narrative, as the Romans on the very front lines against Persia react to the early stages of a fully resurgent Persian military campaign. Ammianus himself helped to deliver a missing child back to his parents in the chaos of the hour, before galloping for his life away from advancing Persian cavalry. In Peter Crawford's label (page 175), it was 'The Return of the King of Kings'.

One of the higher ranking military commanders on the scene for Rome was one Ursicinus, a citizen of Antioch who had risen to the rank of *magister equitum*, or cavalry master. Ammianus, who had served under him (based at Nisibis) since AD 353, was deeply devoted to his superior, and blamed the machinations of local court politics for Ursicinus' ultimate failures against Persia.

Sapor did not intend to launch a fourth assault against Nisibis. This time, he planned to bypass the city and instead strike the comparatively easier target of Amida. This siege would last for seventy-three days, and would apparently cost Sapor in the vicinity of 30,000 dead. The siege was ultimately a success for Persia, but something of a Pyrrhic victory. By the time it was over, winter was approaching and the campaign season of AD 359 was at an end – Sapor had essentially lost a huge army all for the sake of one fortress city and some other relatively minor conquests. Book 18 of Ammianus offers a description of Amida and the forces that were on guard there, while Book 19 opens with Sapor urging the city to surrender. Ursicinus tried to relieve the city, but was dissuaded from doing so by the court official Sabinianus (who seemed worried that any such intervention would be disastrous). Unfairly (in Ammianus' estimation at least), Ursicinus would be blamed for the ultimate loss of Amida (20.2).

A plague added to the misery of Amida during the siege. As with the earthquake at Nicomedia, Ammianus takes the opportunity to offer a digression on the causes and types of pestilence. A sally of Gallic legions wreaked havoc among the Persian attackers; the Romans also set fire to the siege engines the Persians used against the walls. Many of the Roman leaders in the city were slain after the capture, while others were held in captivity.

It is thanks to Ammianus that we have a detailed account of the Amida operation. No doubt numerous other such descriptions could have survived for other engagements in the long history of Rome's wars with Persia.

By AD 360, Constantius was on his way in person to deal with the crisis in the Near East. But the man of the hour was increasingly his Caesar in the West, the future emperor known to history as Julian the Apostate.

Julian had been born in Constantinople in AD 331 or 332. He was appointed Caesar in 355, and had distinguished himself in campaigns against the Alamanni and the Franks – he was destined to be one of that elite group of emperors who would experience fighting on opposite sides of the Roman world. There is good reason to believe that Constantius was increasingly jealous of the man who was hastily climbing the imperial ladder; Ammianus (20.4) indicates that the decisive event came when Constantius demanded legions from Julian to use in the Persian War. Julian's Gallic legions responded by declaring him Augustus in February 360, thus raising the spectre of renewed civil war.

Sapor meanwhile needed to take full advantage of the campaign season of the spring of AD 360. Ammianus records (20.6) that he proceeded to invade Mesopotamia with an attack on Singara. This would be another successful Persian operation, though again at high cost to both sides.

Ammianus reports that the Legio I Flavia and Legio I Parthica were defending the city, as well as many native contingents; these are said all to have been killed or captured. The bulk of the Roman military was guarding Nisibis – after three sieges, there was no question in some people's minds that Sapor would strike there again. Ammianus notes that Singara was essentially impossible to defend, since the countryside around it was waterless and bleak. The settlement was there to alert the Romans to the first signs of Persian incursion into Mesopotamia, but in Ammianus' estimation this was a poor strategy given that the defenders of Singara always had to be sacrificed since it was impossible to relieve them in time of crisis.

Sapor was not interested in Nisibis, given the memories of his miseries there. He instead proceed to Bezabde/Phaenica, in south-western Anatolia in modern Turkey. The Second Flavian, Second Armenian and Second Parthian legions were stationed here, together with a sizeable number of auxiliary archer units. There is a story from this siege that Ammianus discounts, namely that a Christian bishop made an attempt to negotiate for peace with Sapor, but was in reality giving him treacherous advice on where to strike the city. Regardless of the truth or falsehood of the story, Sapor did manage to take the site and it was soon the scene of ghastly atrocities and destruction as the Persians spared neither woman nor child. Sapor prudently sought to rebuild the defences of Bezabde and to station a large force there, certain that the Romans would seek to retake such a strategic citadel.

Virta was the king's next target, in no small part, Ammianus notes (20.17), because it was said to have been built by Alexander the Great. Yet here he suffered a defeat – perhaps a victory for the spirit of the Macedonian conqueror.

Constantius, meanwhile, was busy attempting both to negotiate with Julian and to proceed to the relief of the East. He parleyed with King Arsaces of Armenia, seeking to ensure Armenian loyalty and support in the coming struggle. He then advanced through Cappadocia, eventually crossing the Euphrates and arriving in Edessa in Syria (20.11). At Edessa he mustered his available forces and prepared to proceed to Bezabde.

Sapor had prepared well for any eventual Roman attempt to retake the town. The rest of Book 20 of Ammianus is dominated by an account of Constantius' frustrated attempts to successfully besiege the Persian garrison. Losses were frightful, and Ammianus notes that Constantius tended to do better against Persia when fighting with his generals as proxies – in person he did poorly. Constantius retired to Antioch to spend the winter of AD

360/361 – his last Saturnalia season – regrouping and preparing to continue the struggle against Sapor, always with an eye to what Julian was doing in the West.

Constantius was caught in something of a vice of problems: Julian represented a challenge to his Augustan authority that was not going away through letters and courteous attempts at diplomacy, and Sapor – though like Rome having suffered grievously in the campaigns of AD 360 – was still a potent threat and in occupation of Roman trerritory. Constantius seems to have decided to deal first with Persia – at least firmly enough to permit a departure west to confront Julian.

Ammianus relates (21.6) that Constantius learned that the Persians were indeed on the move as the campaign season of AD 361 commenced, though it was uncertain where Sapor intended to strike first. Crossing the Euphrates, the Roman emperor advanced to Edessa. Constantius was in a state of total indecision and confusion by this point (21.13). Intelligence reports were giving little if any useful information on what Persia intended to do. Bezabde was still in enemy hands, but another costly campaign there might leave Mesopotamia exposed to a devastating new Persian strike.

Reports may not have been particularly useful about Persian intentions, but the steady drumbeat of news about Julian was increasingly worrisome. What was actually happening with Persia was that the spring of AD 361 was a time more of retrenchment and regrouping than of major campaigning – once again there was a need for recovery after the devastating losses of the previous season. Constantius eventually decided to leave the usual garrisons behind to defend Mesopotamia, and to head back west to deal at last with Julian. Ammianus notes that the emperor was consoled in this trying time by the memory that in civil wars at least, he had always emerged the victor.

Constantius would live long enough only to proceed west to deal with his imperial rival and former colleague. He would die at Mopsuestia in Cilicia in early November AD 361, aged only 44. The cause of death was fever; the toll of the constant warfare that ended his long reign must have been a contributory factor in any ill health. There is a report that Constantius was baptized before his death, and that he recognized Julian as the rightful heir to the empire. It is quite possible that he was more or less sanguine that Julian would now have to pay the price for his usurpation – he would need to face Sapor's Persia, alongside the myriad other problems of the empire. Book 21 of Ammianus includes a lengthy appraisal of the virtues and vices of the emperor who had managed in some fashion or other to be in power for nearly a quarter of a century of the most turbulent period in late Roman imperial history.

Julian arrived in Constantinople and assumed the purple without further struggle (22.2). By AD 362 he was in Antioch, passing through the ruined region of Nicomedia that had suffered from its aforementioned earthquake. Relief of the devastated area was a priority, though clearly Julian was preoccupied mainly with the joint tasks of securing the loyalty of the Roman East and facing Sapor. Persia could not be expected to remain quiescent for long, and a change of emperors had been the critical moment for renewed hostilities more than once before.

There is good reason to believe that Julian viewed Persia as an opportunity to solidify his control over the empire – a classic instance of using a war as an excuse to deflect from other problems of rule. That said, Sapor was obviously still a threat, and Constantius had left his war quite unfinished.

The continued quiet of Persia during 362 is a testament to the losses Sapor had suffered in his previous campaigns, and also perhaps to the king's strategic plan to wait and see what the new emperor would do. Julian was thus afforded plenty of time to prepare himself for renewed war, and it appears that Rome's new ruler viewed his reign as a chance to conquer Persia once and for all.

Ammianus' Julian (22.12) is desirous for glory, eager to do something – indeed anything – against an inveterate foe of Rome. His counsellors are depicted as doing their utmost to delay a renewed war. Ammianus memorably compares Julian's men to the Pygmies assailing the great hero Hercules.

AD 363 was Julian's fateful year. Arsaces of Armenia was ordered to prepare a large force to support a Roman invasion of Persian territory, and Julian left Antioch at the start of the campaign season in the spring. He may have commanded anywhere from 65,000–90,000 men in all. Not surprisingly given the outcome, the omens are said to have been bad for this March advance.

It is not entirely clear what Sapor's intentions were in this period. His extended period of quiet may be attributed entirely to the aforementioned twin plans of recovery and waiting to see what Julian would do – he may have felt that time favoured the defender. Ammianus says that Julian's advance (which commenced on 5 March) was so rapid that the Persians were caught quite by surprise (22.2). The emperor crossed the Euphrates on a bridge of boats, and arrived at Batnae in Osroene with a large force that included Scythian auxiliary units. He proceeded to the ill-omened locale of Carrhae. From there, Ammianus notes, there was a road to Persia through Adiabene and across the Tigris, and one through Assyria and across the Euphrates.

On the night of 18/19 March, Julian's sleep is said to have been disturbed by troubling dreams and nightmares. The emperor was thus especially cautious on the following day. Later, Ammianus reports, it was learned that the temple of Palatine Apollo in Rome had suffered a devastating fire, and that the precious Sibylline Books kept there had nearly been consumed by the flames.

Julian was preparing for his own departure on campaign when he learned from reports that the Persians had now taken the initiative. In response, Julian put 30,000 men under the command of his kinsman Procopius. Forces were to guard against Persian attack on this side of the Tigris, with orders to join up with Arsaces of Armenia in relief of Julian's planned advance through Assyria.

Julian himself feigned a crossing of the Tigris, but turned instead to the right. The death of a favourite horse named Babylonius was taken by the emperor as an omen of the fall of Babylon.

Ammianus was there with Julian's army as it celebrated the rites of the Trojan Mother Goddess Cybele on 27 March. Julian marched through Mesopotamia and received the acclaim and support of the Saracens as auxiliaries. A Roman fleet of some 1,100 ships bridged the Euphrates. It was in some sense the zenith of Julian's power. That early spring of AD 363, he no doubt thought of himself as another neo-Alexander, determined to do better than his predecessors in the seemingly endless conflict with Persia.

It is not the concern of this volume to deal with Julian's religious administration of the empire, but his persecution of Christians and reversion to the practice of paganism made it easy for later, Christian writers to denounce him for vainglorious pursuits and being deluded by hopes of immense conquest.

Book 23 of Ammianus is famous for its extended digression on the Persian Empire, both its geography and anthropology. It is one of the most important sources in extant Latin literature for our knowledge of Roman understanding of Persia. It repays close study and enjoyment, not least as the earnest record of a man who had first-hand experience of war in the region.

Book 24 resumes the narrative of Julian's campaigns. His advance was careful: 1,500 mounted units rode ahead to provide reconnaissance and ferret out any threat of ambush. Julian's main force consisted of anti-cavalry infantry, which he personally commanded. The cavalry were posted on the wings, their ranks thinned so that if the Persians caught sight of the army, they might be cowed into thinking that the Romans and their allies had a far larger force – a device, Ammianus notes, that was first used by Pyrrhus of Epirus. Julian advanced near what is today the Iraqi town of Anah in Al-Anbar Province. There is an extraordinary story that a Roman was rescued here – a man who had been a soldier many decades before in a previous campaign. He had many wives, according to the custom of the region, and was now bent with old age and surrounded by the many children of his polygamous life. Nearly 100 years old by then, he declared that he had announced long before that he would find a grave in Roman earth.

Dust storms and intermittent skirmishes did not seem to deter Julian's progress. He was now advancing deep into Mesopotamia, in what in a much later age would be the playground for a terrible period of ISIL terrorists in northern Iraq. He was soon at the gates of Pirisabora/ Bersabora, the modern Anbar in the very heart of today's Iraq. The city had a double wall of fortification for defence, that may well have been built by the labour of Roman prisoners. Julian was now only some 50 miles from Ctesiphon.

Pirisabora would be sacked and destroyed after a short, highly successful siege. This was the Roman revenge for the siege of Amida in AD 359. Julian now had spoils with which to enrich his army, and a great victory to his credit. His progress across the deserts of Mesopotamia had begun to reap appreciable results.

Bithra, Diacira and Ozogardana were also destroyed by Julian's advancing force. Book 24 of Ammianus' account devolves into a dramatic story of the impressive work of the Roman army and their auxiliaries in seizing one Persian stronghold after another. In one engagement, some 2,500 Persians are said to have been killed at the cost of just seventy of Julian's men. Whatever the exaggeration of the numbers, the Roman victories were incredible.

Ctesiphon was finally once again in sight as a Roman target (24.7). Julian's counsellors were of mixed opinion on the wisdom of laying siege to one of Sapor's most fortified and staunchly defended cities. There was significant fear that not only would the siege be a severe drain on Julian's army, but that Sapor might appear at any time to confront the Roman invader. The advice given to the emperor was that the surrounding countryside should be ravaged in an effort to cut off supplies from the city.

Julian – perhaps not surprisingly – was not much interested in hearing how he should refrain from seeking to capture a city that had, after all, been taken so many times before in Roman history (only to be given back). At some point Julian seems to have been urged by treacherous machinations to give the order to burn most of the Roman fleet so as to free up soldiers who were otherwise assigned to transport the vessels and guard them; burning the ships would also be a clear signal to the men that they could not simply hope to use a river escape to flee from peril. While the evidence is relatively scanty, it appears that there was a mounting list of problems. The Roman relief that had been assigned to rendezvous with Arsaces of Armenia had failed to appear, and the Persians – although not yet with the main body of the king's army – were increasingly on the scene to harass Julian's force. And Ctesiphon itself was no easy prize under the best of circumstances.

Julian tried to rouse his soldiers by parading Persian prisoners before them, heaping insult on the nation that was allegedly causing such fear among the Roman ranks. A subsequent council of war was as divided as ever. Many in the army wanted to return, though it was pointed out that the countryside behind them had been devastated during the Roman advance, and that they faced the prospect of a long retreat through desert wasteland. Flies, gnats and heat contributed to the barren scene. Julian was resolute in wanting to push on, but his allies in his quest for glory were few.

Camp was finally broken on 16 June AD 363, with a plan to return west by way of Corduene in modern far eastern Turkey. Book 24 of Ammianus' history ends on a dramatic note: at break of day, a large, whirling cloud of dust was seen, which might have been thought to be from a herd of wild asses travelling in a tight pack to escape becoming the prey of lions. Some believed it was Arsaces and the Roman relief force. The Romans decided to encamp and wait to see what was happening, so as not to be attacked in a vulnerable position on the march.

By dawn, it was clear that Sapor's army had finally arrived on the scene. Battle was soon joined in the desert heat of mid-June. Both sides were quickly exhausted by the ferocious clash of arms. The Romans, clearly outnumbered, seem to have engaged in something of a fighting retreat. That withdrawal was hampered by the aforementioned lack of grain and fodder occasioned by the speedy Roman advance eastward.

The end of the Roman campaign came suddenly in Samarra, in modern north-central Iraq, a little under 80 miles north of Baghdad. The basic facts are simple, and the consequences momentous: the Romans and Persians engaged in a major skirmish, in the course of which Julian was fatally injured – thus joining that grim catalogue of Roman emperors who had died in combat. Julian is said to have removed his armour because of the extreme heat, and to have tried to rally his dispirited troops when he was struck down. Julian would die in his tent after what amounted to something of an inconclusive battle: some would argue that the Romans had actually won, others that the Persians were victorious.

It is almost certain that Julian was slain by a spear thrown by a Persian auxiliary. There is a later, Christian version of his downfall in which he utters the immortal words, 'You have conquered, Galilaean' – a reference to the origins of Christ. In some versions of events, a Christian actually struck down Rome's pagan emperor. Tactical successes aside, the Romans had lost their great would-be Alexander and were stranded without an emperor, deep in the heart of enemy territory.

A senior officer by the name of Jovian would hastily be chosen as the next emperor (25.5). He had been born in what is today Belgrade in Serbia – the ancient Singidunum – in AD 331. Now emperor, he found himself moored in an incredibly perilous position in the desert. His decision to resume the retreat that Julian had commenced is no surprise, and he deserves no condemnation for the plan. The Romans endured a continuing fighting retreat, harassed along the way as they made their way to Dura Europos.

The Romans had no ships, and they were sorely in need of supplies. The River Tigris was now a barrier that kept them from making a speedy exit to the relative safety of the west bank. At this juncture, Jovian was compelled to come to terms with Sapor's Persia – and this time, the humiliation would be Rome's.

Sapor, to be sure, had endured his own frightful losses. He is said to have suffered a greater loss of elephants in this campaign than he had ever before experienced; he was fearful that the Romans would gladly exchange their security for a chance at revenge. For Ammianus, the Roman position was by far the worse, and it was only divine providence that saved Jovian's force (including the historian himself). The Persians made the first overtures at peace – and while the conditions would have to be endured, the Romans were apparently more than thankful that any had been offered at all.

Nisibis and Singara were to be surrendered. Five provinces on the far side of the Tigris in Armenia and Mesopotamia were also to be abandoned. In other words, significant territory was to be relinquished as the price of Julian's failed expedition.

Not surprisingly, there was dissension in the Roman ranks and the nascent court of Jovian as to what to do in the wake of Sapor's demands. Jovian in the end did succeed in negotiating that while Nisibis and Singara would be surrendered, the inhabitants would be allowed to depart for Roman territory. The Persians added the demand that Arsaces should never be allowed to use his forces against Sapor – it was clear (as Ammianus realized) that Sapor intended to eliminate Armenia's independence once and for all, and *in toto*. Hostages were exchanged, and it was agreed that the peace would be of thirty years' duration.

There was tremendous suffering in the Roman retreat, from both hunger and the risk of drowning in the river as a crossing was finally commenced. Jovian had but a few vessels, which had to be used repeatedly in trying to convey as many people as possible to safety. The Persians were discovered planning to attack the sick as well as exhausted Roman animals; this was prevented only by a timely intervention.

The Romans arrived at Hatra, which, Ammianus notes (25.4), had once been the object of attacks by both Trajan and Septimius Severus. The march continued, as word began to spread of the Roman defeat and the humiliating conditions of peace that had been imposed. Nisibis learned of its involuntary surrender – the only hope for that city being that Jovian could somehow be persuaded to change his mind and to break the peace.

Conditions were so dire for the retreating Roman army that Ammianus reports that cannibalism was contemplated. Jovian eventually reached the outskirts of Nisibis and made a camp outside the city. The people of Nisibis were unable even to persuade the emperor to enter the gates. The Persian Bineses arrived soon with orders from Sapor to take custody of the new spoils of war (25.9). When the inhabitants of Nisibis were told that they must leave at once, voices were raised in condemnation of Jovian for giving up the city without a fight. Ammianus leaves little doubt as to his own thoughts on the matter, writing that this was, without question, one of the more disgraceful days in the history of Rome's involvement in the Near East.

Jovian and his army proceeded to Antioch (25.10). Ammianus is clear that the emperor was eager to exit the region. He had incurred great unpopularity for the terms of his peace, and he could not have forgotten that he had the rest of an empire to try to manage. He proceeded to Tarsus in Cilicia, the site of Julian's burial. Tyana in Cappadocia was also on his itinerary.

But his final major destination would be Ancyra, the modern Ankara, capital of Turkey. His son Varronianus was made consul as his colleague in office, even though the boy was a mere infant at the time. And then – at Dadastana on the borders of Galatia and Bithynia – Jovian died on 17 February AD 364, at the age of just 33. It was thought he may have suffered carbon monoxide poisoning from a charcoal fire, or have been suffering from acute indigestion. Some might speculate that he had been murdered. Whatever the cause – and Ammianus notes that there was no inquest – Jovian's brief reign was over.

The military officer Valentinian – the man known to history as Valentinian I or Valentinian the Great – would be the new emperor, assuming power at Ancyra before the end of the month. By the end of March, he would agree to share power with his brother Valens.

The problems that would confront the imperial brothers were immense, and were centred on the West. AD 365 would see the invasion of Gaul by the Alamanni as they swarmed across the Rhine. There would also be an attempted revolt by Procopius – one of the last of the Constantinians – in Constaninople. That revolt would be put down by Valens, with Procopius being killed in the spring of 366, and Valens would also have to contend with the Goths who had sent aid in support of the usurper.

Valentinian proceeded to deal with the western crises. By AD 367, Rome was in the throes of suffering from what has been called the Great Conspiracy, with the Picts, Scots, Saxons and Franks launching attacks in both Britain and Gaul. There was every reason to believe that Britain might in fact be lost to the empire. It was as if everything in the far west of Rome's holdings was unravelling; the peace that has been so ignominiously secured in the East had been followed almost at once by the total breakdown of order on the other side of the Roman world. Significant problems in Africa, both foreign and domestic, also plagued Valentinian's reign.

Matters were comparatively quite peaceful in the Roman Near East for some time. But Sapor II was not finished entirely with his grand plans. Now in his sixties, his life had paralleled a century of almost constant major crisis with his Roman neighbour.

Ammianus reports (27.12) that Sapor struck at Armenia – as had been expected – in what must have been sometime between AD 368 and 370. Arsaces would be captured, imprisoned and ultimately killed. In the ensuing troubles in Armenia, there was the inevitable appeal to Rome for help, but Valentinian's brother Valens (who had been entrusted with responsibility for the eastern provinces while his brother sought to manage the West) was not interested, at least initially, in stepping across some tripwire that would spark a new eastern conflagration. Tempers would flare, both in Persia and in the eastern Roman Empire, over the renewed strife in Armenia – but there was no great eruption of war on a grand scale between the two empires, merely Armenian intrigues, however serious they admittedly were for the region.

Valentinian I would die in November AD 375 of apoplexy while angrily dealing with envoys from the Quadi. His death in what is today the far north of Hungary (on the Slovakian border) ended the reign of one of the most successful men of his age, a man some would call the last great western emperor. Valens would be doomed to die on the dark day of 9 August 378 at the Battle of Adrianople in what is today European Turkey, when the Romans suffered a castrophic defeat at the hands of a massive Gothic army. The harrowing story of that battle is the climax of Ammianus' history – he was well aware that it marked the beginning of a new page for Rome, indeed the clear beginning of the end for the western empire.

As for Sapor, he died in AD 379 at the age of 70, having seen enormous success as one of Persia's most militaristic of kings. Armenia was under Sassanian control, and beyond doubt Sapor handed on an empire that was in a far stronger and better state than when he had received it 'in the womb', as was said, so many decaded before. His brother Ardashir II would succeed him as regent until his young son Sapor III was ready to take power. In the end, both brother and son of the great Sapor II would have nowhere near the success of their predecessor. Both would be murdered by Iranian nobles (Ardashir in 383, Sapor III in 388). In terms of Rome, both would be preoccupied with troubles in Armenia. Persia had entered another of its own periods of instability. The internal dissension in Persia was no doubt a godsend for Rome in the critical years of the Gothic crisis. Armenia would be definitively divided on the basis of a new treaty – one might call it a supplement to Jovian's far-reaching agreement with Sapor II – whereby the two empires would more or less seek to prevent any future conflict over that problematic buffer zone. This treaty of 387 – signed by Sapor III – was made with Theodosius I, the Roman emperor who holds the distinction of being the last man to rule over the 'combined' western and eastern empires. By virtue of the settlements of 387, both powers agreed to cooperate in the defence of the Caucasus region against raids by plundering nomadic tribes.

In the aftermath of Julian's failed Persian War, Amida became the new capital of Roman Mesopotamia. Roman Arabia remained comparatively unscathed by the long history of war with Sassanid Persia.

Roman relations with Persia during the early fifth century AD were perhaps surprisingly cordial. Sapor III's son Bahram IV was assassinated after his own brief reign, while his brother Yazdegerd I would enjoy the rare blessing of a long and comparatively peaceful reign from AD 399–420, years in which the kingdom enjoyed a respite from problems both domestic and foreign.

There would be a renewed war between Persia and Rome in AD 421–422, one largely fought because of the question of religious persecution (specifically the plight of Christians under Persian rule). The result of the war was that everything was restored exactly to the *status quo ante bellum* – that hasty treaty of Jovian (as foundation to the agreements of Theodosius in 387) had lasted in many key regards far longer than its initial thirty-year duration. Disputes over the question of Roman assistance to Persia in defending the Caucasus region led to another short-lived war in 440, but there, too, the results were relatively minor: Rome agreed not to build any new fortifications in Mesopotamia. By then, Rome was more than preoccupied with Vandal incursions. To give a sense of how lasting the peace between Rome and Persia would be, there were no wars at all until 502 – a remarkable sixty-plus years of quiet. By then the western empire had fallen, and the problems of Rome and Persia pass into the annals of Byzantine history.

In some important regards, then, the last Roman emperor of great significance in Roman–Persian relations was Julian the Apostate – if by 'Roman' we refer to the 'complete' empire, that is, both West and East. Julian the Apostate was certainly the last emperor of the combined realm to contemplate the conquest of Persia in accord with what we might call the vision of Alexander the Great. His decision to stop before the gates of Ctesiphon was a fateful one. In many ways he had no choice but to make his doomed retreat. But somewhere in the deserts of what is today central Iraq – another of those Near Eastern regions that has rightly been called the graveyard of empire – a Roman dream died. It had been a dream held by such as Lucullus and Pompey, not to mention Julius Caesar and Mark Antony, in the tumultuous last century of the Roman Republic. It was on the mind of Augustus as he inaugurated the constitutional settlement that paved the way (for better or worse) for what we would come to call the Roman

Empire. It was a strategic vision inherited from Alexander of Macedon, and to some extent his father Philip before him.

The fact that Julian was a pagan interlude in a Christian age, and one of the most literate emperors of his day, adds to the mystique and interest of the man. In some ways he was the likeliest of imperial candidates to revisit dreams of Persian conquest. Orphaned at a young age and educated in part by a Gothic slave, his life is of profound fascination for students of the age. He was convinced that a return to the Roman values of former times – complete with devotion to the traditional pantheon of Roman gods – was essential to the success and survival of the empire. In other words, like students of his times today, he perceived that the Roman Empire was in a state of profound decline and near collapse. His efforts to turn the tide of fate and to restore something of the grandeur of Rome's past were astonishingly ambitious and accomplished, especially given the brief compass of his reign.

Those interested in exploring Julian's extant writings will find the three-volume Loeb Classical Library edition a convenient starting point. Robert Browning's 1976 University of California Press study, *The Emperor Julian*, remains a good foundational biography, especially alongside Glen Bowersock's 1978 Harvard work *Julian the Apostate*. H.C. Teitler's 2017 Oxford volume, *The Last Pagan Emperor: Julian the Apostate & the War against Christianity*, may also be highly recommended. Julian has enjoyed a rich afterlife, not least in the existence of the so-called Julian Society of neo-pagans that thoughtfully offers miniature statues of the emperor for sale through its internet souvenir shop. One can only imagine that Julian would be bemused at this and other survivals of his legacy at the start of the third millennium of the Christian age he held in such suspicion.

Along the way, emperors such as Julian, Trajan and Septimius Severus did much to advance the goal of moving Roman frontiers to some always 'over the next ridge' new border. Other, perhaps wiser and more cautious rulers like Hadrian – and indeed the mediocre Jovian – were eager to move in the other direction, withdrawing Roman forces from the lands between the two rivers. Throughout, the goals of Roman conquerors and diplomatic negotiators alike was to control the lucrative trade and commerce between West and East, the routes by land and sea to India and beyond.

The story of Rome's long and violent involvement in Mesopotamia and Arabia is interesting in and of itself as a source of pleasure taken from the study of the annals of times past. It is also a peculiarly relevant and timely source of historical commentary, cautionary warning and sober analysis about the actions of empires across time. Those powers – western and other – involved militarily in the modern countries of Syria, Iraq, Jordan, Saudi Arabia and beyond would do well to master the manifold lessons of Roman involvement in the beguiling sands of the Near and Middle East.

Index